MADDIE'S BEACH

THE THINGS THAT MAKE US

THE THINGS THAT MAKE US
LIFE, LOSS AND FOOTBALL

NICK
RIEWOLDT

With PETER HANLON

SYDNEY·MELBOURNE·AUCKLAND·LONDON

First published in 2017

Copyright © Nick Riewoldt 2017

All rights reserved. No part of this book may be reproduced or transmitted in any form or by any means, electronic or mechanical, including photocopying, recording or by any information storage and retrieval system, without prior permission in writing from the publisher. The Australian *Copyright Act 1968* (the Act) allows a maximum of one chapter or 10 per cent of this book, whichever is the greater, to be photocopied by any educational institution for its educational purposes provided that the educational institution (or body that administers it) has given a remuneration notice to the Copyright Agency (Australia) under the Act.

Allen & Unwin
83 Alexander Street
Crows Nest NSW 2065
Australia
Phone: (61 2) 8425 0100
Email: info@allenandunwin.com
Web: www.allenandunwin.com

Cataloguing-in-Publication details are available
from the National Library of Australia
www.trove.nla.gov.au

ISBN 978 1 76029 462 5

Index by Puddingburn
Set in 12.75/18.5 pt Adobe Garamond Pro by Midland Typesetters, Australia
Printed and bound in Australia by Griffin Press

10 9 8 7 6 5 4 3 2 1

The paper in this book is FSC® certified. FSC® promotes environmentally responsible, socially beneficial and economically viable management of the world's forests.

For James and Will

Contents

Introduction   1

1   Heritage   5
2   Tassie   25
3   (In)Experience   51
4   Competitiveness   73
5   The Spotlight   95
6   Mentors   125
7   My Baby and My Texas   149
8   Loving and Losing Maddie   179
9   Grieving and Giving Back   203
10   Longevity   227
11   Friendship   243
12   Being a Saint   269
13   Winning and Losing   291

CONTENTS

14	Leadership	309
15	Scandal	329
16	Family	341

Conclusion	357
Acknowledgements	363
Maddie Riewoldt's Vision	365
Index	369

Introduction

I never saw myself writing a book, simply because I didn't think I had a compelling story to tell. I was an elite footballer for seventeen years, but so what? That wouldn't have been enough to make me want to read 90,000 words about myself, let alone write them, so why would anyone else be bothered?

I read fiction, because I want to escape. And I read history, because I'm interested in the world and how we got to where we are. But I've never been a reader of athletes' biographies.

Maddie's illness, her struggle, her loss, changed everything, including my attitude towards penning my story. We'll never get over it but, as a family, even in the hours and days after her passing, we resolved to do everything we could to ensure she didn't 'fight like Maddie' for nothing. My beautiful sister leaves a powerful legacy, and I hope this book plays its part in that.

I hope the book resonates with football fans, and also with people whose interest in the game is only fleeting. I didn't want to write a 'cookie-cutter' footballer's book—chronologically moving from the under 8s through to the big time, full of hard-ball gets, wins and losses, triumphs and disappointments. I chose the title because it made it easy to explore things we can all relate to, no matter what path our lives have taken. Stop and think for a minute, and we can all locate the things that have made us who we are.

I hope there's something in these pages for everyone who's known grief, especially anyone who's lost a sibling. The ache of losing someone can go quiet for a while, but turn around and it's right there. I hope elements of my story will bring some solace to people who have known similar pain.

I hope, too, that my story brings a deeper understanding of a footballer's crazy world. An insight into what goes into making it, what it takes to stay there, and the crippling anxiety that can consume you when your burden is to accept only the best. I hope it paints a picture of what it's like to be the focus of acclamation and scandal, the good and bad of a searing spotlight, and how these experiences can bring out the best and worst in us. I hope it offers a reminder of the power of the mentors and friends who guide our paths, that we couldn't do it without them.

I hope it honours my family—the German and Tasmanian sides, with their stories of struggle and endurance—who are

Introduction

the essence of the book's title. I hope it gives thanks for the love I found on the other side of the world, and the beautiful next generation Cath and I are building together.

I hope above all that it honours my sister Maddie.

These are the things that made me.

1
HERITAGE

Dad wanted to name me Maximilian. Or Helmut. If I was a girl, Dagmar. My brother-in-law, John, still has a lot of fun with that. He calls me Helmut in a German accent. 'Hel-mut! Hel-mut!' I was pretty happy Mum won out and the three of us ended up as Nick, Alex and Maddie—normal, straightforward names.

The older I've got the more I've been drawn to my heritage, the more I've wanted to learn and document my family story. When the elders pass away, their stories go with them. We only get one chance to get it all down. I want my children and their children after them to know where they've come from. I want them to know the things that made them.

Over almost twenty years in an AFL footballer's spotlight, it's a story I've never told. Some of it's harrowing. Some unremarkable. Some of it's almost unbelievable. But it's shaped me. It's given me the resilience to play a demanding sport for so long at such a high level. The flexibility to adapt to change and find a way to overcome each new challenge. The determination to weather the storms and keep going, keep pushing on. The courage to pick myself up in the face of loss so big you're sure it's going to consume you.

I'm a descendant of people who've known hardship. My heritage has given me strength. It's helped make me the person I am.

•

In a *Sliding Doors* world I might have been a young German boy growing up in Berlin wearing lederhosen. Even as kids in Hobart, my brother Alex would joke that I'd marched out of the womb. Alex was blond and curly at the start but he's dark now. I was the Aryan prototype as a child. I suppose that's never really changed.

Christmas was the time I realised the Riewoldt side of our family is different. We'd pile into the car on Christmas Eve, cross the Tasman Bridge over the Derwent River and snake up the hill to my grandparents' big, rambling house on the eastern shore at Bellerive. When I was very young, I called them Mama and Grandpa. Dad's grandparents were living in Hobart too, and they were Oma and Opa. I was the only one of us three who really knew them, and after they'd passed away Mama and Grandpa—Helga and Heinz—became Oma and Opa.

Oma would always do a prawn cocktail, and there'd be beef olives, schnitzel, sauerkraut, red cabbage, all the German staples. The house was furnished in a very European style and there were little things that stayed with me, like the nativity scene that would rotate, driven by the hot air from candles set into its base.

We'd sit around singing carols and then we'd hear the bells and Santa would come in with his sack. We always had a Santa. I don't know where they got him from—whether it was one of my uncles in a suit or if they went down to a shopping centre and gave the resident Santa 50 bucks to come to Oma and Opa's. One by one we'd go up to get our presents, sing a Christmas carol with Santa then sit down to unwrap them and discover what we'd been given. The majority of our presents came on Christmas Eve, then we'd get a stocking with little things on Christmas Day.

The next day we'd get up and make the one-hour drive up the east coast to Orford to have a traditional Christmas with Mum's side of the family, the Millingtons. So we essentially had two celebrations. We still do. Oma and Opa are deep into their eighties now, and they have a 'shack' at Carlton Beach, near Dodge's Ferry (Tasmanians call their holiday houses 'shacks' whether they're sheds or palaces or anything in between). It's an awesome place, really beautiful, right on top of the sand dune with a pristine beach. These days, we drive back to Orford on

Christmas Eve for the Millington/Hean (Mum's side of the family) Christmas the next day.

Dad is Joe but he was christened Joerg, which is pronounced Jor-ick. He was born in Berlin after the war, whereas his younger brothers—Ray, Chris (father of Richmond's Jack) and Peter—were born in Tasmania and given Anglo names. Or at least in Chris's case, versions of Anglo names. Oma was due to have Chris on Christmas Day, and she and Opa wanted to call him Christopher but didn't know how to spell it. On his birth certificate his name is Christover, as in Christ Over. Dad and Ray, who were six and three, respectively, got to choose Chris's second name. They went with Rolf, because they liked Rolf Harris. In hindsight that doesn't sound like such a good choice.

As kids we'd listen to Oma and Opa talking to Dad in German. You'd have no idea what they were saying, but if you heard your name in a sentence you'd think, 'If they're talking German it can't be good, I must be in trouble.' Their accents are so strong; you'd struggle to understand my grandmother, her voice is so deep and thick for such a small woman. Dad's still fluent and regularly speaks on the phone to relatives back in Germany. I can speak *ein bisschen*—a little. If I sit down and listen to Dad talk to his parents I can get the gist. I've tried lessons a few times—one on one, then with language tapes. For a while I set aside a couple of hours a week at the footy club and would go and lock myself in a room and do it. It ended like a lot of hobbies do.

Heritage

But I really wish I could speak it. I tell Dad all the time to speak to my sons James and Will in German, but I think he wants to interact with them just like everyone else does. As the oldest child of postwar migrants trying to make their way in a strange land, Dad didn't have it easy. He has memories of taking eel wrapped in wax paper to school for lunch, telling the kids who teased him that it was snake. His sandwiches would be filled with salami, which nobody else had either. When they studied German, he'd get into trouble because he could speak it so well. Classmates resented him for it, ignorant teachers figured he must have been cheating. He carried his things in a leather backpack, which was very German. Every kid in Australia takes a backpack to school now, but in the 1960s it was a school case or a Gladstone bag. The other kids leapt on that as just another reason to tease Dad.

Home life was marked by discipline, hard work, stoicism, not a lot of laughter. Dad tells the story of he and Ray having a pet lamb, which they imaginatively called Lamby. They loved Lamby, but one day Lamby ran away. A few days later they were at the table having the evening meal, and Oma asked if they were enjoying their dinner.

'Yes, very nice,' Dad and Ray replied.

In her deep voice, matter of fact as could be, Oma said: 'It was your pet.'

Sometimes Dad dug his heels in, refused to eat what was put in front of him. And his parents would make him sit there until he did, even if it took until midnight. 'Won't eat your dinner? Okay, we starved in the war so you'll sit there until you finish.'

Mum discovered pretty early on what she was in for with the Riewoldts. Soon after she and Dad starting dating, she went to their house for dinner. Heinz, Helga, Joe and the other boys were all there, and everyone was served up a plate with the biggest mountain of food Mum had ever seen. All the boys had finished their enormous meals and Mum was still labouring away, just about sweating from the effort. My uncle Peter looked across the table and said to her, 'Fiona, you have to eat everything on your plate because they starved in the war.'

Oma realised what was happening and said to her, 'Darling! You don't have to eat all of that! If you're done, you're done!' The boys had set Mum up.

It must have been a tough house to grow up in, at times seemingly cruel and even brutal. But people are a product of what they've been through. And Oma and Opa have been through things you could barely imagine.

•

Oma's sister, Krystal, died from diphtheria in 1935 when she was nine and Oma was six. She'd been born on Christmas Day, thus the name. If Dad's brother Chris had been a girl she would have been Krystal (rather than Christover!). Oma never

Heritage

spoke about Krystal, but her loss and the traumas of the years that followed had a lasting impact on her. Oma and Opa were fifteen when World War II ended, both living in Berlin but yet to meet. Growing up I knew snippets of their story, and the older I got the more I wanted to learn. One day, not so long ago, over a lunch of schnitzel, sauerkraut and potato salad in their house in suburban Hobart—with Opa insisting I have a beer despite my being in the middle of pre-season training—they filled out the horrifying picture.

Oma lived in a five-storey building with multiple apartments on each floor. It was near an airfield that was a major target for bombing by the Allies. She remembered the first time a house in her neighbourhood was bombed, in 1941—everyone leaving their homes when the bombing had stopped, standing on the street in front of the smoking ruins and saying to each other, 'Look at what they're doing!'

Oma couldn't begin to guess how many times in the next few years the warning siren sounded and her family retreated to the cellar in their building while the bombs rained down above. Sometimes they stayed there for days, fearing they would starve. When the Russians swept through in the Battle of Berlin in 1945 they hid in the cellar again, and it saved their lives.

A neighbour who spoke Russian stood at the cellar doorway and talked to the invading soldiers, somehow distracting them so that they went upstairs and not down.

Oma knew a girl around her age who lived on the first floor. The Russians kicked down the door of her family's home, raped her and killed her.

'That's how bad the Russians were,' Oma said.

'Yes,' Opa replied. 'But the Germans weren't much better than the Russians.'

The Battle of Berlin left Oma racked by another loss she never really got over, that of her beloved father. Like so many Berliners who were too old to fight in the regular army, he was part of the Volkssturm, or 'People's Storm', essentially a motley gathering of mostly ageing citizens who were mobilised in the last months of the war to help defend the homeland.

He'd returned home safely but as Berlin continued to fall to the Russians he announced that it was his duty to return to the streets and stand alongside the other members of the Volkssturm. Oma's family begged him to stay, pleaded for him to realise the war was almost over, but he wouldn't be swayed. It's straight out of the movie *Downfall*, about the last two weeks in Hitler's bunker. Some of the people were so brainwashed they kept fighting when it was unwinnable. When it was virtually suicide.

He called Oma 'my Goldpiece', and before leaving he told her, 'If we don't see each other here, you know where we'll see each other again.'

When the fighting finally stopped Oma's mother went looking for her husband. She tried to get to her parents' house nearby but the Russians blocked her path. She snuck behind the houses in her street and retreated home that way, and from a distance saw the body of a man lying on the ground. She came closer and realised it was her husband.

Oma refused to believe her father was gone. They covered him with a blanket and carried his body on a stretcher to the cemetery where Krystal was buried. Only there, when his arm slipped off the stretcher and dangled towards the ground as he was being carried to his resting place, did she see the ring on his wedding finger. 'Otherwise I would not have believed it was my dad.'

Opa was spared such deep loss but his story is still incredible. He remembers being eight or nine and part of a junior version of the Hitler Youth. He likened it to scouts—going on camping trips, having contests between teams wearing red and blue armbands, singing, joking, helping the elderly cross the road or giving up your seat on a tram. 'It wasn't that you had to be in it,' Opa said. 'But when you're seven, eight, nine years old, if all your mates are going in something, you do it too.'

He recalled that they didn't suffer under Hitler, but had no inkling of the suffering his rule was inflicting elsewhere. The German propaganda machine ensured the majority of civilians were kept in the dark as to what was really happening. Oma and Opa both realised much later that if they'd been teenagers living in London during the war they would have known everything. Living in Berlin, they had no idea. 'We didn't know what was going on in the camps. They only let you know what they wanted you to know.'

Opa thinks he was lucky—he wasn't in Berlin when the Russians came, and he was convinced that saved his life. His whole school class—40 children and their teacher—was evacuated to the south of Berlin before the Russians arrived. They tried to pick up other children along the way, and Opa remembered stopping at a camp and being told, 'Keep going, keep going!' They asked why there were no children there, and were told they'd all been shot.

After a night in Prague they made it to Bavaria, and that's where Opa stayed as the dying months of the war played out. By then his school group had splintered; he was fifteen, virtually alone, and had to find his way back to Berlin, 500 kilometres away. The courage and industry he showed in achieving that still makes me shake my head in awe. Talk about 'the things that made me'.

For weeks he and the few of his classmates who remained in his group worked on Bavarian farms, then, when the father of one boy arrived from Berlin to take his son home, Opa figured he should hang onto his coat-tails. American and Russian troops had been forging further into Germany, and the threat of a swift end was still high.

Having snuck onto a train headed from Nuremberg to Leipzig, housed by the driver in the coal tender, they were stopped just short of their destination by Russian troops.

Heritage

'Someone must have seen us,' Opa said. 'They lined us up; I thought we'd all get shot.' The driver declared that he was Russian, produced a document, and they were spared.

Opa was soon on his own, young and frightened. He came to a river, with the Russians on the other side. He knew he needed to cross to get home to Berlin. He's always been a clever man, Opa, and his ingenuity was to the fore here. He caught the attention of the soldiers on the other side, pointed to his wrist and yelled out, 'Uhr! Uhr!', trying to convince them he had a watch, something of value they might want. They beckoned him to swim over, and when he'd almost reached the other side he kicked off a gumboot, pretended the watch had dropped inside and feigned panic as it disappeared downstream. 'I never had a watch at all,' Opa laughed as he told me.

He was put in a camp, given scraps of meat to eat and charged with keeping the fire burning and stirring the enormous wash-pot that was suspended above it. An older girl helped him escape, and via a train from Utrecht he finally made it home to Berlin. 'Everything was destroyed,' he recalled. 'I walked to our street, could hardly bear to look, and our house was still there!'

His parents, who of course had feared Opa was dead, were beside themselves. Their boy was alive, and he was home. Within two months the war was over.

Opa reckons being such a big boy helped him—at fifteen he stood six feet tall, and he was never afraid of a challenge. Some time after the war a group of American soldiers taunted him that he couldn't climb a huge industrial chimney that stretched high into the sky, with metal rungs cemented into its side. They said they'd give him a carton of beer if he could. Opa climbed the chimney and got the beer.

Opa's father, my paternal great-grandfather, had incredible war stories of his own. He fought in World War I on the front line in the German trenches. It's amazing to think that my paternal grandfather on Mum's side—Pa Hean, who was a member of the Australian Light Horse regiment and survived the landing at Gallipoli—fought in World War I on the opposite side to Dad's grandfather.

Opa's father was in the Battle of Fromelles, and his job was to stand and wave flags signalling whether the enemy was shooting short or long. He took a bullet in the skull—right through the front of his helmet—and that was the end of his war. He was incredibly lucky to survive—when they carried him back to the first aid station, by chance the doctor was a brain surgeon who said, 'Leave this one to me.' By the time that bullet moved enough to kill him, he was 86 and living happily in Hobart.

He also disappeared at the end of World War II. Not long after Opa arrived back in Berlin the Russians put out a directive: anyone who held any sort of office was required to report to a central body. Opa's father was caretaker of the building they lived in. He took that responsibility as being a form of office, and said to his wife, 'Well, I must go.' She told him not to be

Heritage

ridiculous, that they didn't want the body corporate manager of a residential building, but he went and reported in anyway. They didn't see him for four years. He was shipped off to a Russian concentration camp, and when he came home he had tuberculosis and weighed about 45 kilograms. Just amazing.

•

Opa came to Australia first, sailing via Cape Town in South Africa, on to Adelaide and then Melbourne with other unemployed German men seeking work on the hydro-electric schemes of the early 1950s in the Snowy Mountains and Tasmania. He still complains that his passage from Germany cost £220, a small fortune that could have bought him a house in the country he would make his home for the rest of his life. Once he'd started work he sent Oma a letter—'If you don't come over I'll marry an Australian girl.'

The hydro scheme brought immigrants from Germany, England, Poland, Italy, Scandinavia and all over Eastern Europe to a country that was still smarting from the war, but he remembered only one incident of hostility. 'We went to the pub, there were some sheilas there and one of our blokes was showing off,' Opa told me. 'One of the local blokes said, "Bloody Krauts." One of his mates tried to calm him, said, "No, they're good Germans." And he replied, "The only good German is a dead German."'

'One of the blokes I was with said something back and—boom! It was on.' Opa thought for a while as he remembered this story from another age. Then he smiled and said, 'Anyway, we won.'

My dad has a small boy's memories of catching the boat across to Melbourne with Opa, waiting for a couple of days for a big ship to arrive, and meeting his grandparents, the original Oma and Opa, for the first time. They sailed back to Tassie and got on with life.

Opa's father—my great-grandfather, who still had the bullet lodged in his head—settled with my great-grandmother in Battery Point, which is now one of the best spots in Hobart. They lived next to an old digger, an Aussie war veteran who'd also been at the Battle of Fromelles. My great-grandfather used to joke with him, 'You shot me, you bastard!' And his neighbour would say, 'That's bullshit!' It sounds like the Hatfields and McCoys, but they became great mates, would have a beer together and tell their stories. It's incredible when you think about it.

•

Opa is an extraordinarily hard worker, even now. When I bought my shack at Orford in 2004 he was up there in a flash, ripping out cabinets as an almost-80-year-old man, still on the tools and knowing exactly what to do with them. He's very, very clever with his hands, crafty and handy.

Heritage

There's some ripper photos of him as a kid—he was strong from a young age. He's not a big man, but he has a thick trunk. My cousin Jack's thick through the thighs like Opa; I'm rangier. Dad says Opa's the strongest man he's ever seen. He's got what people call old-fashioned man's strength—handy strength, the sort that can carry anything or get the lid off a jar when nobody else can. He's an amazing man. Dad remembers that one of Mum's friends was the granddaughter of a guy named Dicky Baker, who owned Bakers Milk in Tasmania. Opa—whom Dicky Baker called Harry—had built one of his factories. When Dicky Baker met Dad he said to him, 'You're Harry's son? Strongest man I've ever met.'

•

Oma's frail now, the furthest thing from a stereotypical big German lady. Family is huge to her, and she's a very, very proud woman. Very strong, someone who's been hardened by all she's been through. She's religious, broadly Christian, and goes to church every week. Opa goes along with her, but it's really Oma's thing. If you want to show them you're thinking of them but you're not really up for a chat, give them a call on Sunday morning—you'll get message bank.

When they're home they don't answer with, 'Hello, Helga speaking', or 'Hello, this is Heinz'. They pick up the phone and bark, 'Ree-volt!' That's all they say.

THE THINGS THAT MAKE US

The pronunciation of my name has never really bothered me, but from a young age I thought, 'If Oma and Opa say it with a *v*, it must be with a *v*.' I think the first time it got any airplay around footy was when I said my name as a panellist on *The Footy Show* one night years ago. I said, 'Ree-volt', and Eddie McGuire was like, 'Hang on, you just said it differently. How do you say it?' And I said it was with a soft *v*, no big deal.

I'm incredibly proud that Riewoldt was a big name in Tasmanian football long before myself or Jack came along. Dad was the trailblazer in everything Australian so he had to deal with Oma and Opa's apprehension when he took up this strange and foreign sport. The boys all played for Clarence, whose home ground is Bellerive Oval, just down the street from their house. At one stage they all played in the same team, which is a pretty amazing feat for the sons of German migrants.

Dad was a reasonable player. They're all big blokes—Dad's the smallest at about six foot in the old measurement, Ray's six foot one or two, Chris six-three or -four, Peter's about six foot five. Chris was the most decorated, a ruckman/forward who held the Tassie games record until Scott Wade, the father of Australian cricketer Matthew, broke it.

Chris played a lot of state footy and even signed one of the old 'Form Four' clearances to come across to Victoria and play for St Kilda. Dad remembers the legendary coach Allan

Heritage

Jeans coming to the house, which must have been bizarre for Oma and Opa—not to mention for Allan Jeans, and not least because Oma, with her still-developing grasp of English, always called him Jean Allans! Chris never made the move because he'd already done a year of university and they weren't going to recognise it in Melbourne. He's never been too bothered. Ray signed a Form Four with Fitzroy after he was named in the All Australian Schoolboys team, but he didn't go either. Dad and my uncles reckon the lure of the old VFL, as it was then, wasn't so big compared to playing in the TFL when Tassie footy was at its peak.

By the end of their sons' careers, Oma and Opa had become extremely passionate about Australian Rules. The pinnacle obviously was having two grandsons playing in the AFL, playing well, being household names. They've got a few bits and pieces about me and Jack around the house. They don't really say anything, being people of few words, but they're clearly very proud.

Years ago, when Jack and I first played against each other, the *Weekend Australian* magazine did a piece about us. They interviewed Opa and asked him whether he'd been any good at sport. He said something outrageous along the lines of 'We didn't throw balls, we threw grenades!' It was so inappropriate, but I think he got a chuckle out of it.

My heritage has opened doors I'd never have imagined, brought a whole group of people into my life that I wouldn't have otherwise been exposed to. Mum and Dad had been to stay with one of Dad's cousins, Andreas—which, being Australian we shortened to Andy, of course—in the mid-2000s, so at the end of the 2007 season, on my way to a holiday in London, I stayed with him and his wife Bianca at their place in Switzerland. I flew into Zurich, Andy picked me up at the airport and we drove the couple of hours to their little village. I'd never even met them before.

I stayed for two weeks, went running in the countryside, went for drives with Andy and Bianca to Lucerne and Zurich. Their English is good, their house was modern and comfortable, we got on. The only awkward bit was at night when we'd have a beer—which wasn't kept in the fridge. I'm not a huge beer man, but it's got to be cold. They had Sambuca shots for a nightcap, and in the morning served a breakfast of spreads, breads, cheeses and meats. By about the third day I'd have given anything for a bowl of cereal.

Without my German heritage I wouldn't have had that experience, and I wouldn't count Andreas and Bianca and their gorgeous little girl Fabienne as family. When Cath and I were married in Texas in 2012 they came to the wedding and had a ball. They live in Dubai now, where Andy works for Siemens in technology development. They'll always be part of our lives, a special link to Riewoldts past.

The older I get, the more Germany prods me. I've long had a fascination with movies set in the world wars—*The Pianist* with Adrien Brody, the old classics, the modern series like *Band of Brothers* about the 101st Airborne produced by Hanks and Spielberg. It doesn't really matter what it is, I can't help watching. I don't feel any association with the German side, because clearly they were the instigators of unimaginable atrocities. But the stories . . . it's hard to believe it all happened. I picked up pretty early that the Germans were always the bad guys, that pop culture painted them in a negative light. At school kids might jokingly call you a Nazi, but I didn't consider it racist. I was an Australian kid growing up in Australia—aside from the name there was nothing to indicate even that Dad was born there. It wasn't like I had a German passport.

As an adult that's changed. When I realised that because of Dad's birthplace I was entitled to one I filled out the forms, drove up the Punt Road hill to the big white building of the German embassy, and a man named Wolfgang handed me my passport. I love it—the red cover with the gold eagle on the front, the words, 'Nationality—Deutsch' on the inside. The only time I use it is when I'm in America and you go to a bar and get asked for ID. Take out your Australian driver's licence and they go, 'What's this? This isn't real, it's a fake!' But they know a German passport when they see one. It's cool.

If there's a German competing on the international stage—in the Olympics, or anything for that matter—I'll go for them. Soccer's handy because they're so good. I have an affinity with anything German really—cars, appliances, whatever. They do a lot of things pretty well.

Germany is part of who I am, and I feel special because of it. Dad's front and centre in that, but Oma and Opa are my link to another time and another world. What they went through, the things they saw, it's hard to fathom. They learnt to deal with hardship in an almost clinical, unemotional way: it's happened, it's awful, but now we must move on.

My father had an uneasy childhood with parents who were still suffering, whose scars were raw. Dad could easily have raised us in the same type of 'get on with it' environment. But he broke that mould, and Alex, Maddie and I enjoyed an upbringing that couldn't have been more filled with love. Mum and Dad did everything they could for us, and I'll forever be grateful.

2
TASSIE

As influential as my German history is on the person I've become, it's dwarfed by the pride I feel in being a Tasmanian. I really love it. I love the place, what the people stand for, the fact that it's not connected to the mainland, that it's an island. I love that you can go to the other side of the world and say you're from Tasmania and people are like, 'Wow! Is that its own country?' I feel like it's cool to be from Tassie.

It will forever be the place I was born, the scene of my most precious childhood memories, the second home I return to every chance I get. It's where I have my shack, at Orford on the east coast. This is my special place, all the more because it became Maddie's too. It's where she spent the happiest days of her life.

There's a lemon twist of sadness now—it's where Maddie so desperately wanted to return, where she dreamed of being well again, of feeling the sun and sea air on her face, of feeling alive. All the time she was so unwell in hospital, she'd say, 'I want to go to Orford, I want to go to Orford. I want to swim at the beach.'

It was where Maddie and Mum would walk every day they were there—out the front gate, along the street towards the mouth of the Prosser River, through the cut to the sand, all the way out and around the point, up the road and back home. All they wanted was to do that again, together.

That's where we scattered Maddie's ashes, so she could be there in her happy place forever.

•

While the Riewoldts' Tasmanian story is relatively recent and short, Mum's side goes back generations. Her mother—my nan, Fay—was a Millington. There's a Millingtons Beach at Orford. We now call it Maddie's Beach. In getting to the heart of my Tasmanian story, there's no better place to start.

Nan is in her late eighties and has been visiting Orford all her life, but the family roots go back way further than Fay. She can remember visiting her grandfather's house at the Quarries, out past Spring Beach, where Princess Mary's family have a shack. James and Will are the seventh generation of our family to visit

Orford. I find that amazing. Unless they're indigenous, not many Australian families have roots that deep in a specific place.

Nan grew up in Hobart, in Lower Sandy Bay. They had a beautiful home with an amazing view of the Derwent, and when her father, Harold Charles Millington, decided to go into the funeral business it broke Nan's mother Kitty's heart, because they had to move into a flat above the funeral home.

The great thing that came out of the move was the shack at Orford. Harold wanted somewhere he could take his wife and three daughters at weekends. Early in their marriage they had holidayed further north at Swansea. Driving back to Hobart one day, rolling across the Orford bridge, Kitty said, 'Why are we going all the way to Swansea? We could stay here.'

Harold bought the block for £25 from a man called Mr Fieldwick, whom Nan and her sisters called 'Iggle Diggle'. Harold built the house that became known as Sunways with the help of family and friends—anyone they could convince to lend a hand. They lived on a boat moored to the bridge while they built it, and Nan's memories of her childhood there are so strong and warm.

There was no Tasman Bridge in Hobart then, and every weekend they'd drive their Hudson car onto the ferry at the wharf, roll off at Bellerive and head up to Orford. It's still a pretty sleepy place now, but it must have been something else then. Their phone number was 'Orford 6', which shows how many people had the phone on! Maybe they were wary of the postmistress, Miss Turvey, who also doubled as the telephone exchange operator and knew what everyone was up to because she'd always listen in to their phone calls. Nan remembers a man named Mr Patmore driving through in a van selling ice-cream; when eventually a store opened, it was run by a tiny woman named Mrs Drake who doubled as the school bus driver. There were very few shacks in Orford then, only residents.

At one stage Nan's school in Hobart was forced to close its doors due to a polio epidemic, so her parents packed up the family and relocated to Orford for three months. It's a time Nan remembers fondly, except for her father lining them up in the kitchen and administering a dose of castor oil, which he told his girls they could either take with orange juice or Worcestershire sauce. 'I chose orange juice and I haven't been able to look at a green plum since,' Nan said. 'I can still taste it.'

They'd go mushrooming and collecting cowpats for compost for the garden Kitty was growing at Sunways. Their father built motor boats, and his children would be sent off into the bush to collect timber shaped just right to fashion into keels. Fear of invasion by the Japanese (who didn't exactly get close to Tasmania in World War II!) meant they weren't allowed to go floundering with spotlights at night, but Nan's dad was in with the policeman at Triabunna who turned a blind eye to their nocturnal fishing. Nan and her sisters would row the boat in the little bay at Swanport while their father readied himself to strike with the spear. 'If we got the spear and didn't get the flounder there'd be hell to pay,' Nan recalled.

She's told me stories of going over to Maria Island, which from 1825 housed a convict settlement. Maria has always fascinated me; I've got a few books at the shack that tell its many stories, like the Italian silk merchant Diego Bernacchi attempting to turn it into a wine-growing mecca, and the sceptical mainlanders putting the story around that when the media made the trip over to see Bernacchi's vines they were faring so badly he'd glued grapes onto them in the hope the visitors wouldn't notice.

When Nan was still young, tragedy struck the family: Kitty died. Harold remarried, and Nan used to go across to Maria Island with her father and stepmother, Vy, to visit a fortune teller called Mrs Hunt. Vy would take Mrs Hunt a bottle of sherry and some bread, and in return she'd read their palms. Mrs Hunt told Vy she could see that she'd been married three times, which was true. And she told Nan she saw cancer in her hands. Much later in life, Nan battled leukaemia.

Nan's always said that my mum had it easy by the time she was spending her childhood weekends at Orford. 'They had nothing like we had to do as children, we did everything.' I guess the expectations placed on children has diminished generationally.

Some people thought the beach should have been named Meredith Beach, after Louisa Meredith, the famous English botanical illustrator who moved to Tasmania. I'm so proud it's called Millingtons Beach after my great-grandfather, who was instrumental in setting up a Progress Association in Orford, organised sailing regattas, raised money and donated a piano so the locals could hold dances. On top of it all, he'd been a pretty handy sprint cyclist way back when bikes had wooden rims, winning races not only in Tassie but also in Victoria. From what I know of him he must have been an amazing man.

Nan's pretty chuffed with the honour too, especially as there's a sadness to her Orford story: after falling out with one of her sisters, her share of Sunways was sold around the time we moved to Queensland.

I already knew how much the place meant to her, then one night, when she was staying at my shack, Nan produced a letter and read it to me.

> Orford has always been a part of my life, a place that has grown from a small seaside village to a fast-growing township. My father saw the potential in Orford as a place for his family to enjoy holidays, and so he built Sunways. He and many friends and family would spend weekends, adding a room at a time whilst living on the boat which was moored to the Orford bridge.
>
> It became known as 'Mushroom Cottage', for obvious reasons, until my mother renamed it Sunways. So over the years generations of this family came to know Sunways as their second home.

Tassie

My memories properly start in the 1930–40 period, going to the shack most weekends and school holidays. When Friends' School closed for the duration of the polio epidemic we spent months at Orford, one long holiday. Although we had no electricity in those days, we soon became used to kerosene lamps, candles, hot water bottles—none of the luxuries enjoyed today.

Having no sons, Dad let us know the value of being capable. He taught us how to use a cross-cut saw, an axe, collect firewood, pulling up the heavy Chapman Pup dinghy onto the davits—not so easy for girls. Waking us up at 6 a.m. to go fishing at his favourite spots, where we were tied to kelp and started hauling in king flathead, setting the pots for crayfish. No wetsuits or life jackets, but we were never afraid of the water. In fact our lives probably revolved around it.

Out the gate, over the road to a beautiful beach on the Prosser River where Dad had built his jetty. Sadly the beach and the jetty are no longer there, but the memories are.

Mother loved her garden, and when electricity was put on Dad was able to have installed our electric pump. Water was obtained from the spring in the garden, hence Spring Bay. I think we've all inherited our mother's love of the garden, but sadly she suffered a massive stroke whilst gardening and died later that night.

I have wonderful memories of her cooking on the Fior stove, testing the heat with her hand and producing meals that would have won her prizes these days. Scallop pies, scones, cakes, roasts and the beautiful lunches we would take on our picnics. Never complaining when we had the place filled with school friends and later boyfriends.

My children Fiona and Craig were given the same pleasures, but in a different time. Orford had become more affluent, so no riding bikes to nearby farms to get milk and cream. We now had a shop in the village where everything was available. But they enjoyed the same routine, most weekends and holidays unless school activities kept us in Sandy Bay.

Then came dances and parties, so it was probably not until they became parents themselves that they rediscovered Orford through the eyes of their children, and their love for Sunways.

So it was with tremendous sadness that circumstances caused me to sell my half-share of the family home that I dearly loved. Times were tough and I felt a great sadness that I had lost part of my life and my grief was immense.

Now here comes Nicholas, aged 11, already an outstanding and caring youngster. Seeing his grandmother in tears and said, 'Don't cry Nan. When I'm a big boy I'll buy you a home at Orford.'

True to his words, and by now an outstanding football star in the AFL, he obtained the ownership of a house that I used to visit as a very, very young girl. So thanks to Nick,

Orford has now become a haven for me. A loved and loving home to family and friends. Our happy place, and in times of sadness a healing place.

So another generation is enjoying the same activities as I had in my youth, middle and old age. My father Harold Charles Millington, being a great athlete himself, would have been so proud of Nick's success. But I doubt if he would even have barracked for St Kilda against his beloved Collingwood.

It is a family story, and we are privileged to have a beach at Orford named after my father—Millington's Beach—in honour of his generosity and leadership for the community.

When Nan finished reading the letter she had tears in her eyes as she said to me, 'Now you know why I love you so much—you've given me all this back again.'

•

My Tassie story began in Duke Street, Lower Sandy Bay, a middle- to upper-class Hobart neighbourhood—the same street that was home to a young Errol Flynn. Mum tells the story that a young Errol set fire to her great-grandmother's plaits one day in church. Which means my great-great-grandmother had a brief but heated relationship with Errol Flynn! Now there's a 'degrees of separation' story for you!

We had a three-bedroom weatherboard house with a huge walnut tree out the back. Mum and Nan would pickle walnuts, and there were jars and jars of black stuff all over the place. When I was a child, the backyard seemed huge, like a jungle. We played cricket there, and there's a famous family story of me absolutely cracking it with Nan when her bowling didn't come up to my standards. 'If you're not going to play properly, don't play at all!' I apparently screamed before storming off. I guess my competitive nature started there.

We still drive past Duke Street every now and then, just to check it out. It hasn't changed much. Not as much as when we lived there, and a growing family was becoming so squeezed for room that Opa stepped in and built an extension containing a family room and a new bathroom. Opa has always taken DIY projects to another level.

When I was six, we moved to Cheverton Parade, up above the Wrest Point Casino in that amazing, hilly part of Hobart. It was a stunning house, just magnificent, and the views . . . It had a balcony that ran all the way along the house, uninterrupted views up and down the Derwent River—almost all the way down to the Iron Pot Lighthouse and back up to the Tasman Bridge. I remember that house really well, walking down Churchill Avenue to Waimea Heights, coming home cold and wet from footy training with Sandy Bay juniors.

But even from a young age, my strongest and best memories are of Orford. We'd go there most weekends, just as Mum had, and Nan before her, setting off straight after school on Friday afternoon with a fresh uniform packed for the drive back early on Monday morning. We'd catch fish, put craypots out, build cubby houses, disappear on bikes all day long. It was me, my brother Alex, our cousin Alex Thompson (who lived next door to Nan and is her stepbrother Leith's son), another cousin Biddy who had the house behind that. We'd just go, disappear, do whatever.

We weren't allowed to go over the bridge, and if we went out on the boats we weren't allowed to go past the lighthouse. But we'd go for miles. Sometimes the grown-ups would take us camping across on Maria Island, either in the tin dish or the Bertram that belonged to our cousin's family. It was a decent-sized boat you could sleep on.

Dad, my uncles and cousins taught me to fish. We always caught stuff, a lot of flathead. I used to hate going under the bridge that crosses the river; just the shadow the bridge cast, how dark it made the water seem, always frightened me. I have a vivid memory of going under there in the tin dish as a kid and saying, 'Gee, I hope I don't catch a fish while we're going under the bridge.' And bang! I hooked onto a pike. It's funny the memories your mind retains—insignificant, yet priceless in so many ways.

Tasmania's convict history is right on your doorstep at Orford. The last ten minutes of the drive into town are stunning. Look to the left and you can see the old convict-built road, this rocky, rugged, incredible thing built by men who would have been cold, wet, hungry and weak. Port Arthur's 50 kilometres down the coast. Maria Island sits there staring at you in the distance, half an hour away by boat, a big grey mass of land rising out of the ocean with its ruins of the old penal settlement and their stories of suffering.

The Monday morning drive home has always stayed with me, a reminder of an obsession with being on time. My whole school life I felt like I was late every day, or I'd get there two minutes before the bell. I just hated being late.

There was a tree halfway between Orford and Hobart that had a splodge of white paint on it. On the way to Orford it was always part of a game of spotting landmarks as we got closer to our destination. You'd get a raspberry lolly from Nan if you were first to see the painted tree—or the bell at Buckland, the huge triangle of rock that's perched above the road a few kilometres out of town, and finally the bridge over the Prosser that showed you were there at last.

On the way back I'd sit in the back seat looking out for the tree, and when we passed it I'd work out how long we'd been driving, double it and think, 'We should be at school by this time.' It never worked out (probably because the tree wasn't exactly halfway), but I fought that battle in my mind on so many Monday mornings. I was always stressed about it. Cath's like that too; we're both really time conscious. It's something Ross Lyon was big on as well, which we all knew too well when he was coaching St Kilda. Rossy's thing was more like, 'If you're not five minutes early, you're five minutes late.'

•

When I was eight, Alex was five and Maddie was two, Mum and Dad separated for a while. It was a difficult time, but I guess at that age you just get on with things. Mum and Dad have always said that was when I became a leader, that I took on the mantle of being the man of the house. I was very aware that I was the oldest and it was my job to make sure Alex and Maddie were coping.

We lived with Mum in Cheverton Parade and every second weekend we'd stay with Dad, above the pub he was running in Battery Point. Mum remembers looking out the window as Dad came to collect us, and me standing in the driveway holding Maddie on one hip, with my other arm around Alex and a big bag of disposable nappies in my hand. Apparently before we left, I'd say to her, 'It's okay, Mum, I'll look after Alex and Maddie.' As I said, it wasn't an easy time.

Dad met someone else and after a while they decided to open a small business together. They saw the bank about a loan on one day, had it approved the next, and the day after that she was killed in a car accident. Thankfully when you're so young these things wash over you, but it must have been just awful. For everyone.

Look hard enough and you can find some light in every dark time. Mum still gets a laugh out of something I said in the car one day during that period. The driveway at Cheverton Parade was really long, and I'd made it my job to wheel the bins down on rubbish day and bring them back up to the house after they'd been emptied. We'd been out somewhere and Mum stopped at the gate when we got back so I could hop out and wheel the bins up the driveway.

Apparently I turned to Mum and said, 'Before I get the bins, Mum, I have to tell you something. I know what sex is.' Mum wondered what would come next, and then I said, 'Don't tell anybody else. It's when a man and a woman rub bottoms.' Looking back, I'm amazed I've got children.

•

Mum and Dad eventually got back together, and in 1992 we moved to the Gold Coast for a fresh start. Leaving Tasmania wasn't easy, but leaving Orford behind was devastating. I was ten, and for the next six years we only went back once. I missed it, but at the time we didn't have anywhere to stay because Nan had been forced to sell her share of Sunways. I don't remember the conversation Nan refers to in her letter, but she swears I told her, 'Don't worry Nan, I'll buy your place when I'm big enough.'

Not long after I started playing for St Kilda I was on the

lookout—if anything came up I was going to get it. It couldn't be at Shelly Beach around the corner. It couldn't be at Spring Beach or across the river. There are fewer than fifty houses in the pocket around Nan's, and some of them I wouldn't have wanted to know about. But it had to be there.

I was playing footy, earning a wage, in a position to buy something. I was going down a bit to stay at Uncle Leith's place to spend time with my cousin Alex Thompson, and a guy I know down there, Chris Dillon, knew that I was looking. His wife was taking meals around to an old couple who lived on the corner opposite Nan's old place. They were entertaining the thought of selling and he told them he had a buyer.

I put in a bid, filled out some forms. It was done under my company name, Roobound Enterprises, which nearly became a problem. The old couple said they wouldn't sell to a company, couldn't bear the thought of someone coming in, knocking down their house and building apartments. Chris assured them that wouldn't happen, that the buyer was a young guy who loved Orford and whose Nan had virtually grown up in the house across the street.

I hadn't even been through the house. I knew the block, of course; I'd walked past it every day I'd ever been to Orford. After settlement, I organised to fly down and check it out, meet Alex Thompson and another cousin, Jarrod Nation, make a start on beautifying it. Mum was flying in the next day and Nan was driving up from Hobart.

I didn't realise one of the clauses I'd agreed to in the contract was that the owners could stay on for an extra month rent free. So I've landed at the front door carrying a few tools to start renovating, and they're still in the house. They were lovely people—took me in, showed me around, said, 'Oh, you're the boy who's bought our house!' And I'm standing there trying to hide a hammer behind my back.

We haven't done a huge amount to the place—painted it, beautified it, brought in some nice furniture. Mum did the decorating, and Dad found a beautiful old table top and had it fully restored so we have a great kitchen table. The carpet was loose in all the rooms, so we've taken that up and had the boards polished. Pulled out some cabinets, opened it up a bit. It's really comfortable now.

As much as I love the place, it's really Nanna Fay's pride and joy. She's essentially the caretaker and she runs a tight ship—she gets cross with me and Cath about the state of the place, and it's our house! There are rules for when you leave—the rubbish can't go in the wheelie bin because it could sit there for weeks; it has to go in the public bin across the road. The firewood has to be stacked and the fireplace loaded, ready to go, so all you have to do is flick a match. The stove has to be off—not just at the stove but also at the fuse box outside. The TV has to be off at the wall and at the antenna, which is way across the other side of the room.

It's a military operation, but she loves it and we love her for it. And there's always orange cake in the freezer or soup that she's made, waiting for us to get there.

The last few seasons of my career I took the St Kilda first-year players down there in the pre-season. The boys would traditionally spend a weekend at Portsea or somewhere local. I said to Tony Brown, our player welfare manager, why don't we go to Tassie? Dad would come every year, which made it a lovely way for two of my worlds to collide. We were spoilt with the weather—no wind, mid-twenties, just gorgeous. It was a great way for everyone to get to know each other a bit better, with Alan Richardson and the coaching staff there but in a really informal setting. I think everyone got a lot out of it.

There's a bunkhouse out the back with three bunks and a double. I made them with my cousins and they're all right, just slabs of wood with mattresses on them. I had the mattresses specifically cut to size. Cath takes the piss out of how uncomfortable they'd be but our bedroom's in the house, so I don't have to sleep out there to find out. She reckons there's spiders as big as your open hand and won't go near it anyway. We've had a few surprises.

But really, it's absolutely fine. I got it carpeted, had power put out there. It was for Maddie and Alex. Maddie never stayed out there, not once. She wasn't going anywhere there might have been spiders or other creepy-crawlies.

With the St Kilda boys we'd go down there on the Friday, have dinner at the pub and a couple of beers. Saturday morning we'd be up early and out all day fishing and diving. I never went diving as a kid, only when I started going back and staying with my cousins after I got drafted. We don't dive to look at stuff, we dive to fish—the full 7-millimetre suit, hood, weight vest, catch bag, knife, torch. The crays hide up under rocks, in cracks, and it's dark in there, really dark.

It was a hit from the start—everyone got in the water, caught crayfish, calamari, abalone. We put nets in and caught flathead. Went back to the shack and cooked it all up, had a feast. Dad had a 44-gallon drum cut in half, put each half up on Besser blocks and there was your fire. Dad has loved the opportunity to hang out with my teammates and coaches, develop relationships so that when he bumped into them later in the year at the footy there was some commonality, a lasting link. It was great.

I've loved making stuff down there, especially with Dad and my cousins, who are incredibly handy. If the compressor's not working, they can fix it. If there's a problem somewhere around the place, they'll find a solution. I had a heap of blackwood trees along the fence that weren't growing, so we drove to Bunnings in Hobart, bought an irrigation system and put it in over an afternoon. We did it for 200 bucks; it would cost thousands if you paid someone. The trees are growing beautifully.

Not long after we'd been down with the Saints boys the second time, there was an awful tragedy. A man from Hobart had given his daughter a diving course for her birthday and they'd gone diving on the last day of the scallop season, just off Maria Island. I've had a dive at that exact spot a hundred times—it's exactly where we took the St Kilda boys, the same point, within 100 metres.

He was taken by a shark while diving with his daughter. It's unimaginable, just so sad. I haven't been back in the water since—haven't had another dive. I don't know if I will. Cath says if I want to stay married to her, I won't. It's different now that I'm a dad.

The first two times Cath came to Australia after we'd met, there wasn't enough time to get down there because she had to get back to the States for college. But once she moved out here, when we had the split round that season we were straight down to Orford. We went out to the Ile des Phoques, which is a rock in the middle of the ocean between Maria and the Schouten Islands. It's about the size of a football ground, rising up out of the water like a mountain. There are caves you can drive a 50-foot boat into and they're full of seals. That's probably why there are sharks. The water inside the caves is this neon, electric blue. It's stunning.

Another time we camped on Maria. It went from being like a lake to blowing 40 knots in the space of an hour; we had to get out of there. Our tents were punctured: the wind ripped big holes in them. It was a pretty hairy trip back.

I can go to Tassie at the drop of a hat with my phone and wallet and nothing else and I won't need a thing. I've got so many clothes there—shoes, runners, toothbrush, bathroom stuff. Nan might meet me at the airport and we'll drive up in her little car, or I'll get a cab to Oma and Opa's and pick up the ute. Once we're in Orford, there's an IGA 200 metres up the road, a great pizza shop, a cafe. I was a bit dubious about having a cafe there but it's been good to be able to go and grab brekkie or a coffee. There's a post office, a real estate agent, the primary school, the pub, and that's about it.

We usually go to the pub in Triabunna, which is a few minutes' drive up the road. The Spring Bay is a beauty, a grand old two-storey place looking out over the marina where the ferry leaves for Maria Island. It's been there since 1838, and been run by the same family for 30 years. I went to school with Liza, who lives upstairs with her husband Geoff and their young family. It's such an easy place to walk into—always a couple of locals in the bar who'll say 'G'day Nick', ask how life is on the mainland, then leave you to grab a drink and a feed.

I try to take the St Kilda boys there during their stay, and there's always a challenge laid down when it comes to dinner. There was a bloke named Woody who worked as a mechanic at the local woodchip mill (he sold me my ute). He used to go into the Spring Bay and ask for a Scotch fillet. 'But I want a double—this thick,' he'd say, holding his thumb and forefinger a couple of inches apart. After a while people started asking for the same thing, so now there's a steak on the menu, a thick-cut Scotch that's called a Woody.

Tassie

I tell the boys when we go there, 'You've gotta have a Woody.' We've gone through stages where we'd have a Woody with two fried eggs on it, onions, curried scallops, goodness knows what. It's just a 'How big a man are you?' contest. I haven't had a Woody for a while, but I still love getting down to the Spring Bay. And I still love scallops on my steak.

•

Every time I arrive in Orford I just get out of the car, throw my head back and breathe. There's no stress there. Okay, phone reception and internet reception are an issue. Or if there was a sporting event on and we didn't have Foxtel, and Maddie would have to go over to cousin Alex's to watch Liverpool, that could get a bit stressful. But it was all part of the charm of the shack.

I love going to Texas and staying at Cath's family's ranch, and essentially the shack is my ranch. In our living room in Melbourne we have two paintings on the wall—one of Nan's shack in Orford, which has been such a huge part of my life, and one we asked David Bromley to do of Cath's family ranch in Texas. The jetty is in the foreground of the painting of Nan's shack. I walked along that jetty a hundred times a summer as a kid, and it's amazing to think I can do that now with James and Will.

I'm so excited to be able to take my kids down there and do all the things I did as a kid. I think it's so important to be able to do that—particularly now, given the changing world we live in. To get away for a couple of weeks, no Foxtel, no screens, just be outside and do stuff.

Spending my childhood there shaped my love of the outdoors. The closeness I share with my extended family has a lot to do with Orford. I'm rapt that we only started going back there as a family once I bought my shack. Mum and Nan and everyone are so grateful that I did it, the joy it's given us. It's been amazing for our family.

For Maddie, from 2004 when I bought it through to the end of her life, that was her Tassie. I guess she was really a Queenslander—I was in Melbourne for nine years, away from my brother and sister, and by the time they moved to Victoria I already had the shack. Every summer, from Christmas until January, Mum, Maddie and Dad would be in Orford. As soon as training was finished, I'd get down there, and we'd all drive up to Oma and Opa's shack for Christmas Eve, then back to Orford for the rest of the holidays.

All of my best family memories are there, and I think that's the same for all of us—especially Maddie, because she spent so much time there in her last ten years.

•

Playing footy in Tassie was always different, even before Maddie died. Even just visiting there with footy as the premise.

Years ago we had a community camp there and organised some promotional activities. Grant Thomas was coach and I told him as we drove into town from the airport, 'I grew up here. We used to live above that pub.' So he stopped the car, we walked into the pub, and there were Dad's old mates sitting at the bar. And me, Thommo and Aaron Hamill just piled in, had a beer and a chat, then kept going. That's the sort of bloke Thommo is; he's big on that stuff.

I did a clinic at Dodge's Ferry with Justin Koschitzke and took him to Oma and Opa's shack. It was odd, the blending of two worlds you never thought would collide—your childhood and your career.

The first time I played in Tassie after Maddie's passing was probably the hardest game of my career. I cried before most games that season; would have to find somewhere quiet to go and let it out. I never told anyone, and I didn't think anyone knew, but Billy Longer looked at me before that game at Bellerive against North Melbourne and he knew. I was in tears up until five minutes before we ran out.

We were staying in town, across the bridge, up on the rise, looking across to Bellerive. I could see the funeral home where Maddie's funeral had been. Just around the corner was the factory where they made her coffin. It was in my face the whole time. That was tough.

Robbie Tarrant was playing on me and he was just into me from the start. It was one of the few times in my career where I thought, 'I don't have any fight in me today. Just leave me alone. I can't do this for two hours. I can't fight back.'

I never saw Dad play footy—he'd already finished, but I know he was a decent player, first with Clarence then Richmond in the country just north of Hobart, then Hutchins Old Boys. I saw Uncle Chris play. The local footy was televised by the ABC back then, and I went to games at Bellerive and North Hobart Oval. I had a scrapbook; if Chris was in the paper, I cut it out and pasted it in. I knew Chris was a big footy name in Tassie.

I never really heard Dad or my uncles talk about whether Tasmania should have a team in the AFL, but I'd love them to. If Tasmania got everything Gold Coast and GWS have been given, I don't subscribe to the argument that it wouldn't work. I understand the decision the AFL have made: it's a captive audience, you've got them already, why put a team there when we can go and capture an audience we don't have? But really, if you can make Gold Coast and GWS work, Tassie will work.

Potentially that's the team I would have wanted to play for. When I got drafted, I was big on the idea of coming to the mecca of footy, but at that stage my affinity to Tassie wasn't as strong as it is now. Since coming back to Orford, spending so much time there as a family, it's something that's grown. If a Tasmanian team had come in when Gold Coast did in 2009, who knows?

One of the things about being Tasmanian is you realise how small the place is, how many people you know. When the Port Arthur massacre happened in 1996, it shook us because my Aunty Mandy knew someone who was killed. Someone else we knew had interacted with Martin Bryant not long before, remembered him being strange. Hobart's pretty small—if I go back to Hobart, I bump into people. You just do.

James Henderson, Ricky Ponting's manager and another expat Tasmanian, started up a regular gathering in Melbourne a while ago as a way of networking. I took Dad along to the first night and it was a pretty impressive room: Brendon Gale, Matthew Richardson, Ricky Ponting. I go to something like that and I feel 100 per cent Tasmanian.

I was picked in the Queensland team of the century after I'd been at St Kilda for only a couple of years. I don't feel I'm being unfaithful to Queensland by saying that I don't feel emotionally connected to Queensland at all. I don't get the feeling going there that I get going to Tassie. I'm Tasmanian.

3
(IN)EXPERIENCE

I think I've always known what's right, the way things should be, how to act and behave. It's only upon reflection that I've realised how naive I've been at various moments through my life.

Sometimes it's been a blessing, shielding me from the pressure that would undoubtedly have accompanied having my eyes wide open. Sometimes the way I've acted, the way I've presented myself—on and off the field—has painted a picture that doesn't stack up with the person I am. I can understand people getting the wrong impression. If a young player acted now like I sometimes did, I'd think, 'What a dickhead.'

I was nineteen and in my second year when I first went on *The Footy Show*. There was one night in particular, and it makes me cringe now, that I went on there and tried to be funny. I'd seen an earlier show where the audience were talking over someone, drowning them out, and I remembered either Jason Akermanis or Shane Crawford telling them to shut up. I tried to do the same thing and the crowd turned on me, booed, were yelling out 'shut up' while I was trying to talk. Thinking about it now I get the sweats: it was horrible. At the time I just thought I was being funny. I should have known better. I'm not a funny person.

Another time Clinton Casey, who was the Richmond president, was a guest. He was talking about redeveloping their Punt Road headquarters, how they needed some huge amount of money to do it, and I said something like, 'Why don't you tip in? You've got a stack of dough.' It was an incredibly disrespectful thing to say. I was young, wide-eyed and caught up in the moment.

I spoke to Dad on the way home and he told me how embarrassed he was, that I'd let myself down. The next day my coach, Grant Thomas, said the same thing. Dad rang again and told me I needed to track down Clinton Casey's number, call him and apologise. I did, and he really appreciated it. 'I know you're a young man,' he said. 'It's taken a lot to make this call.'

A couple of nights later I went to the Hall of Fame dinner as a guest of Carl Ditterich. On the next table, with his back to mine, was Clinton Casey. If I hadn't made that phone call it

(In)Experience

would have been the most awkward situation imaginable, but it worked out fine. I was so lucky. I learnt from it: how to read situations better, how to be myself and not someone I thought others wanted me to be.

With maturity I realised how naive I was when I started out. That was a blessing and a curse, but it's made me better. Or at least those experiences have.

•

My earliest football was unremarkable. I started with the Sandy Bay juniors, which was great because they were the Seahawks and wore Hawthorn jumpers and I was a Hawthorn supporter. When you went up to the next age level it was the Seagulls and you wore North Melbourne jumpers, but for my first year of footy I wore a Hawthorn jersey with No. 19 on the back, just like Jason Dunstall—my favourite player, whose poster was on my bedroom wall.

Dad barracked for St Kilda, wanted me to be a Saints fan too. But I said, 'Nah, they never win, I'm not going for them.'

The first time I played was a game at Kingston. I was a bit scared, a bit shy, didn't really know if I wanted to play. There was a kid with curly red hair called Aaron Buckland who was a gun. I was a bit intimidated. Aaron was playing under 8s. I ended up playing under 7s.

I played three years and Dad was coach each year. He was ridiculously fair. We had the awards each week, and the best players would appear in the Hobart *Mercury*. Every kid had a turn of being in the best, everyone got a run in different positions, and everyone had to spend time on the bench. Dad treated it as team policy, figuring that every kid and every kid's parents got a big kick out of seeing their child's name in the paper. There was a little kid who spent pretty much the whole season making mud pies during games, but one week he somehow managed to kick a goal. He was named first in the best that week.

Parents used to come up to Dad and say, 'It's really unfair that you never put Nick down as one of the best players.' But he'd defend his policy to the hilt. I didn't mind that so much, but I lost it one day when he left me on the bench and put everyone else on the ground. We were playing at Parliament Street, up the road in Sandy Bay. I started the last quarter on the bench with some other kids and was supposed to go back on halfway through the quarter. Everyone else got back on except me. There was this park at the back of the ground with a huge slide that went down to the creek below. I jumped on the slide, went down to the bottom and just sat there. I didn't shake hands with anyone, wouldn't talk to Dad. I was convinced he only did it because it was me. I was filthy.

Mum says I wasn't a sulky kid and it was really out of character, but that day I just lost my mind. Dad maintains he

(In)Experience

wasn't hard on me, but he will admit he was more focused on looking after the other kids. I guess he was so conscious of not being seen to play favourites.

I was fairly tall, but not one of the biggest kids. I didn't watch much footy; as a young kid I probably didn't even know the difference between AFL and TFL. I had a scrapbook with cuttings of Uncle Chris taken out of the local paper, and I collected footy cards. I've still got my tin out in the shed at home. But I wasn't obsessed with footy.

I played soccer for school on Saturday mornings and was really into that. Footy was Sunday morning, but the bit I enjoyed most was going to watch Dad's old team, Hutchins Old Boys, at Memorial Oval in Sandy Bay on a Saturday afternoon. Dad's circle had boys around my age—my cousin Alex Thompson, and Tom Gibson, who ended up rowing for Australia. We'd run around the Hutchins campus being absolute menaces, then go up to the clubrooms at six o'clock, find our dads, get them to finish their beers and eventually head home.

There was a rowing cage at Hutchins that sticks in my mind; it was like an outdoor Ergo with an actual boat in the water. We'd climb in there and have a go. In the depths of winter the water would freeze on top; you could lift huge plates of ice off and smash them over your head, pretending you were breaking plates of glass. I remember doing that and getting yelled at.

Sounds and smells stayed with me. Walking past the rooms when the seniors were warming up, hearing the count as they sprinted on the spot—'one, two, three, four!'—and the stops on their boots clattering on the concrete floor. The Hutchins theme song after games they won, a primal war cry that doesn't actually have any meaning at all but was always so rousing. I remember the smell of the change rooms—the Deep Heat and liniment—and the big tubs of PK chewing gum. AFL rooms don't smell like that. Suburban rooms do, but rooms in the AFL are so big and sterile, and no one uses Deep Heat anymore.

We'd have a footy and have a kick, but we could just as easily spend three hours running around playing. At Queenborough Oval, the Sandy Bay ground, there was a huge hedge all the way around the perimeter, a massive thing. We loved going to games there because it meant climbing through the hedge all afternoon. One time Alex Thompson's sister, Elle, went missing for hours. I'm pretty sure the police were called. And about 6 p.m. she just walked out of the hedge, wondering what all the fuss was about.

There was something magical about just being at the footy, without even taking notice of the game. Suburban footy is special, so different from the controlled environment of the AFL where you can't have a kick at half-time, can't go on the ground. Can't climb in a hedge.

After we moved to Queensland when I was ten, I didn't play football for a couple of years. I played soccer instead for the Burleigh Bears. I guess I just liked it more. I was playing

(In)Experience

cricket with Broadbeach Junior CC, went down there with Tristan Showers, a mate from school. A few of the guys in our team also played footy at Broadbeach, and one day, around the time the seasons overlapped, we were at cricket training and a few mates were waving and calling out as they ran a warm-up lap in their footy jumpers. I was like, 'How long's this thing been going on?' That rekindled my interest in footy.

I started Little Athletics when we moved too, in the under 10s. I wasn't the fastest, wasn't the best long-distance runner, but I was pretty good at everything. I won the club champion award a couple of times, but only because the best sprinters were hopeless at the longer stuff. The 400 and 800 metres were my main events. I went to state championships with those one year, up to Townsville for a week with Mum. I did okay, nothing special. I could run, but I didn't know what it meant to work hard and push myself. I hadn't worked that out yet.

•

It's always annoyed me that when the conversation about footballers who could have made it as cricketers comes up, I never get a mention. It's always the same ones—Jonathan Brown, Luke Ball, Luke Hodge, James Gwilt, Jimmy Bartel. No Nick Riewoldt. I never sneak in there. But I played in all the representative teams from the under 13s; made the Queensland under 15s and topped the batting averages on a tour of New South

Wales; and was in the Pace Australia squad with Mitch Johnson, Shane Watson and Nathan Rimmington as an under 16. I was a better cricketer than footballer, and I definitely put more time into it.

I bowled left arm—not super-quick, but I could swing it and land it pretty much on the same spot. My stock ball was a big left-arm over-the-wicket in-swinger, and I got a lot of guys out lbw or bowled. Occasionally I'd hold one across the seam and push it across them. If I was playing for Gold Coast or South-East Queensland, I'd usually open the bowling, but I'd come on first change at higher levels.

One day, when I was about sixteen, I took 7 for 17 in a game, including bowling a kid with a big in-swinger that somehow broke the stump into three pieces. I had the bits of the stump and the ball in my cricket bag for ages, then they went missing. I looked for them everywhere and had pretty much forgotten about them, then that Christmas Mum and Dad gave me the broken stump and ball mounted in a wooden box with a glass front. It's a pretty cool memento of a different time in my life.

My bowling coach was Frank Tyson, the Englishman who got the nickname 'Typhoon' when he scared the life out of Australia's batsmen and took 28 wickets on the 1954–55 Ashes tour. He liked it so much here he emigrated, and I was glad he had. I could always swing it, but he taught me how to bowl with swing and control. He had these amazing drills—I'd sit at home for hours holding a cricket ball with the seam upright and practise running my index and middle fingers down either side. He had these special, tiny little cricket balls—he reckoned if you could control one of them it would be easy with a regular ball.

I had a batting coach too, an incredibly tough man named Ray Frost. I batted in the middle order, and he turned me into a good player. I practised for hours and hours—I've still got a video at home, the piece of rope tied to a beam, a sock on the end with a ball inside, me hitting it back and forth, back and forth, back and forth. It was monotonous. Alex always thought I was a bit of a loser but I was just determined to improve.

I don't think Ray was very well liked, just because he was so hard. We'd train at Kerrydale, home of the Gold Coast Dolphins. He didn't have a bowling machine, so he'd stand halfway down the pitch and throw balls at me. Hard. I remember showing up once; it must have been a chilly day because I had a footy jumper over the top of my cricket shirt. Ray said, 'Take that off, son. You're gunna be sweating.'

There were times when I'd walk into the nets feeling scared, even though I had all the gear on, helmet included. It got to the point where Ray would stand half-pitch with a bat, toss the ball up in the air and hit it at me. It wasn't about technique; it was all about protecting yourself—get your bat in the way, don't let the ball hurt you. Dad would come and watch every session. God knows what he must have thought.

I became technically very proficient. I wasn't a slogger, didn't pull or hook, but I could cut, was good off my pads and drove the ball well. I played straight. At that age I didn't put any extra work into my football—I'd already worked out that you could make up for technical flaws in footy, but not in cricket. Cricket was more of an art: you're either technically good or you're no good. I guess it was that '10,000 hours' theory that you hear the great coaches espouse.

I'd never made a hundred before Ray's coaching, and I came out in the first game after I'd been with him all winter and made a ton for Gold Coast in the Lord's Taverners. Then I got another one in the second game, all on the back of Ray. But his impact was even more profound. At sixteen, I'd never been a great footballer compared to my peers, just okay. After training for cricket with Ray Frost, being submitted to his unusual and downright frightening methods, I came out and marked everything once the footy season started. My reflexes, the hand–eye stuff that's so important, had improved out of sight. And it was all down to a cricket coach.

I loved cricket and still do, but it wasn't always a barrel of fun for Alex and Maddie. When I started making representative squads and the like, the games would often be played a couple of hours or more from the Gold Coast. More than once they were at Boonah, which was a two-hour trip west. One day Maddie spotted Mum and Dad packing the Esky, getting everything ready, and asked where we were going. Mum said, 'To Nick's

(In)Experience

cricket.' Maddie groaned. 'Oh, not Bastard Boonah again!' That's what Boonah has been ever since—Bastard Boonah.

•

I made the Queensland under-16s football team later that year and we headed down to Melbourne for the national championships. We played at Oakleigh then Sandringham, a game at Punt Road, and trained at the ground opposite the zoo. It was an early eye-opener to the big world out there—we stayed in a backpackers' in the city, and blokes walked up and down Swanston Street going to the $2 peep shows.

I played full-forward, thought I had a decent carnival but knew that wasn't necessarily enough. Michael Osborne, who became a Hawthorn premiership player, was a star and won the Division Two medal. Luke Weller, who played a few games for Brisbane and Richmond, and Michael Davis, who went to Essendon, made the Australian Institute of Sport team as well. I was devastated to miss out, thought that was it. I probably hadn't played well enough, but I thought I was good enough.

At the time the Brisbane Lions fielded a reserves team in the QAFL called the Cubs. Along with their senior-listed players who weren't getting a game, they'd select promising young blokes who weren't getting a senior game for their club side. In 1999 I was playing reserves for Southport as a sixteen-year-old and that season I played at least half a dozen games for the Cubs. It was great experience; my teammates were Simon Black, Luke Power, Daniel Bradshaw, Tim Notting—guys who became stars of the Lions' power era—plus guys like Brett Voss, Marcus Picken and Shannon Rusca, who all played senior AFL footy.

I played some decent footy in defence. We had a team rule: when the ball wasn't in your vicinity, you had to stand with your arm across your opponent's chest. We played Maine in a Lions' curtain raiser at the Gabba one day and they had these brothers, the Tapps, who were amateur boxers. I put my arm across this Tapp bloke's chest and he said, 'If you don't take that away, I'm gunna punch you right in the face.'

From behind me I heard a teammate yell out, 'Team rule—put your arm up!'

I'm thinking, 'Christ, here we go . . .' So I put my arm up and this bloke Tapp says again, 'Next time the ball comes down, I'm gunna kill you.'

So the ball was kicked into their forward line, I turned around and ran back with the flight, and whack! I don't know if I was concussed; all I can remember is sitting on the bench, trying to get myself together and Leigh Matthews turns to me and says, 'Good courage, son.' I hadn't lost my memory anyway, because it was the first thing I said to Dad after the game: 'Leigh Matthews told me I had courage!'

•

(In)Experience

Winning a football premiership ended my cricket career. It was for Southport reserves in 1999; the seniors won as well, and it was on.

Southport had two ovals, and they set up a marquee on the second one. There was a refrigerated truck with all the beer in it, and at some stage during the night someone snapped the hinges off with bolt cutters and hooked into the contents. The premiership cup ended up in a bonfire; a couple of blokes were on crutches from injuries they'd copped in the grand final, and their crutches ended up on the fire too. Someone went and bought a car for 500 bucks and started rally-driving around the oval. It was loose. Those blokes knew how to party.

Dad had always encouraged me to keep going with cricket, figuring two eggs in a basket were better than one. The day after the Southport grand final was the state under-17s trials in Brisbane. I didn't want to go, but Dad convinced me that if nothing else it might help my footy. 'Look at a guy like Brad Green. He got drafted to Melbourne, they still talk about him being a good soccer player and a good cricketer. It just adds a bit to your pedigree.'

So at some stage Dad came and dragged me away from these mad premiership celebrations and the next morning we drove up to Allan Border Field—except I wasn't playing at Border Field. Eventually we got to the right ground and they'd already finished warming up. I was thrown the new ball. I hadn't played for a while and wasn't exactly brimming with confidence—not to mention not feeling overly flash.

I put my fingers across the seam to try to minimise the swing, was hoping just to land the ball in a half-decent spot. I bowled five wides in a row, and that was it. I remember one of the officials asking me, 'What happened to that beautiful in-swinger?' I didn't have the heart to tell him it had been chucked on the bonfire at the Southport footy ground.

•

By that stage I'd played in the AFL under-18 national carnival and played well. Against Tasmania I played on Danny Roach, an underage star who ended up being drafted at pick seven by Collingwood, and had a really good game. I'd been lucky to get a game at all—Robbie Copeland would have played instead of me but he hurt his ankle in a practice game. I played well and kept my spot. I was bottom-age and still ineligible to get drafted, but that was when I started thinking I might at least get rookie-listed the next year by Brisbane.

The first game of the 2000 national under-18 championships the following year was at Princes Park in Melbourne. I played centre half-forward at one end, and Justin Koschitzke was centre half-forward for New South Wales–ACT at the other. I'd never heard of Kosi before then, but we took about fifteen marks each, kicked a couple of goals and straight away

(In)Experience

we were on the radar. The next game was against Northern Territory in Geelong. I was playing well, had taken a couple of strong marks backing into packs, but I hurt my quad just before half-time and that was the end of my championships.

By that stage Brisbane had been in touch, given me a pair of Puma King boots that I thought were great, and a Brisbane Lions footy bag which I proudly (and stupidly) used in front of everyone, like a knob. There was clearly a bit of interest and I was starting to think I might get drafted, but I still had no idea how high.

When Vic Metro played Vic Country in Division One at the MCG, I went along with Michael Davis, who played for Queensland but was living in Melbourne. Everyone was talking about Laurence Angwin, a big kid from the Dandenong Stringrays who was tipped to go No. 1 in the draft. I remember watching him and thinking, 'Oh, that's him then . . .' Mick introduced me to player manager Paul Connors and we started talking about the draft. And Paul said, 'Don't worry, you'll go top 10.'

It was like getting whacked in the head. I was like, 'Top 10? What the hell is he talking about? This bloke's mad!' I was playing Division Two; these blokes were playing Division One on the MCG. I didn't think I was anywhere near their level.

I recovered from the thigh strain and finished the QAFL season strongly. My form must have been good enough for a whisper to go around that I'd won the Grogan Medal for best and fairest in the competition. It didn't happen, but I'd attracted enough attention for a few AFL clubs to come and watch without me knowing they were there.

Draft camp was the first time I thought, 'Shit, I'm gunna go pretty early.' I sat down with Collingwood officials and Mick Malthouse, who was coach, asked me who I thought I played like. That was a really hard question. Years later at St Kilda, the same question was asked of a kid we were interested in and he said, 'I'm a combination of Lance Franklin and Cyril Rioli.' Like, really, you're the best player of all time?

I said, 'Chris Tarrant.' He was a young, mobile forward who'd started kicking a few bags of goals.

Malthouse just said, 'It doesn't matter anyway—you won't still be around by the time we get a pick.' And Collingwood had pick three.

I met with Brisbane—Leigh Matthews, footy manager Graeme Allan and recruiter Kinnear Beatson—and they floated the idea of not nominating for the draft so they could push to get a rule changed that limited their zone to players living within 50 kilometres of the Brisbane GPO. I was down on the Gold Coast, about 75 kilometres away, and the Lions were arguing with the AFL that their zone should be expanded to a 100-kilometre radius. They got it changed the next year, but ironically missed out on David Hale, who lived at Coolangatta, 102 kilometres from the GPO.

(In)Experience

I came away from the meeting with the Lions wondering what all the fuss was about. I was thinking, 'You've got the wrong bloke.' I had no base for comparison. I knew I was one of the best players for my age in Queensland, but I was like, 'It's Queensland—it's not Victoria, it's not South Australia, it's not WA.'

In the end, it was as if going at No. 1 happened almost without me knowing it. I just didn't see it. Being at Griffith University helped shelter me. I used to borrow Mum's or Dad's car in the morning or get a lift with a mate, go to my classes or tutes, walk the couple of kilometres to Southport footy ground for training and head home. That was my year. Most of my mates knew I played footy, but they didn't even know what the AFL draft was, let alone that I was about to be taken at No. 1.

I was doing an exercise science degree and the first semester I was fully engaged. The second semester I had to put off some exams to head down to Melbourne for the draft. I told a few friends and they were like, 'What are you talking about?' I sat an exam on my own after I got back, but I hadn't properly prepared, had hardly even looked at a book. I still have nightmares about it, about not being ready, feeling stressed out. And then thinking to myself, 'It doesn't matter, I'll be playing footy anyway.'

Halfway through the exam, I think it was some sort of biological studies, I just got up, handed the paper to the professor and said, 'I'm sorry, I don't want to waste any more of your time. That's all I've got.' I got through ten units for the year, somehow. But getting drafted put an end to my student days.

I was the first top 10 pick to come out of Queensland, not to mention the first No. 1. And you still had to dig half a dozen pages into the sports section of the *Gold Coast Bulletin* to find it. A bloke called Terry Wilson wrote the story. He's still there; he interviewed me ahead of my 300th game in 2016.

I was incredibly naive. My friends didn't comprehend what it meant; even my family didn't get it. I don't think we had any idea what was to come.

•

Mum and Dad went down to Melbourne with me for the draft, and we stayed at the Buckingham Motor Inn on the Nepean Highway. I knew by then that St Kilda were going to take Kosi and me at picks one and two, but didn't know in which order. Mum still talks about her first encounter with John Beveridge, who was the Saints' recruiter. She'd only spoken to John over the phone and was taken by his command of language, the way he articulates everything so beautifully, and most of all by his strong voice. She pictured him as a huge man.

John arrived at the Buckingham to meet Mum and Dad. Mum heard the knock at the door and looked through the peephole to find this small man with Coke-bottle glasses;

(In)Experience

she reckoned he looked like Mr Magoo. She thought it was someone who worked at the motor inn, answered the door and said, 'Yes, can I help you?' John put out his hand and in that wonderful voice of his said, 'Fiona, lovely to meet you.'

John took us around a few different host families, looking for somewhere for me to live. It was awkward. We'd go through their house and it was like, 'Yeah, I don't really like the bathroom . . .' or whatever. I felt like a real estate agent. Kosi was in Year 12 and in the middle of exams so I had to make the decision for both of us. We ended up going with a lady in Brighton, Virginia Dunleavy, who had two spare rooms and was prepared to take both of us. I didn't want to live by myself.

The draft was held in a function room at Rod Laver Arena, broadcast on Channel Seven. I was called up on stage, gave Mum and Dad a hug, then Kosi came up as pick two with his family. It was weird. He had to fly home for an exam, so I did some media and we flew out that night.

By this stage I'd hired Ricky Nixon from Flying Start as my manager. That process was another eye-opener. It was a choice between three. John Longmire, who's now the coach of Sydney but back then was with the management group IMG, took Dad and me to Indy on the Gold Coast. I'd done work experience with IMG and loved it, and Indy was a great day. We were in a suite on pit straight, had it all laid on. It was the first time I met Sam Newman, who was up there racing his car.

Paul Connors was also keen to sign me. He came to the house and picked me up, took me and a few mates out on the town. Clearly that resonated with me, as I came away from that night wanting to sign with Paul.

Ricky knew what he was doing—he came around and had a meal with Mum and Dad. They stepped in and strongly recommended I go with Ricky. Then they made me make the phone calls to John and Paul myself. Paul was the hard one; I think I might have got upset on the phone breaking the news to him. I felt like he thought I was a sure thing, that I was letting him down.

My first day at St Kilda, I walked into the Trevor Barker Room at Moorabbin trying to look as cool as I could. Talk about naive. I had my best Gold Coast kit on—three-quarter cargoes with the string on the cuff that you could tighten, a half button-up white T-shirt, a ratty, surfie hairstyle even though I was never a surfie. The older blokes must have thought, 'Who the fuck is this bloke?' It was just horrific.

There were eleven new players at the club: Stevie Lawrence, Matthew Capuano, Fraser Gehrig, Aaron Hamill, Craig Callaghan, Robert Powell, Daniel Wulf, Brett Voss, Mark Gale, Kosi and myself, plus Stephen Milne and Brett Moyle promoted off the rookie list. Everyone had to get up and say a bit about themselves. And there's me trying to be Mr Cool and looking like a complete dick. I said something about where I was from and how I was into surfing. The truth is I couldn't even get up on a board, but I thought everyone would expect someone from the Gold Coast to be a surfer. What the senior blokes like Robert Harvey, Barry Hall, 'Spida' Everitt and Nathan Burke must have made of me, it frightens me to think.

Malcolm Blight was the new coach, two years on from winning back-to-back premierships with Adelaide. He mapped out the plan for the pre-season, said we wouldn't be riding bikes, because the last time he looked there was no velodrome on the footy field. And we wouldn't be swimming, because there was no pool out there either. We wouldn't be touching footballs until after Christmas. All we'd be doing was running. And more running. How excited was I?

We did our whole pre-season at Monash University, three days a week. Tuesday, Thursdays and weekends were for golf—this is Blighty—and we'd do weights at 9 a.m. Monday, Wednesday and Friday, then run in the afternoon at 3 p.m. We'd drive out to Monash, me and Kosi in his old EB Falcon—Kosi driving and me next to him with the Melways. We'd do weights, come home, have lunch, maybe have a snooze, play some table tennis, then drive back in the afternoon and run one-kilometre time trials. That was pre-season—essentially an hour and a half twice a day, three days a week. Nine hours a week all up.

Not long after I'd arrived at the club a few of the senior players thought they'd do the right thing and take me out. Kosi must have gone back to the farm, but Stevie Lawrence,

Fraser Gehrig, Cappers and a few of us went out to the Spy Lounge in the city. Our major sponsor at Southport was Cocktails and Dreams in Surfer's Paradise, so I'd obviously been out to nightclubs. But this was different.

We walked in and someone handed us a drink card. It was the best night ever, and I'm there thinking, 'How good is this? Is this what goes on? This is unbelievable!' I didn't think for a second anyone would have any idea who we were.

The next day I rang Michael Davis, who I hung out with a lot in my first couple of years. 'You wouldn't believe this place I went to last night! Wanna go tonight?' So we walked into the Spy Lounge again, asked for drink cards, had another awesome night. Mick had a heap of school friends, girls, it was awesome.

Monday morning I walked into the club and footy manager Brian Waldron called me into his office. I didn't have a clue what it was about, and he asked, 'How come you were out two nights in a row on the weekend, getting drink cards in a nightclub? Are you a party boy?'

It was mind-blowing. I couldn't believe he knew. I wasn't in trouble, but he just laid it out for me that I was a public figure now, that I couldn't just do as I pleased. It was the first time I thought, 'Things are different now—my life's changed.' Not to say the penny dropped there and then, but it was the first time I realised I'd been naive. And that I would have to wise up.

4
COMPETITIVENESS

I've always been a bad loser. I don't think that's necessarily a bad thing. It's okay to hate losing, for it to bore so deep into you that you never forget the hole it leaves. That you'll do everything to make sure the feeling is different next time. It's when losing strays into the sphere of blame and excuses that it gets ugly. When you're thinking, 'I lost, but it's not my fault. It was his fault.' Or, 'I had a cold.' I've never been one for excuses, but I've been a bad loser.

It comes down to competitiveness. Without doubt it's been a trait that's made me, but equally it's made me vulnerable at times, isolated me. When I retired, journalist Mark Robinson made a comment that I'd played with 'a resting bitch face' for seventeen years, been wound up like a top, but when

I announced that I was finishing up people finally saw me smile. He had a point. That competitiveness has been there as long as I can remember, even before that day when I cracked the shits because Dad didn't put me on the ground, and I went down the big Parliament Street park slide and sat brooding at the bottom.

It's not just about losing—it's measuring so much of your self worth by how you do things, and feeling inadequate when you haven't done something as well as you know you could have. I've had games where we've won and I've played okay, but I might have shanked a shot at goal or made some other basic mistake. That night I wouldn't be able to sleep. It made me feel dirty, and I'd want to keep talking about it until someone said, 'Don't worry about it, you still played well.' I'd search for something to help me cleanse. The whole week, I'd just feel dirty.

It got to the point when we were kids that Alex and Maddie wouldn't even play Mario Kart or FIFA on PlayStation with me, because I just couldn't handle losing. I'd throw the controls, break stuff. I look back and think, 'What an idiot.' Carrying on like that because I'd lost a meaningless game. I didn't have a clue what real loss felt like. Alex reckons there was a mercy streak underneath the competitiveness, that I'd let him win sometimes, but I can't remember at what. Maybe the odd video game, but certainly never anything physical.

Dad's competitive; so was Maddie. Mum reckons she's always felt sorry for Alex, who was surrounded by people who would

Competitiveness

do anything to win, while he was happy just to be playing the game. We grew up making up games—you couldn't just throw a frisbee, it had to be frisbee golf. Tennis would be American or Canadian—two against one so everyone was involved. If we were playing golf, I'd say stupid stuff when Alex was about to chip or putt like, 'A thousand bucks if you get it in.' We had one of those miniature houses in the backyard for James to play in, and I once bet Alex a grand he couldn't put a footy through the window. He put it straight through, but I reminded him that he owed me $2000 from the bond on a house we'd shared way back: 'You still owe me a thousand.'

When I lived with Kosi (Justin Koschitzke) and Joey (Leigh Montagna), they stopped playing backyard cricket with me because I took it too seriously. I'd try to bat all afternoon. If we ever had a hit at the club, when it was my turn to bat, Schneids (Adam Schneider) would say, 'Oh, here we go—it's a Test match now!' He'd get in my head about how seriously I took it, and straight away I'd be thinking, 'Stuff you, Schneids!' And I'd try to slog it and get out. He'd laugh, and I'd be like my head was about to pop off. He's good at winding blokes up, Schneids. Alex reckons you knew when a game with me was over—when I'd had enough, I'd hit the ball over the fence, in the water, wherever it couldn't be found.

Schoolwork was different—I tried really hard, I was a good student, but I wasn't competitive about it like I was with sport. I was dux of Robina Primary School which went up to the end of Grade 7, and I did the hard subjects at secondary level—physics, chemistry, maths. But we had some freaks at All Saints Anglican School. In Queensland back then you got what was called an Overall Position, or OP score, which was on a scale of 1–26. A score of 1 was the top 1 per cent, and we had a dozen kids get that. I got an OP6, which equated to just over 90 per cent. Solid. It's not a 99.

I got the marks I did because I worked hard. Dad talks about taking me and Michael Osborne, who went on to play for Hawthorn, up to state underage training in Brisbane, at least once a week from under-16 through under-18 level. I'd make Dad drive back to the Gold Coast with the interior light on in the car so I could study. Mum reckons wanting to succeed at everything I do is in my DNA. She'll tell people I wanted to be a marine biologist. I reckon I only said that because I thought it sounded cool.

With academic stuff, it's either right or wrong, whereas in sport there are degrees to how you perform. If you're an A student you're generally going to get an A. You're not going to have that day a batsman has in cricket, where no matter how good you are you can cop a great ball and you're out for a duck. The fact that there's nothing you could have done about it never made me feel any better.

I was playing First XI cricket for the school when I was in Year 8. We played a big game one day against a touring school; it went for the whole day on a Friday. There was a big crowd

Competitiveness

around the oval at lunchtime and again after the last bell when I came out to bat. I was so pumped up, playing in front of everyone. And I got a first-ball duck. Cleaned up, bowled.

I felt a humiliation that I couldn't shrug off. Walking off, I wanted to be anywhere else; I just hated it. I couldn't see beyond a foot in front of me; I just wanted to crawl into a hole and not come out. It didn't matter that I was a thirteen-year-old playing against seventeen- and eighteen-year-olds. All I felt was embarrassment.

A couple of years earlier, in late primary school, there had been an athletics carnival in which another kid and I were level on points for the age champion award going into the last race. We cooked up a plan to dead heat so we'd both be age champion. It was the 200 metres, around the bend, and I was so anxious and apprehensive at the start. Nervous about not doing well. And this other kid got me on the line. I cracked it. We'd tried to manufacture the result and I still lost. I was furious.

There's no question the way I'm wired has made me hard to be around at times. In 2003 we played North Melbourne in a Saturday afternoon game and hung on to win a close one. It had been pre-arranged that everyone would come back to Kosi and my place and have a few beers. I hadn't played well, so even though we'd won I made up a story, said I was crook in the guts, and went to my room. I don't even know how many people were there, because I didn't come out all night. I didn't want to be around anyone. I was filthy on myself, embarrassed. And we'd won.

I know behind my back they would have been saying stuff denigrating me, and fair enough. For a while I was like, 'What do you want me to do? Isn't it a good thing that I'm pissed off?' The feedback was that it's okay to be critical of yourself, but it's harmful to be so consumed by your own performance. Especially when we win—it's just a bad look.

That period didn't last long; I got better at channelling my competitiveness. But along the way it made life more difficult than it needed to be.

•

When Kosi and I started living together, we weren't exactly two peas in a pod—me fresh out of the Gold Coast, him off a farm at Brocklesby, a town of barely 200 people just over the New South Wales–Victorian border. Kosi was carefree, didn't try to be anything he wasn't. We hit it off straight away, which in hindsight was almost surprising. Although we would become so much more than teammates and housemates, there was this deep-seated, fierce competitiveness between us that many friendships don't survive.

When we first arrived at the club Kosi had an issue with his groin and had to do a lot of swimming. He was a terrible swimmer. I could swim well, and I was out running and

Competitiveness

preparing well for our first season. Then on the last day of pre-Christmas training, doing nothing more strenuous than a quad stretch, I felt something go 'pop'. I'd torn the meniscus in my knee. There were lots of complications over the coming months, and I didn't play until round 15.

Mum and Dad were down in Melbourne, which was good because I was so upset when I got back to the house. Kosi came home, grabbed his goggles from his bedroom, came out and threw them to me on the couch. 'Here, you'll need these,' he said. Everyone laughed—it was funny—but inside I just wanted to punch him in the face.

When he made his debut in round 3, I was insanely jealous. It was weird. Seeing him play when I couldn't ripped me apart inside, but our friendship only became stronger. At the end of that 2001 season we went to Bali with Stevie Lawrence, Fraser Gehrig and Caydn Beetham. It was the first time either of us had been overseas and we had a ball. Back home we did everything together, and when I got a girlfriend for the first time since I'd moved to Melbourne and Kosi started seeing his future wife Alicia, we'd all hang out together. But right at the start there was tension. The tension of competitiveness, buzzing just below the surface.

In our second season, the wheel turned. Kosi had won the Rising Star award in 2001 while I'd watched through gritted teeth. In 2002 he hurt his back in round 4 and didn't play again all year. I took his spot at centre half-back and won the Rising

Star. I was so distracted by my own stuff—my performance, realising I could play AFL football and play it well—that I didn't even notice how he was coping, just as I don't think Kosi noticed how I was holding up the year before.

In truth there was competition within the whole group. We were so young—the emerging leaders group that Thommo put together included myself, Kosi, Joey, Bally (Luke Ball), Dal (Nick Dal Santo), X (Xavier Clarke) and Goose (Matt Maguire). It was a healthy competitiveness, not a sniping, call-a-bloke-names-behind-his-back thing. Clearly it never hurt Kosi and my relationship, didn't stop us from becoming friends for life. But it was there.

Thommo was all over it. He'd swung me forward in the last game of 2002 and I'd kicked six against Melbourne, so when we lined up for an intra-club practice match at Moorabbin late in the next summer, Kosi was at centre half-back for one team and I was centre half-forward for the other. Talk about a grudge match. We were living under the same roof but, as we prepared that day, we didn't speak a word to each other. We even took separate cars to the ground. Everything between us was fine, but when I found out we were playing on each other I was like, 'Right, I'm gunna smash him.'

At the start of the game I turned and gave him a massive double-handed shove in the chest, ran into the centre square, grabbed the ball and kicked it forward. I was away and played a good game. In the last quarter Kosi took a few strong grabs;

Competitiveness

I remember Thommo saying after the game how good that was for him. And I knew he was right, that it was good for Kosi and for the team. But I still didn't talk to Kosi all day. Our competitiveness overrode everything.

•

The downside of being wired like me is that it's made game day a living hell—and me a nightmare to be around. Night games were especially awful, waking up at the same time as you would for a day game, feeling the same queasiness, but having to ride it all day. Watching the clock tick away, minute by minute, hour by excruciating hour.

Like everything, experience has made me better—I found a way to just go out and play. Whereas before I'd have the same meal the night before, then on game day go to the same cafe and get pancakes, I settled into eating whatever I felt like on game eve. For a time Fraser Gehrig and I went to a sushi place every night before a game, even washed our meals down with a shot of saki. But I finally shook off the need for a sameness on game eve that had become almost ritualistic.

Having a family provided a distraction and focus that occupied my mind. You can't afford to be a basket case every weekend when you've got small children. But for such a long time game day was a thing to be endured, a hell to get through before the main event of the week. And it was all because I was so competitive—I wanted to do everything perfectly every time, and I'd get myself in an awful mess thinking about all the ways that might not happen. The perception that I was wound up and intense is a product of that.

When I was living with my brother Alex in South Melbourne before I met Cath, I don't know how many times he had to talk me back off the ledge on game day. Friday nights were tough because he'd be at work, but on Saturdays or Sundays we could hang out together and he could eventually make me see sense. 'Man, you'll be fine,' he'd tell me when I was losing it. 'You say this every week.'

Friday night games, I'd leave home about 5 p.m. and find myself driving past the George Hotel, looking at all the people piling into the pub, so happy and relaxed. And there I was, wound up like a top. Part of me wished I could join them, or just go home. Wished I could do anything other than what I was about to do. I didn't even consider that some of the pub-goers might have noticed me and thought, 'Gee, I wish I was off to play at the MCG in front of 50,000.'

I was better by the time I was living with Cath, but not completely. She moved to Melbourne in 2010, the year we played in the drawn grand final. It wasn't easy for her to understand the person I became on game day. I described it to her once as feeling like I was on death row, awaiting my execution. She couldn't believe I'd been even worse before she got here. She'd come out and find me cleaning the window sills, doing all sorts of weird stuff. She'd know it was game-day morning because she'd catch me brushing my teeth really, really hard, and I wouldn't even know I was doing it. I tried watching *Game of Thrones* episodes back-to-back but I couldn't concentrate, couldn't sit still. Nothing could snap me out of the sense of impending doom.

Routine was always big, but in a lot of ways only perpetuated the feelings of anxiety. It was all so regimented: 'Okay, it's this time of day so I'm doing this, and I need to feel like this.' I wouldn't say the anxiety crippled me because I was still able to go out and perform, but the feeling ate away at me in the interminably long hours before the bounce. I used to talk to Max Hudghton about it—he was similar to me, found game day an almighty struggle. I used to throw up a lot, couldn't keep anything down from a few hours before game time.

The times when I wasn't able to play only made a mockery of the weekly hell I'd put myself through. In 2016 I missed a game after my knee blew up and had to be drained. Cath and I took James to the zoo in the morning, wandered around with all the other parents and kids, then I drove down to Etihad Stadium without a care in the world. Gosh, the difference was incredible, the freedom, the ease of just meandering through the day without this huge cloud hanging over me. But as much as football wound me up so tight, I had to wonder that if I hadn't been like that, would I have been the same player? I might have enjoyed the experience more, but would I have been as good or performed as well?

In my early years I kept an A4 day-to-a-page diary. I wrote in it during the week—a review of the last game, affirmation of the player I was becoming, plans for the next challenge. It was part of my routine. I'd write some stuff in the morning if I could sit down for long enough, struggle through some lunch, try and have a snooze for 45 minutes in mid-afternoon. That was tough, but I usually found a way to nod off. Set the alarm for about 4 p.m., get up, write some more, sort my bag out and make sure everything was ready to go, have a cold shower, get dressed, write some more. Then drag myself to the game.

I still have the diaries. If I look at them now, I can hear the young man I was, feel his commitment to being the best. And remember how much playing this game shredded him inside, week after week.

26 April 2002: I'd just played my tenth game. Bullet points down the side of the page read: 'I am a leader.' 'I am respected.' 'I am a great contested mark.' 'My work ethic is second to none.' 'I am courageous.' 'I will be one of the greats.' Under 'Match Preparation' I wrote that something had been asked of us the previous week against Geelong and that we had failed. Personally I'd kept Ben Graham reasonably quiet, but was 'soft once and am very embarrassed about that. Make it right. Tomorrow I have the chance to do something special.'

27 April, game day: 'I will mark strongly. I will tackle aggressively. I enjoy taking my turn. I always hit the target. I am fitter than my opponent. I will dominate. I am consistent.'

Competitiveness

28 April, in review: '17 touches, 12 marks, 4 score assists. Best game yet for the club. Build on it.'

Yet even as I continued to build a career, the competitor in me rarely allowed me to be satisfied. Every week I would write the same thing in varying ways: 'I am our best player because I inspire my teammates with my strong marking, hard running, courage, work rate and preparation.' It was all about affirmation—wanting to be the best, and wanting to get better and better.

•

The longer I played the more I had people—especially opposition supporters—say, 'I used to hate you, but now I don't mind you.' I understand why people might have perceived me a certain way—I get that. In a playing sense I've been criticised for my body language at times, but however I reacted on the field was a function of wanting to win so much and to personally be a big contributor to that.

If a teammate missed me with a pass or ignored me on the lead and my body language reacted, it wasn't because I was mad at him. It was because I felt so much pressure all my career to perform, that missing an opportunity to get the ball and alleviate some of that pressure was a loss of its own. Playing forward so much, you depend to a large degree on what happens up the field. That's why at times my body language was demonstrative.

It was one of my biggest weaknesses as a leader, and came on the back of this feeling of 'Please, just get me the ball!' Playing pretty good footy at a young age in the AFL didn't help; it only increased that weight of expectation I felt throughout my whole career.

It's so easy to drown yourself in the negativity of the game if you let yourself, but to have played for such a long time there are obviously so many things I've loved. There was the camaraderie for starters, the chippy, antagonistic nature of a locker room, the jokes, the fines that get read out once a month for stupid stuff teammates have done. It's an environment of shared hard work and fun that I know I'll never experience again in the workforce. I'll miss that almost more than anything.

I'll miss absolutely pushing the limits, as hard as that can be from a mental and physical sense. That's something I've really loved about footy—physically challenging yourself every day, every session, whether you felt like doing it or not. And the sense of accomplishment that comes with doing the work. I'll even miss the soreness, particularly when you've played well, put everything in, and got the result.

I'll miss the amazing feeling of playing well, when it seems the game has slowed down just for you, the ball follows you, everything comes off the boot well, the ball hits your hands and there's no way you're going to drop it. Those days don't happen all that often but, when they do, that feeling of being in total control is incredible. The moments within those games, when you've put in a long lead and you can feel your opponent just dropping off you ever so slightly, they're like gold. Knowing the defender can't run with you, that's a great feeling. They're the things I've loved. And of course the recognition, the adulation. Who doesn't like being patted on the back and told they've done something really well? You almost become addicted to that. Pride is a big part of footy.

•

Expectation is often fuelled by outside noise. I've never been on Twitter, so I haven't interacted with people in that forum. If I'm honest, if I could do anything in the world it would be to somehow stop the negative, hurtful side of social media. It has the power to do so much good, as our experience with Maddie's Vision has shown me, but it can also be so damaging.

I've talked about perception and popularity with Jarryd Roughead and Bob Murphy. The three of us became close on the International Rules tour of Ireland in 2015. Actually our wives hit it off, which is the first requirement in making friends after you've hit 30. We quickly followed suit. Anyway, they had one of those 'Best blokes in the AFL' polls the next year, and of course Roughy and Murph finished one and two. I sent them both a text: 'Any tips?'

If I had my time over there are things I'd do differently, and I know there would be a different perception of me as a result. The 'sooky' thing gets to me sometimes, and I feel like I've been misrepresented a little bit. I get it, but really—no kidding, I cried after we lost the 2009 grand final, because I'd just poured everything into something and come up short. And, yes, I cried after I broke my collarbone against Brisbane in 2005, but only because I wanted to be out there so much, only because I cared.

The aftermath of that incident was amazing. It was the first game of the season, a stand-alone fixture on Easter Thursday with my family and friends among a packed Gabba crowd and everyone around the country glued to their TVs. I'd just been made captain, taken the baton from Lenny Hayes. We were premiership favourites, and I was Brownlow Medal favourite. Other little things stick in my mind; I'd just changed boot sponsors, signed a big deal with Nike, and led the team out in new, gleaming white boots.

We were a few points in front in the third quarter. I'd kicked three and was playing well when I led towards Aussie Jones on the forward flank, dived to mark and felt something go in my shoulder. I knew something wasn't right, but I said to a trainer, 'I think I'm okay.' I waved the trainers away, then Mal Michael and Chris Scott came in and bumped me. I can't remember them coming at me, that's just a blur. I was in pain.

I went off, down to the rooms, and they cut my jumper off. The doctor pushed a point in my shoulder and the bone moved. I'd broken my collarbone. After the huge build-up to the start of a season that promised so much, it was devastating. Thoughts were whirring around my head, none of them good. 'Is my season over? Do I need a shoulder reconstruction? I've done all this work, I'm meant to be premiership captain this year, I'm meant to contend for the Brownlow, meant to do all these things . . .' With my good arm, I punched the wall.

I came out onto the ground at three-quarter time in my tracksuit top and Milney (Stephen Milne) grabbed all the boys in the huddle, pulled them together and said, 'Here's our skipper, he's hurting.' I was overwhelmed and became quite emotional. Soon after, the camera caught me slumped on the bench, my face streaked with tears, trying to stop myself crying.

More than a decade later I still get people trying to wind me up by rubbing their eyes in the 'boo-hoo' mime of someone having a blub. The on-field incident divided commentators and horrified viewers. Tim Lane likened it to a driver hitting a pedestrian then reversing over them to finish the job. Robert Walls saw no issue, comparing it to a fast bowler in cricket working over a tail-end batsman.

I didn't feel aggrieved in the slightest, and it didn't even enter my head that Mal Michael and Chris Scott might have done something outside the rules or the 'spirit of the game' until the debate started. I'd travelled to Ireland with Mal a few months earlier and got on really well with him. I didn't harbour any ill-will towards him and Chris Scott, none at all. That sort of approach was why Brisbane were kings. They were ruthless. Good luck to them.

But the amount of mail I received in the following weeks—mostly from women being incredibly supportive—was staggering. The main thread was that it was okay to show my emotions, and that by doing so I'd inadvertently become a role model of a welcome kind. Nobody was happier than Max Hudghton, who'd famously tried to hide his tears by emptying a water bottle on his face in the wake of an especially heart-breaking Saints loss. I was like, 'Thanks, that's very kind, but I don't want to be a poster boy for crying!'

The most jaw-dropping arrival in the post was a parcel from the renowned children's author Mem Fox. I'd read *Possum Magic* as a kid and I was like, 'What's Mem Fox sending me a package for?' I rang Mum and said, 'You wouldn't believe who I've just got a letter from.' Fox had sent me a lovely copy of *Possum Magic* with a handwritten note saying something like, 'Here's a book about a wombat who got picked on.' The fact that it resonated with her drove home how big a story it had become. And all I could think was, 'Gosh, I've made a complete fool of myself.' I guess the fallout from it all has had both positives and negatives.

•

Competitiveness

I hate perfectionism, but it's just the way I am. It can be the most maddening quality. We have a cypress hedge that runs across the back fence at home, and a while ago a small section of it browned off and died. I didn't know it was the same cypress disease that had swept through Victoria, that it would probably kill the whole hedge. But every time I looked out in the backyard that's all I could see. You wouldn't believe how mad that hole in the hedge made me.

At training I could be shocking; it was like I went into a different space. Leigh Montagna would say to me, 'Why do you get so wound up? You don't have to play the game now, you know.' I knew he was right, that I'd go somewhere that doesn't do anyone any good. But I couldn't help it. It was like I became a different person.

Anything but perfection at training always drove me insane, but I came to know that was my issue, not anyone else's. I had another issue too, that was a bit unusual. I'm red–green colour blind and, of course, when we did competitive drills at training half the blokes would wear red bibs and the other half green. I'd completely lose my mind because I couldn't tell the difference. 'How are we supposed to tell who's on which side when everyone's wearing the same colour?'

On reflection, it was pretty funny. I didn't realise until after I'd started at St Kilda, and I can't even remember how the penny dropped (probably a training drill). I still find myself doing those tests you can look up on the internet, where you see certain shapes that are made up of a mass of dots. It might be a circle of green dots with red dots inside it making up a number, but all I can see is a circle of dots.

•

If I see my kids showing the same competitive traits as me, what will I tell them? Probably what Dad always told me: that you can only do your best. That it's important to do that, but that's all you can do. If your best is good enough, that's great. But if it's not, you can still hold your head up.

Adam Kingsley is the best assistant coach I've had. He'll make a great senior coach. His philosophy is 'don't let previous results and the emotions you experience around them dictate your future actions'. In regard to body language, his take is 'if the ball's been kicked over your head, and even for a couple of seconds your body language is poor, that's affecting your next opportunity to get the ball'. It's a great point.

Broadly, as with any setback, perspective helps. The night after the Brisbane incident, a few mates from the Gold Coast came back to the team hotel, we slipped the concierge a few bucks and, even though it had ticked over into Good Friday, beers and toasted sandwiches were brought up to my room. The next day we went straight from the airport to the Royal Children's Hospital for the Good Friday appeal. I had my arm in a sling, was feeling pretty miserable, but what the kids in there were going through was the slap in the face I needed.

Competitiveness

The next day I had surgery at Vimy House. While I was convalescing, a newspaper photographer was caught scaling the drainpipe on the wall outside, trying to take a photo of me in my room. I was 22, at the start of my fifth season, but it was another penny-drop moment. The spotlight on me was only going to burn brighter.

5
THE SPOTLIGHT

The wonderful way in which I've been able to provide for my family while doing something I love is ultimately thanks to the attention playing football has brought me. I've spent half of my life in the public eye, and the media, the fans and all that comes with living in the spotlight have helped make me. I appreciate the positive impact it can have. But there can be a downside too.

At various stages the spotlight affected me profoundly. When we first started seeing each other, Cath reckons that when we landed back in Melbourne after spending a few months in Texas she could see my shoulders hunch over, my cap come down an inch lower to shield my face and my hoodie go up over my head.

Early in my career, I didn't cope well with the spotlight being on me. In certain situations I developed mechanisms to avoid contact or people recognising me. Silly things, really. If I drove up to a red light and there was already a car there, I'd pull up so that the person driving or the passengers had an obscured view of me. I'd make sure I was one back, or pull up so that the panel that runs down between the doors was blocking their view. If a car pulled up next to me, I'd roll forward a bit more or turn my head. I just tried to avoid the interaction. Upon reflection it was irrational, but in those early years I felt like every interaction was going to be negative. Ninety per cent of the time it was probably going to be nothing—or good. But I couldn't see that.

The spotlight that was on me also impacted my family. It burned brightly on game day, and at times members of the crowd would become abusive and Mum, Dad, Alex and Maddie found themselves in unpleasant situations. I'd hear later that someone would have been getting stuck into me and Dad would say, 'Mate, I know him pretty well—would you like to say that to his face? I reckon I can organise it . . .'

Things would just happen and you'd be expected to wear them as part of the territory. I got home from a game against Carlton one night when I was living in South Melbourne and the entire house had been egged—not just a few eggs, a few cartons. It was a three-storey townhouse, and it was covered in them. It took ages to clean that up with a high-pressure hose.

The Spotlight

At the same house I received letters in the mailbox that had my face scanned onto a page with a bullseye or cross-hairs over the top, and threatening words pasted together with individual letters that had been cut out of magazines. It was like the death threats sent to Whitney Houston's character in *The Bodyguard*. We took them to the police.

Regardless of whether it's positive or negative, the spotlight is not an easy thing to get used to. When I was first drafted, Maddie and Alex would come down from the Gold Coast to stay and we'd be walking along the street. Someone would say, 'G'day, Nick!' And I'd say, 'G'day, mate.' Maddie and Alex would be like, 'Who's that?' And I'd say, 'No idea.' They thought it was so weird.

Attention is a double-edged thing. When it's positive, who doesn't like attention? But when I was young the supporters' side of being in the spotlight was something I struggled with for a long time—the constant, constant, constant having to be 'on'. By the end of my career, I made sure I was the last one there signing autographs, but early on I used to take a back exit just to avoid people. I don't know what it was; it wasn't that I was worried about what they were going to say, I just felt claustrophobic in that setting. I'm not a shy person but I'm not a massive extrovert either. I could feel my whole body tense up when there were lots of people around hunting autographs or asking for photos. I felt like I had a shell around me that didn't enjoy it.

I find it really hard at times to be in a room full of people I don't know. Even with my mates, I'm not someone who can just sit around and have twenty beers and talk rubbish. I wish I could but I find that stuff hard. I need to be doing something.

I saw someone for a while about helping me through that stuff. I'd just feel the shell come up around me; it was crippling at times. Talking about it with a professional helped. Just maturity as well, getting older, being a parent. Before I had kids I'd never have done something like take public transport, but now I can jump on the train with James and Will and, while you know people are looking, recognising you, wanting to say something, I'm far more accepting of that. I'm sure as the boys grow up they'll take some enjoyment in their old man being recognised, and I will too.

•

I got an inkling of what was ahead even before I'd played a game. Mum and Dad had a close friend, Kirsty, with whom they used to stay when they came down to Melbourne, and when they were in town for the draft we all went to the Malvern Hotel for dinner. A journalist who knew Kirsty walked past, and she introduced him and said, 'These are the Riewoldts. They're here because their son hopes to get drafted tomorrow.'

A few days later in the *Herald Sun* this journo wrote something about bumping into Nick Riewoldt, the No. 1 draft pick, in a pub the night before the draft. No mention that I was with Mum and Dad, in the dining room, having a family dinner. He did write that I was drinking Coke, and added something pointed like 'I certainly hope it was Coke.' It was so unnecessary, teasing the reader to let their imagination run away.

My second season, 2002, was when the spotlight started to kick in. Even though I'd been the No. 1 draft pick, missing so much footy in 2001 meant there wasn't much to focus on. Then I had a big year, won the Rising Star award, the St Kilda best and fairest, was a panellist on *The Footy Show* for the first time, went to the Brownlow. It all started to happen.

Some of the attention made me uncomfortable. The *Herald Sun* ran a fan-driven competition during the 2002 season called 'The One You Want'. They came up with a list of 50 players, pitted you against someone else, and the readers voted on who went through to the next round. The first round I was up against Luke Darcy and went through something like 52 per cent to 48 per cent. Next round Andrew McLeod, 51–49. Michael Voss was at the peak of his powers; Nathan Buckley, Anthony Koutoufides—absolute stars—were still playing. And I ended up being 'The One'.

I guess it was under the guise of, if you were starting a team from scratch to play for the next ten years, who was the player you'd want? But I was so embarrassed. I'd barely played twenty games. I was nineteen. The *Herald Sun* came down to

Moorabbin afterwards to take a photo; the boys pushed me out the front of the group at the end of training. It was mortifying and, in my opinion at the time, misguided.

Even at the end of that year, I had no idea what winning the best and fairest of a footy club meant. I'd never won one in junior footy, let alone at an AFL club. I started to become aware that things had changed, that I'd become a target for the spotlight. I tried to make myself comfortable with it, but I wasn't necessarily prepared for it.

At the start of 2002, playing as a forward, I didn't set the world on fire. I'd played on Wayne Carey in a practice game at Moorabbin and done pretty well. It was actually the last game he played for North Melbourne before he left the club. Grant Thomas wanted to play me back and throw me some big assignments. Against Sydney in round 5 we hadn't won a game. I took a dozen marks, caught the opposition's kick a lot. We won and I got a Rising Star nomination. That was my break-out game.

Sponsors started to kick in. I was wearing Puma boots and started to get some favouritism, invitations to the warehouse in Keys Road, Moorabbin, a bit of special treatment. 'Come in, we've got these cool new shoes,' and I'd be sent out the back to see the guy who got his hands on all the new stuff.

Ricky Nixon organised a car for me through Zagames, an MG ZT. It wasn't one of the old coupés, but a modern, stylish thing that was pretty cool to drive. MG were making a big push back into the market. At one stage I was going to be driving a little Lotus Elite—a low-to-the-ground, two-door sports car with a hard top. I might as well have turned up at the footy club in a Ferrari. The boys already gave me the same sort of grief I'd give a twenty-year-old now if they showed up in a sponsored MG. I'm sure there was a bit of jealousy, but there was also an element of me enjoying the spotlight a bit too much.

I was really conscious of the fact that my teammates were onto me about those things, about always being in the spotlight. One day at training a newspaper photographer turned up to take my photo for an article I'd been interviewed for. All the boys were out on the track; we were about to do the warm-up lap then get into the session. The club media person came over and asked if I could go and do the photo.

I said, 'No, I'm not doing it now, it's time to train.' It was in front of all the boys. Part of my objection was, 'it's work time'. Part of it was 'please don't make me go and do a photo now in front of all the boys, you've got no idea how much shit I'll cop'.

Thommo called me over and said, 'Go and do the photo.' I protested, said I'd do it after training, and he said, 'No, go and do it now.' After training he called me aside. He took me into what we called 'the players' room', which housed a full-sized snooker table (funnily enough, it found its way to Thommo's farm in Johanna when he left the club). The room had been the venue of many a famous Thommo heart to heart, and this was no exception. 'Is there anything you need to say?' he asked me. I replied, 'About you making me do that photo before training? I didn't appreciate that.'

He said, 'No, you owe me an apology. Don't you ever question me in front of the group like that. If I tell you to go and get the photo taken, you do it.' I was like, okay, fair point. He was just teaching me a lesson. He looked for an opportunity to provide a lesson out of every occasion.

When I was out socially the attention I'd get—from men and women—escalated pretty quickly. Ninety per cent of it was great; 10 per cent of it was blokes wanting to bait you or belt you. Occasionally it nearly got ugly, until I learnt to walk away. I've never been a fighter, but learning not to react still took time.

Stringing together some good performances was a factor, plus starting to get a bit of a profile in the media. But there's always just been the fact that I'm a big bloke with white hair: I stand out in a crowd. I probably didn't help myself the way I dressed. I look back at some of the kits I got around in . . . we were all the same, but I was at the far end of the spectrum, incredibly consumed by my appearance. Double denim, leather jackets—just no good. Kosi was Kosi—country boy, never really gave a shit about that stuff. But I got pretty consumed by it.

If adulation, a car, sponsors were the upside, the downside of the spotlight, the thing that irritated me, was the personal stuff. At the beginning of 2005 I started dating Stephanie

The Spotlight

McIntosh, who was in the middle of a five-year stint playing Sky Mangel in *Neighbours*. Steph's family are well known on the showbiz landscape: her mum, Sue, was an actor and ABC newsreader; her father, John, is a television producer; and Jason Donovan is her half-brother.

A footballer dating a soap star meant the spotlight shone especially bright around that time. We had stuff written about us quite often: I'd be called Steph's handbag, she'd be attacked in the junk media for no reason. That stuff really got to me. Steph had one particular journo who used to smack her at every opportunity, just give it to her. I'd get caught in the crossfire, feel bad for Steph. It drove me insane. That was the first time I didn't enjoy the spotlight and developed some animosity towards the media.

At times the spotlight was a lot of fun, but as good as the good was, when the spotlight was negative it was a pain in the arse. I got dragged a little bit into that tabloid, showbiz stuff. Steph would get whacked for the dress she was wearing, or be called a prima donna in the media for no reason. She signed a deal with a record label and they said she couldn't sing. Cheap little shots, just enough to wear you down. It was just upsetting to see someone you cared about going through that stuff.

We broke up at the start of 2009, really just because our lives were taking different paths. Steph was in London and then Los Angeles pursuing a music career; I was captain of St Kilda, trying to win a premiership. We did the long-distance thing for a year when she was in LA but it was too tough in the end. Our relationship now has come full circle. Steph reached out when Maddie was sick, and again when she passed away. She has a little girl, four days older than James. When she's home she'll drop around to visit; she and Cath will sit having a cup of tea while the kids play on the floor. It's a bit of a spin out. People on the outside would say it's weird that my wife and ex-girlfriend could be so amicable, but it's better than the alternative. Given the circumstances that triggered the reconnection, it's something I'm really grateful for.

The time I spent with Steph also showed me that living with the spotlight is a matter of degrees, that as big as the focus on football and the people who play it in Melbourne, it's just a little book-light compared to Hollywood. I had time on my hands when I was there, and Steph would usually be auditioning during the day, so I hung out with a lot of her friends. A girlfriend Steph had made over there lived with Adrian Grenier, who was Vincent Chase, the lead in the HBO series *Entourage*. I ended up spending a bit of time with him, going to the movies, whatever. *Entourage* started in 2003 and by then it was in its fourth season and massive. Adrian was in the spotlight for playing a guy who was in the spotlight: it was life imitating art. It was a novelty to hang out with him. We stayed at his joint a couple of times, crashed there after nights out.

Steph's godmother is Olivia Newton-John. Her parents are also friends with the Farrars: John Farrar was in The

Strangers and Cliff Richard's backing band The Shadows, and wrote 'You're The One That I Want' and 'Hopelessly Devoted to You' for *Grease*. They live in an amazing place in Malibu. Their eldest son Sam was bassist for a band called Phantom Planet, and his best mate was Adam Levine from Maroon 5. We'd all go out for big group dinners. I think the fact that I was Australian was a bit of a novelty for them. They were school friends, a really tight group, and we were included in their group.

Celebrity was almost a way of life for them, and it's not the real world. For people like me from the outside, you'd come in and think, 'What is this? This is just a zoo.' It was crazy. Every year Adam Levine throws legendary Halloween parties—invitation only and always extravagant dress-up affairs. One year Adam, myself and another guy went as gladiators. It just became a normal part of the annual routine while I was there. When I'd get back to Melbourne and try to explain it, I'd sound like a liar or a dickhead.

Nick Dal Santo and Leigh Montagna came with us one year, on the way home from the footy trip. A movie called *Tropic Thunder* had just come out, featuring Ben Stiller, Jack Black and Robert Downey Jr playing actors who were making a war movie. We got ourselves done up as soldiers for the party. You'd meet at a warehouse, get on a bus and be taken to a secret location. It was just an empty house. Steph and Holly Vallance were good friends, and we went with Holly and her boyfriend, who she's ended up marrying. Russell Brand was there, from memory just dressed as Russell Brand. There was a two-person camel, like the old horse or cow get-up. Dal thought it would be a good idea to jump on the camel's hump and go for a ride. He leapt on and this voice from inside the camel suit screamed, 'Hey, hey, it's a girl in here!' The camel's hump came off and it was Katy Perry. That's the sort of crowd it was. Dal asked her for a photo, and she said, 'You can have a photo if you stop speaking in that ridiculous accent.' He got the photo in the end. Looking back, I feel like it all happened in a movie, which isn't that far from the truth.

•

The spotlight on my footy has always been pretty consistent, in that it's been overwhelmingly positive. I might have had a bad game and a commentator or journalist would say my man was best on ground, just for running around punching the ball away all day. Fair enough, you wear that. There's a massive industry now in people having opinions and generating debate about footy, and as a player you have to wear the good with the bad.

Broadly, I think there's a significant lag between what's happening at 'club land' in terms of terminology, structure and game plan, and when the media—and therefore the public—catch up. It worries me, listening to some of the commentary that comes from people who are well respected for their standing in the game, and their take on what's happening is years out of date.

I've spoken to guys like David King and Nathan Brown who make a point of visiting footy clubs to research and do a virtual refresher course on what's happening in the game. That's what everyone should be doing; it's irresponsible or just plain lazy not to. As someone who will probably spend time in the media, I think players who are now fresh out of the game are more conscious of staying relevant, staying informed, simply because of the hypocrisy of not being as well prepared as you can.

Overall, when I reflect on my time in the spotlight, the thing that stands out the most has nothing to do with on-field performance. Losing Maddie is obviously the worst thing that has happened in my life. But of everything that has resulted from me being a footballer, the most regrettable thing was also beyond my control. Other than letting a teammate take a stupid photo of me on a footy trip, it had nothing to do with me.

That didn't stop people lining up to take a shot at me, diving in when they saw an opportunity to whack me. For more than a year it crippled me. It coincided with my worst year of performance as a player. Much worse than that, it happened just as we found out Maddie was seriously ill. By the end of 2011, I was so broken I seriously thought about giving the game away. I was still only 29. And I would never have found myself in such a miserable place if it wasn't for the saga of 'The St Kilda Schoolgirl'.

Cath and I were driving to her parents' ranch, on the Interstate 10 highway somewhere between San Antonio and Rocksprings, Texas. It was a few weeks after we'd lost the replayed 2010 grand final. We'd known each other for a year, and Cath had been living with me in Melbourne for about four months.

My phone rang. It was Ricky Nixon, my manager. I remember thinking it was a surprise to have any mobile reception—West Texas is incredibly desolate, and we were only 80 kilometres from the Mexican border. Ricky asked if I had a minute. I had all the time in the world. He asked about a girl two of my teammates had had 'a thing' with. I said I didn't know her.

'She reckons she's got a nude photo of you,' Ricky said.

Cath was driving. I asked her to pull over, got out of the car and stood on the side of the road. I remember having a weird feeling that I might get bitten by a rattlesnake.

I said, 'What are you talking about? Mate, I've never met her, wouldn't even know what she looked like.'

Ricky said he'd seen the photos—there was one of Nick Dal Santo as well; the girl had brought them into his office. He assumed they had to be fakes. I asked him to describe the one of me. He said I was standing in a room, naked, next to another teammate, Zac Dawson, in front of a studded white leather wall.

The Spotlight

I said, 'No, that's real. I know exactly where that is—the Delano Hotel in South Beach, Miami.'

The previous year, after we'd lost the 2009 grand final to Geelong, a group of sixteen of us went on the end-of-season trip to America. I can honestly say I don't even know the exact circumstances of the photo being taken, it was so inconsequential at the time. I don't know which day of the footy trip it was. When you're on the other side of the world with a group of mates after months and months of leading an incredibly disciplined lifestyle, you tend to let your hair down. Details can become a bit fuzzy. Some might say that's convenient. It's just the truth.

Ultimately, all that happened was, in a room full of blokes, one man (Sam Gilbert) took a photo on his phone of another man (me). That's it.

People might think men taking photos of other men naked is weird, but you need to consider the context. We shower together under twenty shower heads with no partitions pretty much every day. Seeing other men naked isn't strange for a footballer, it's normal. The shower is a place you not only get clean, it's where you have a chat. Why the photo was taken, I have no idea. I imagine it just seemed like a funny thing to do at the time. I also imagine anyone who's been on a footy trip at any level will understand that.

I assume the photo—along with every other photo Gilbo took on the trip—ended up on his laptop. It was just so inconsequential at the time that the photos were taken. It certainly wasn't a big moment of, 'Oooh, we shouldn't have been taking these photos . . .' It was just a non-event.

In our round 1 game at the Olympic Stadium against Sydney in 2010, there was a girl in the crowd wearing a St Kilda jumper that she'd cut down to show off her midriff. She went to the team hotel after the game, I assume in an attempt to meet St Kilda players. I had no knowledge of her visit to the hotel.

At some stage in the coming months the girl found the photos on Gilbo's laptop and emailed them to herself. When contact between the pair ended she was angry and tried to sell the photos to the media. Even the *Herald Sun* refused to buy them, reasoning that she wasn't in a good place and it would be wrong to take advantage of her. All this had been going on for the best part of a year, and now I was about to be dragged into it.

Standing by the Texas road, trying not to step on a cactus, I told Ricky I had no idea how she had the photos. He replied, 'She says she took them.' He assured me he had it under control, that she wouldn't do anything with them. Cath had been living in Melbourne long enough to know what a circus it would be if the photos got out, but we weren't too worried. We figured the photos were stolen, which would stop her from publishing them. Social media wasn't as big then as it is now, certainly not in my world anyway. I wasn't on Facebook or Twitter; Instagram had only just been launched.

The Spotlight

I had no inkling of what was about to happen. Back from Texas months later, I was doing weights in the gym at Moorabbin on the last day of pre-season training before the Christmas break. One of the boys came out of the physio room, which was next door, and said, 'Come and have a look at this—quick.' I walked into the room and found a group of my teammates sitting around a computer looking at an image of me, naked, with Zac Dawson next to me. It was captioned, 'Merry Christmas from the St Kilda Schoolgirl'.

The girl had posted the photo on Facebook. Holy shit.

Within a couple of hours I was sitting in a lawyer's office in Richmond with Ricky and the club CEO, Michael Nettlefold. The photo scandal had just exploded. I was absolutely devastated, knowing straight away what it would mean to my reputation. That's something that means a lot to me: I'd maintained a clean image throughout my career, which is essentially the person I am. I'm not that person who goes out and hits someone, drinks and drives, is followed by controversy because of the way he behaves. I'm pretty straight. To be dragged into something like that was humiliating and absolutely beyond my control.

Cath had stayed in Texas to have Christmas with her family. Maddie actually called her in tears and told her before I had a chance. Cath was able to explain to her parents what had happened, the fact that I was innocent of everything except allowing a dumb photo to be taken of me on a footy trip.

They knew the real story before the media spun it the way they wanted. And boy did they spin it.

Even so, I'm sure if I'd met Cath after that, rather than a year earlier, we wouldn't be together. If I'd met her after the scandal her family would have said, 'No, not him.' They had googled the life out of my name to find out who I was. Her grandma found photos and articles going back to when I was sixteen. Fortunately for my future with Cath, I was squeaky clean.

Cath was amazing through the whole thing. She drove a really hard line with the club to get the images removed from Google, which is so hard to do. Years later, my concern is still that my children might look up my footy career one day, type my name into a search engine and that stuff will come up. At the end of the day it's just me naked, no big deal. But it was all the implications that were attached to it.

The thing that pissed me off the most was knowing that I hadn't done anything wrong. I just watched this event snowball. It's not as though I was naked in a photo with another girl, or engaging in something I shouldn't have been, cheating on my partner, doing drugs, or whatever. I was just standing there, naked. Big deal.

But the way it turned, the way the story was spun by the media was to make out the girl had taken the photos, that she was in a hotel room with me and the others, and I'd been doing the wrong thing; it was all just so hard to watch it happen around you. The media helped perpetuate this. Not only did she steal the photos and lie about taking them, she said she was pregnant to an AFL footballer (a claim that did not implicate me). She said she was having twins, made all sorts of outrageous claims, and the media lapped it up, threw fuel on it. By the time she admitted she'd never been pregnant, it was too late; she'd already brought the footy club to its knees.

Maddie was amazing. She was really sick at the time, mostly bedridden, and the day the photos were posted online she and Mum were at the shack in Orford. Maddie said to Mum, 'This is so wrong, those photos clearly aren't taken in Melbourne, she wasn't there.' She became obsessed with clearing my name, trawling the internet until she found the photos of rooms on the Delano Hotel website. Not many hotel rooms have studded white leather walls in their rooms. You'd be able to ascertain pretty quickly that the photo hadn't been taken in a Melbourne hotel. If someone had checked the girl's passport (if she even had one), they would have seen she hadn't been in Miami in 2009. But that didn't fit with the mission of derailing someone's life.

I need to take responsibility for something that I'm sure contributed to the glee with which the *Herald Sun* covered the story. At the end of the 2010 season we'd lost the grand final in a replay and I'd had post-season surgery on my knee. Cath and I were living in a three-storey terrace in South Melbourne—two doors down from a house where a woman alleged she'd been sexually assaulted by two Collingwood players on the night of the grand final.

Early the next week there was a knock at our door. I made my way down two flights of stairs on crutches and opened the door to find a *Herald Sun* reporter and photographer standing there. The reporter asked me for a comment on the rape allegations, for no other reason than I lived two doors away. I slammed the door in their faces then, after the photographer had put his camera in the back seat of their car, I opened the window and gave him an almighty spray. 'Leave me the hell alone!', with a few profanities thrown in.

Apparently he'd been at the *Herald Sun* forever, was an incredibly respected and much-loved employee. And I'd given it to him deluxe. When the naked photo story broke it was their chance to go 'whack!'. I'd made a prick of myself to one of their people, I admit that, and in return they dived in.

There are two other moments in the whole saga where I wish I could have my time over. The first came out of that lawyer's office meeting the day the photo of me and the one of Dal were posted on Facebook. I said we needed to get on the front foot, that telling the truth would diffuse the whole thing. All it did was make me the poster boy, and intensify the spotlight on it.

I fronted a media conference the next morning and read a prepared statement, talked about my reputation, said how disappointed I was to be dragged into such a situation by someone I'd never met. I thought people would think, 'He's been caught up in something here that wasn't of his doing, he's a respected player, he's had ten years in the game without anything untoward, we'll let this go.' That's how I was hoping it would be received.

I couldn't have been more wrong.

I fronted the cameras and said I'd asked Gilbo to delete the photos and he obviously hadn't. Looking back, that was unfair. I threw him under the bus a bit, which I should never have done. I didn't ever specifically say to Gilbo, 'Delete the photos', but everyone who goes on a footy trip knows the unspoken rule that 'what happens on footy trips stays on footy trips'.

Gilbo was incredibly apologetic, and there was definitely a bit of tension between us for a short time. We're mates—great mates. There's nothing lingering there. The club went to New Zealand on a training camp in January 2011, barely a month after the whole thing blew up, and I asked if we could room together. We knew it was going to come up, so to be able to say we'd roomed together in New Zealand would hopefully put that part of the story to bed. St Kilda were flag favourites; we didn't need anything getting in the way of what we were trying to achieve.

My other regret is addressing it at the St Kilda AGM in February. A group of us were being awarded life membership and I was the one put up to speak. We were under siege as a club, getting absolutely hammered by the media. Someone had come out and given Gilbo another whack that day. I just saw it as my responsibility as captain to say, 'Enough's enough. Back off. We're a good group.' It was the wrong thing to do, I know that. But as captain I just wanted to say, 'You've got it wrong.'

My other mistake was trusting Ricky to fix the mess. I had full faith in him, and that speaks to a bit of naivety. I should have made absolutely sure it was being handled properly, rather than leaving something so combustible to someone else. In a situation like that, nobody is going to look after your interests as well as you'll look after them yourself.

I started to smell a rat when I was driving to our new training base at Seaford one morning early in the New Year. Ricky called me and said, 'You're not gunna believe what they're saying now. They reckon I'm involved with her, that I've been sleeping with her.' Then the photo of him on a bed in his undies came out. Part of me still wanted to think, 'No way, it's not him, not possible.'

Ricky was still really strong in his denial, but he started to become evasive, went to ground. It turned really quickly when incriminating footage emerged, complete with audio. It was obviously Ricky and he had nowhere to hide.

I went into self-preservation mode because I had a bit of money tied up in his management company, Flying Start. I needed to reconcile that in case things really went pear shaped. The company had been going down the path of setting up a lifestyle and leadership type of business. I'd had money coming in from endorsements, appearances, my Additional Services Agreement, plus some other funds, and I'd advised Flying Start to use it as equity in the business.

I got in touch with the woman who did the books for Flying Start and she said, 'Oh Nick, I'm sorry, there's no money, it's all gone.' Ricky owed me a lot of money. I severed ties with him straight away. I got a legal letter midway through 2011 saying he was threatening to sue me for management fees and lost business. He was arguing that he'd negotiated my contract in 2009 for the next four or five years, so he was entitled to that percentage all the way through. I responded along the lines of, 'You're not providing me with a service. In fact you've done the opposite—you're meant to be handling this situation and all you've done is get involved with the girl at the centre of it. Plus you owe me that money I'd already earned.' There was a mediation and I ended up getting some of it back.

Ricky was amazing for me as my manager. A good friend who opened a lot of doors. He was incredibly good at his job—until he wasn't.

I don't know if there were signs along the way I should have picked up. There was a time he got pneumonia because he tripped and fell in the spa; there were some stories around that. There was something that happened in the States. But I just never saw anything but the professional manager. None of the stuff that I heard about happened in my presence.

As for our relationship now, we have none. He lobbed at my doorstep a couple of years ago to get a jumper signed. It was weird. I look at him now and I feel for his kids, for his wife. They're a great family. I can only imagine what it's done to them.

•

The effect the whole saga had on me was profound. You hear people liken catastrophic events to a car crash, but a car crash is over pretty quickly. This just kept gathering momentum and snowballing. I was called a liar in the media by people who refused to believe the circumstances of the photo were innocent. People made what they wanted of it.

That's a horrible thing to have to carry, because I know how it looks when you see other people in the spotlight denying things. You're like 'yeah, yeah, sure'.

The photos were posted on Facebook less than a week before Christmas, and our usual gathering of family and friends in Orford was a nightmare. The first time I saw my cousin Alex Thompson, he made a joke that I didn't find funny at all. Mum and Dad were devastated by what had happened; my brother and sister wore it as hard as anyone. They'd find themselves in circles where people would bring it up and they'd leap in to defend me. It was hard on everyone.

Our annual Boxing Day barbecue is a time when we all get together at Alex's place across the road. There's a pig on the

The Spotlight

spit, a couple of kegs, backyard cricket, everyone having a ball. That year I had my laptop set up, running the music. There were people there I didn't know—Alex's friends, some friends of friends. All of a sudden the laptop went missing. I had a complete and utter meltdown. I was convinced someone I didn't know had nicked it, knowing it was my laptop.

It turned out that Simon Taylor, who'd been to school with Alex at Hutchins and went on to play for Hawthorn, had accidentally spilt a beer on my laptop and put it on a shelf somewhere to dry. And there I was running around like a paranoid madman. I wasn't myself. I've got no doubt I was suffering from something. The photo scandal had rocked me.

After an awful Christmas, day one back at training was our first day at Seaford. Nobody wanted to go there. I remember driving down the new Eastlink freeway and coming up alongside Joey Montagna. I looked across, shook my head and rolled my eyes, to a degree that just summed up how I felt. 'All this has happened. We're driving to bloody Seaford. This is as bad as it gets.'

It carried on all year. Not only was it the worst I've ever performed personally, but the season was a disaster for us as a group. Round 1 we were up by two goals with two minutes to go and Geelong came back and beat us. Round 2 we were playing Richmond, who were a bottom-of-the-ladder team. Lenny Hayes went down with a ruptured ACL and the game ended in a draw. Round 3 we got smacked by Essendon. After seven rounds, we'd had one win. Remarkably, we somehow ended up making the finals but got knocked out in the first week by Sydney.

It was Cath's first full year living in Melbourne, and we hardly left the house all year. One night in March I went down the road to get fish and chips. Clarendon Street was a block away and there was a Hunky Dory fish-and-chip joint. We ordered fish and chips and about six o'clock—because I couldn't face walking—we drove around. Cath stayed in the car; I went in and grabbed the food.

I came out and there were two blokes about my age sitting at an outside table. One of them called out, 'Oi, fuckhead!' I turned around. 'Oi, fuckhead. Is this you?' He was holding up his phone with the photo on the screen. They'd obviously seen me walk in, got the photo up on their phone and were waiting for me to come out.

Normally I'd keep walking—I'm no fighter. But I thought, 'No, I'm not copping that, I've had enough.' I walked over and grabbed the bloke by the shirt and said, 'What did you say? Have some fucking manners!' He grabbed me back, his mate got involved, the plastic bag with the fish ended up tangled up around my fingers. They ripped my shirt off me. I backed off, realising there were two of them and it was time to get out of there. There were no punches thrown. It all happened really quickly.

Cath was screaming when I got in the car. We drove home, 30 seconds away, and went inside. I rang our footy manager at the time, Greg Hutchison, and told him what had happened.

The Spotlight

He said to sit tight and we'd see what happened next. We were upstairs on the third storey with the windows open about ten minutes later, eating dinner, and a car drove past with one of the blokes hanging out the window, screaming, 'You're fucked, Riewoldt! We know where you live!'

They went to the cops and wanted to press charges against me. Reporting of the incident made out like it was late at night and I was on the way home from a day on the grog and had ducked in for a grease attack. I'd ordered grilled fish, brown rice and a Greek salad. They weren't interested in that.

I was a defeated person. I didn't think it was that bad when I was in it, but I was in a bad way. I've never had depression, but I can imagine that's what it would be like. I was under siege and became volatile. It was an awful time.

Eventually the girl at the centre of the scandal did a paid TV interview and came clean on the whole thing, said she'd been lying the whole time, had never been pregnant, hadn't taken the photo, had never actually met me. By then the experience had changed me. Every time I walked into a room I felt like that photo was the first thing people thought of. I was paranoid, no doubt. At the start of 2011, when we had a vote about leadership and captaincy, I looked at the young players who'd just arrived at the club. Adam Kingsley had just started as an assistant coach. I couldn't help but think, 'That's all they've heard about me. How am I meant to be captain when that's all they know of me?'

By the end of that year I wasn't far away from pulling the pin on my career. I was 29. My form dropped off dramatically. Ross Lyon, who replaced Grant Thomas in 2007, had printed off stats of the great modern-day forwards—Carey, Neitz, Lloyd, Brown, Tredrea—when they were the same age, showing they'd dropped off. He was almost saying, 'Hey, it's all right, this is what happens to key forwards.' He was trying to get me out of the doldrums, but I was starting to think my best footy was behind me. It had beaten me.

My anxiety was even worse that year, because I knew I wasn't playing well. It was different to going to a game anxious because you're scared of not playing well, and then you play well anyway. Fear of failure becomes a lot more real when you *are* failing. That's a much worse place to be.

•

Until you've experienced what it can do for you in a positive sense, and how it can bring you down in a negative way, I don't think you can fully understand what the spotlight is. If you'd asked me about it prior to 2011, I would have given a completely different answer. The things I would get shitty about were so small, in hindsight I couldn't care less. But at that stage they were my only exposure to the negativity of being in the spotlight.

It was an incredible lesson in the power of a groundswell: the way that, once a ball gets rolling, you can be powerless to

The Spotlight

control a situation. There have only been two times in my life where I was utterly powerless to control what was happening. That was one. What happened to Maddie was the other.

People who live their lives mired in controversy—I don't know how they do it. It's just so exhausting. Early on in my career I know I trotted out the line, 'I don't care what people think.' But I really do; it's important to me. I don't want to be 'that person'.

The spotlight has the power to pump you up, and the power to bring you down very quickly. But I know that so many of the incredible opportunities I've enjoyed have resulted from the positive impact of being in the spotlight. Players wouldn't get paid what they do without it, wouldn't play the game in front of tens of thousands of people, wouldn't get to do what they love for a living. Foremost for me has been the support Maddie Riewoldt's Vision has received. I've done a lot of media work throughout my career, and there's every chance I'll go down that path in the future. How ironic is that? To step out of the spotlight and start shining it on others.

6
MENTORS

If you spend a long time at the one football club you come into contact with a lot of people from many different walks of life. I've been incredibly fortunate. I know I retired from the game having met people who have not only made me a better footballer but also helped to round me as a person and prepare me for life after footy.

Over the journey I've been exposed to some incredible business people. I first met Gerry Ryan, the 'caravan king', early in my career. He's a big St Kilda man, still heavily involved in the direction of the club. I've greatly appreciated the advice he's always been happy to offer, the sounding board he's been for me.

Brandon Chizik is another Saints supporter I've leaned

on for advice on real estate, business and all things financial. He came away on a pre-season trip with us to Colorado one year and we struck up a friendship. He's been a mentor. Then there's the Fox family, who've probably been greater friends than mentors. David, Lindsay Fox's youngest son, is one of my best mates. He's a bit older than me, in his forties, but we've always hit it off. Lindsay's 80th 'Conception Party' fell during the 2016 footy season but I'd have loved to be a fly on the wall there. Lindsay hired a boat and they did a Mediterranean cruise. The boat was full of billionaires.

Paul Yeomans and Jarrod Nation, who is my cousin through marriage and godfather to my son William, are both entrepreneurial guys close to my age who have served as personal and professional sounding boards, providing me with a great deal of insight and inspiration into what can be achieved in the business world. They're both terrific mates.

In football my two greatest mentors are the two coaches I've played under longest—Grant Thomas and Ross Lyon. I'm still extremely close to both of them and have much to thank them for—as a footballer and as a person. I'm well aware that my bond with both men has been hard for people who don't know me or them to 'get'. That's understandable. I'll attempt to capture a little of the Thommo and Rossy I know and love here.

But as for footy mentors, let's start at the end. I'm blessed to have finished my career under Alan Richardson. Richo's terrific.

Mentors

In a respect he's probably the most old-school of all my coaches, perhaps because he was in the system for so long before he got a senior gig. There's never been a more apt nickname for anyone than Richo being called 'Citizen'. He's just the model citizen. He very rarely says anything bad about anyone; he's just an honest, genuine person, and his glass is always half-full.

I'm really fortunate that he's been my coach the last few years. Richo, Joey Montagna and I formed a really strong collaboration around the importance of legacy, of teaching the young players the right way to play. Mark Neeld went into Melbourne in a similar situation to the one Richo encountered at St Kilda and swept a broom through the place. James McDonald, a much-loved veteran player, was out on his ear. Depending on who came in when Richo did, that could have happened to me, or to Joey. We'd still been playing really strong footy and were being given the opportunity to play a really active role in the transition of our club. Richo was really accommodating and supportive in that.

And challenging. He challenged me as much on my leadership as any other coach I've had. We had the conversation every year about the handover of the captaincy. At the end of 2014, around Christmas time, I said, 'I don't know if I can do it. Maddie's really sick. If things go badly for her I don't know if I can keep being captain.' He just said not to make the decision based on what might happen. He told me I was the best person for the job, and ultimately I stayed in the role.

In 2016 I thought the club would go in a different direction, and he said, 'No, I want the best leader to be leading.' We had that conversation in Houston during the off-season. Richo was doing a course at Harvard and came back through Houston, spent a night with Cath's family. We went to a high school football game together to watch Cath's cousin play, then had a beer at a bar that had horse saddles for seats. He said he wanted me to keep captaining the club. After that we had a barbecue for lunch and I drove him to the airport. He was only there for 24 hours, but he filled me with a real sense of optimism and positivity about where we were going as a club and the role I still had to play as captain.

Richo is an incredibly supportive person. He was my coach through the most challenging period of my life, let alone of my football career. He brought in little things that feel like they bring big results, such as taking the first-year players down to my place in Tassie every year. I loved doing that, even more so because I could see how much Richo was into it.

While everyone calls him 'Citizen', he has a really good balance of work at the right time, enjoyment at the right time, camaraderie. For example, he's happy for the players to have a beer in the airport lounge after the game. He sees the importance of that, which is less common in the modern game. I see the position we were in when Richo took over as similar to when Grant Thomas became coach. They're very like-minded in their philosophy: they see their responsibility as producing not only good footballers, but also great people.

•

I knew very little of Grant Thomas before Malcolm Blight was sacked and all of a sudden he was the St Kilda coach. He had been director of footy at the club, but I hadn't really had anything to do with him. I was living with Kosi at Virginia Dunleavy's in Brighton at the time, and straight after he was appointed he came over to talk to us and make sure we were okay.

I don't think the senior players and Blight's relationship was all that strong, so change for them was probably a good thing. But I was an eighteen-year-old kid, and for me Malcolm Blight was a huge footy figure. We stayed in touch after he left St Kilda and every time I catch up with him it's great. But at the time my head was just spinning; I didn't know what day it was.

Pretty quickly it struck me how much of a St Kilda man Thommo is. He just loves the football club. There were only six games left in the season when he started, but it felt like he had the group straight away. There was a bit of banter about him and club president Rod Butterss being mates, some jokes about the interview process. I remember boys doing skits about whether Thommo even interviewed for the job. But early on it was pretty clear they were all going to play for him.

Butterss was a pretty slick customer—the big palace in Brighton, all that sort of stuff. That year or the next we had a barbecue there and Shane Warne was out on the tennis court, bowling leggies to whoever was game enough to face him. At one stage I was wicketkeeping and the batsman danced down the pitch. He missed it, I stumped him, and then I celebrated like we'd just won the World Cup, ran down and gave Warnie a high five. It's fair to say I got a bit carried away.

Mental strength was the big thing Thommo pushed me on. At the end of 2001 he conducted player interviews. He got me in and asked me what I thought my strengths were. 'I think I'm mentally tough,' I said. He asked what made me think that. I just said some of the stuff I'd been through, some of the challenges I'd faced as a young person.

He said, 'Okay, you're mentally tough. What's that going to look like with respect to your footy?'

From then on, that was what he smashed me on: being mentally strong, being the hardest trainer, the best preparer. That conversation was almost the seed for the relationship we developed. I felt he respected the way I went about things and our relationship grew out of that.

I think back to footy then and it was just fun. Thommo made it fun. He provided us with life experiences that made us more rounded as people. It was all about the team, getting out of your comfort zone, doing stuff as a group, experiencing stuff together you hadn't done before that just galvanised us as a group and made us stronger mentally. He introduced pre-season camps, starting in 2002 when we went down to Warrnambool, where Thommo had enjoyed great success as playing coach. The next year it was Anglesea, the next year London, then South Africa, then China. Incredible experiences. We were so fortunate as a group.

We caught the train to Warrnambool together as a team. We'd train in the morning then go to hospitals, schools, nursing homes, get out and about in the community. We also trained bloody hard, using the ocean to do a triathlon, working on skills at the Reid Oval. We'd do all our values and trademark stuff, then we'd go and serve the community in the afternoon. Thommo was really big on that humility side of things, which was great. We were a pretty young group and it helped our growth enormously.

Thommo loved togetherness. We were going terribly in 2006, so when we got to the mid-season break, he said, 'Right, we're going to Bonnie Doon.' *The Castle* had come out a few years earlier, so you can imagine the bus trip up there: 'We're goin' to Bonnie Doon . . .' The first time it got a bit of a chuckle, the second it was like, yeah. By the 30th time it had worn a bit thin. We stayed in a lodge, got up and trained our backsides off in the morning, went for 10-, 15-kilometre runs up hills. Then at the end of the day we sat around a fire and had beers, red wine, talked, held each other accountable, had a crack at each other. It was awesome.

It was effectively the sort of high-performance management training that Leading Teams offers, without involving Leading Teams—halfway through a season. We came out and won our next five and made the finals. We just resolved that we were going to have a crack.

Thommo's an enormous man: everything is in excess. I mean, he's got eight kids! If you go around for dinner it's a brontosaurus steak, the biggest spread of all time. We used to go around as young blokes for dinner once a week—to the coach's house! There'd be eight or ten of us. Every year while he was coach, the Sunday after the last game was at Thommo's. He'd put up the marquee, have a spit, and all the players and their partners would be invited. His eight kids would be running around. He and Kerry are very inclusive, very generous people.

I'm sure people thought the fact that Thommo would have the boys over all the time wasn't normal behaviour for an AFL coach. He'd go away on a family holiday, and me and a couple of other players would look after his house. In 2005, Geelong were playing Sydney to see who'd play us in the preliminary final. He had all the boys over to his place to have a steak and watch the Geelong–Sydney game. We got there and he said to me, 'Right, you're in charge, I'm taking the kids and Kerry to your place.' He went and sat at my place for five hours while 40 of us sat in his house, eating steak and watching the footy. He'd do stuff like that.

Mentors

If we'd played a bad game, we'd be at his place at 5 a.m., go down to the Brighton Baths and tread water for ten minutes in the middle of winter, then back to Thommo's for bacon and eggs. Logistically, how they pulled that stuff off is staggering. Kerry is amazing: wife of the year, mother of the year, every year. He could let her know at the last minute there were 40 footballers on their way over, and it would just get done.

We always had the review the day after the game. If we played Friday night, we were in the lecture theatre with him on Saturday morning. He would have gone home, watched the game and coded it ahead of our review. He always wore a hoodie, and he stood out in front of the boys with both hands in the hoodie pockets, jiggling these mints. He always had those extra-strong mints in his pockets. He was up there one day, a massive man in this huge hoodie, and Cathal Corr, a young Irish bloke who was on the rookie list, fell asleep. He was sitting there, head dropping, and he was out.

Thommo was up there talking to the group, took out a mint and threw it full pelt. 'Doink!' It hit Cathal smack in the middle of the forehead. Thommo didn't break stride, just kept talking. He grabbed him afterwards and said, 'If you ever fall asleep in one of my meetings again, you're out.' He was different in that regard—brutally honest—but he had our respect.

Some people in the media questioned Thommo's match-day coaching, but footy was a different game then; you were still able to just go out and play to a greater extent than you can now. Our game plan was pretty simple. We wanted to move the ball quickly, and had a strong emphasis on bringing it back inside and getting it in direct to Fraser Gehrig. It was a pretty simple plan but it stacked up: it worked. What we did really well was play with outstanding effort.

I don't think Thommo gets the credit he deserves as a coach because he was polarising; he was very opinionated, he fought City Hall—was happy to take it up to Andrew Demetriou, to the media. If he had a strong opinion, he'd just give it. There was no diplomacy with Thommo at all, and that opened him up to a lot of criticism. But our actual footy results were really strong.

Thommo's policy of rotating the captaincy was one of the major things people wanted to criticise, but I think it was right for us at the time. The stuff he said probably didn't help. He used to say some funny things. After his line about eating pressure for breakfast, the *Australian* sports writer Patrick Smith started calling him 'Cornflakes'. I've got no doubt people thought we were a bit brainwashed by him. He just did things differently; he was unconventional, and that frightened a few people.

I speak more glowingly of Thommo than do some others who fell by the wayside but, if you did the work, he respected you. He wasn't for everyone. He holds people more accountable than anyone I've ever known, and some people can't handle that kind of honesty. At various stages throughout my career, right up to the day I retired, he'd send me a text after a game: 'Make sure you don't have zero tackles ever again.'

Mentors

A couple of years ago I spoke to him after a game. We'd played Port Adelaide over there; my GPS was off the charts—I'd run 16 kilometres at really high intensity. We'd been thrashed but I'd kicked four and played a bit of a lone hand. Thommo said, 'How'd you think you played?' I said I thought I'd played a pretty solid game. He said, 'I think you're kidding yourself.' Sometimes I know he just does it to needle me. But that's why he's not for everyone—a lot of people can't handle that. With me, it gets a response every time.

The end of the 2011 season, when I went through that really difficult patch, I spoke to Thommo about maybe not playing on. I said I just wanted to enjoy my footy. He said, 'Give it away if that's your attitude. If you just want to enjoy it, stop playing. You won't prepare properly, you won't put in the effort, won't put in the hours. You'll chip away at a reputation that you've worked really hard to establish. You'd be better off giving it away.' He's very confrontational, which is why he's not for everyone. But it was what I needed to hear.

Thommo got the sack at the end of 2006, after we'd made the finals, which was extraordinary. He'd been the first coach since Allan Jeans to get St Kilda to three consecutive finals series and he got the sack. The breakdown of his relationship with Butterss obviously played a role there.

The day Thommo was sacked, I was at Aaron Hamill's house and got a phone call from Kacey Thomas, Grant's eldest daughter, in tears. We'd done the Sunday at Thommo's the day before and were having a barbecue at Aaron's place on the Monday. Kacey rang and said, 'Dad's just been sacked.' It wasn't on the radar. We'd been talking about our next training camp. It came out of nowhere.

I got a phone call from Butterss. He didn't go into reasons, and I was pretty short on the phone. I was devastated. We went to the club for a meeting and there were media everywhere. I got asked, 'How do you feel?' I replied, 'Angry.' I was criticised for sticking my nose in business a player supposedly shouldn't have been commenting on. I just got door-stopped, and I said how I felt.

That afternoon I went straight round to Thommo's and stayed all night. I walked in the door and gave Thommo a hug, had a tear, and that set Kerry off. They were all in on St Kilda, his whole family.

We'd done things that hadn't been done before: the altitude camp in South Africa, training camps in London and China. All those experiences that made footy so much fun, and we were successful. We arguably should have won a flag in '04 or '05. Seven points up at three-quarter time against Sydney in a prelim; a goal up against Port in a prelim. Lost both of those.

I kept in touch with Thommo more than anyone else did. That made that dynamic a little bit hard. It's all fine now, but for a few years it was a little tricky. Even when Ross Lyon was our new coach, trying to be respectful to Ross while still having a relationship with Thommo was tough.

In the backyard at Duke Street with Mum and Dad, on the morning of my first day of school at Princes Street Primary in Sandy Bay, Hobart. (Author's collection)

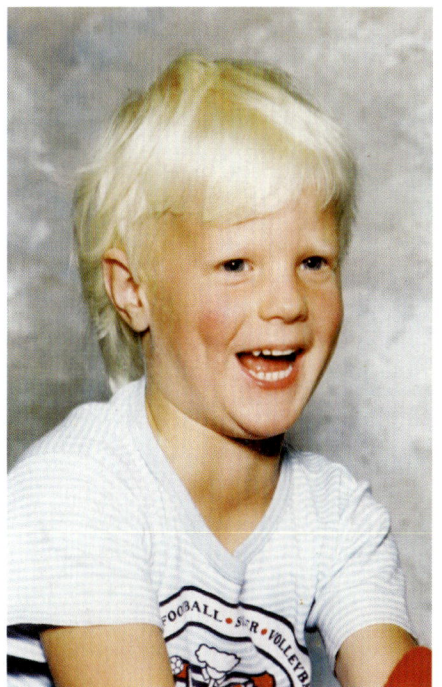

I was a happy little fella. And yes, I had white hair. (Author's collection)

Helping Maddie put on the pads, while she's wearing my Queensland Schoolboys under 12s footy jumper. (Author's collection)

Bath time for the Riewoldt kids in Duke Street, Sandy Bay. (Author's collection)

With my grandparents, Oma and Opa (Helga and Heinz), on Alex's ninth birthday. (Author's collection)

A photo Mum stage managed when we were living on the Gold Coast to send back to family in Tasmania. (Author's collection)

Getting ready for my first grand final, with the Broadbeach Cats under 13s. We beat Palm Beach. I played in grand finals every year from here until I arrived at St Kilda, winning all but one. (Author's collection)

The moment we became an AFL family—draft day, 29 October 2000. (Author's collection)

Me and Kosi on draft day, with new St Kilda coach Malcolm Blight, who was sacked the following July the week after I made my debut. (Sean Garnsworthy/ALLSPORT/Getty Images)

The first of seventeen official AFL portraits, pre-season 2001. (Allsport Australia/ALLSPORT/Getty Images)

Still with some meat to put on the bones, during an intra-club practice match in 2002. That season I won the first of six St Kilda best and fairests. (Author's collection)

With Aaron Hamill after winning the 2004 Wizard Cup grand final against Geelong. 'Sammy' taught me the meaning of hard work and how much of it was required to make it. (Mark Dadswell/AFL Media)

'That' mark, SCG, 2004, vs the Swans. Mum rang straight after the game to tell me never to do anything like that again. When I announced my retirement thirteen years later it was hailed as the signature moment of my career. (Glenn Campbell/Newspix)

With Justin Koschitzke, Fraser Gehrig, Max Hudghton and Aaron Hamill, South Africa, 2004. During the Grant Thomas era we were fortunate to grow not just as footballers but as people. Pre-season camps to London, South Africa and China were a huge part of that. (Author's collection)

At training with a very lean Grant Thomas during the 2004 finals. Thommo was a constant friend and mentor throughout my career. (Stuart Hannagan/Getty Images)

Brisbane's Mal Michael smells blood in the water after I injured my shoulder, round 1, 2005. We began the game as premiership favourites, me as Brownlow favourite. The night was a lesson in not taking anything for granted. (Ryan Pierse/Getty Images)

Shane Warne, the greatest wicket-taker in Australian cricket history, has often said he'd prefer to have played footy for St Kilda. His resilience in the face of a searing spotlight has provided lessons for me through some tough times. (Ryan Pierse/Getty Images)

Diving for crayfish and abalone off Orford, Tasmania, with two of my best mates, Alex Thompson and Jarrod Nation. (Author's collection)

With Lenny Hayes, Brendon Goddard and Justin Koschitzke after a successful dive off Maria Island, Tasmania. (Author's collection)

One of the best feelings I've had in footy—kicking the last goal of the 2009 preliminary final, which sent the Saints into the grand final. (Sebastian Costanzo/Fairfax)

With Cath in Las Vegas—I'd met the girl who would become my wife. (Author's collection)

Off to a flying start in the 2010 season—marking was a huge part of my game, and I'm proud to have finished having taken the most marks in AFL history. (Ryan Pierse/Getty Images)

Round 3, 2010, and the hamstring injury that would cost me fifteen weeks. It also contributed to Maddie and Cath becoming firm friends. (Quinn Rooney/Getty Images)

Marking over Bob Murphy in the 2010 preliminary final. Five years later, with the help of our wives, we became great mates on an International Rules tour of Ireland. (AFL Media)

Parading my best 'resting bitch face' alongside Collingwood captain Nick Maxwell, grand final eve, 2010. (Quinn Rooney/Getty Images)

After an early goal in the 2010 grand final. We finished the draw with all the momentum, but it wasn't to be. If only extra time had come in a few years earlier! (Quinn Rooney/Getty Images)

Every footballer's window on hell—with Ross Lyon and the boys after losing the 2010 grand final replay. (AFL Media)

Farewelling the legendary Darrel Baldock. Ross Lyon (on my right) remains one of my closest friends and confidantes. He coached with passion and the hard edge we needed. (AFL Media)

Nanny Fay and I share a love of Orford and a pride in the mark the Millington family has left on the area. I love her dearly. (Author's collection)

Tassie winter fishing with Maddie. Orford will forever be her special place. (Author's collection)

On a pre-season training camp in New Zealand, early 2011; a welcome distraction from a scandal that upended the football club—and my world. (Author's collection)

On the burst against the Lions at the Gabba, 2011. (Jonathan Wood/Getty Images)

To lead St Kilda in 220 games over eleven seasons humbled me enormously. (Mark Dadswell/Getty Images)

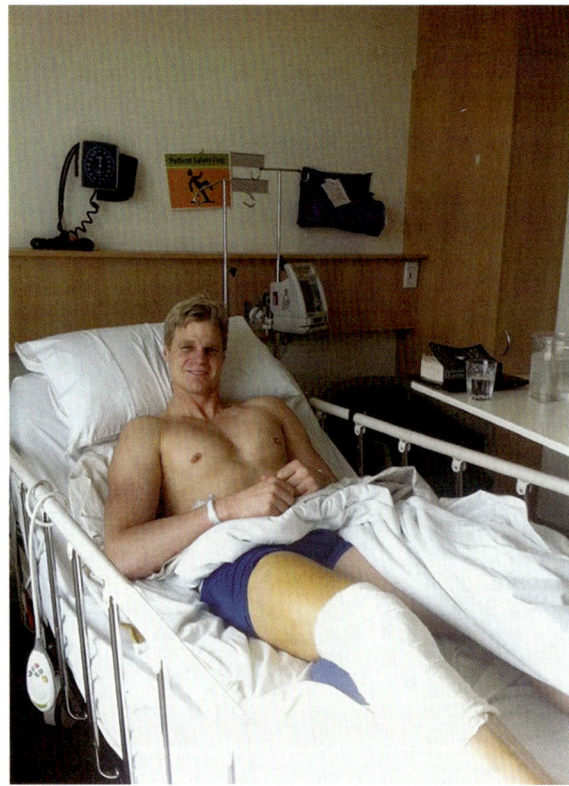

Recovering from one of the twenty-plus surgeries that dotted my career, this time after a post-season knee operation. (Author's collection)

Mentors

My wedding was almost like the breaking of bread for a lot of those relationships. The reception was under a huge marquee with everyone sitting at long tables. At one stage Rossy and Thommo were sitting on the same table talking to each other. All of us Saints boys found each other and were just sitting there watching. 'Can you believe this is happening?' There we were at a wedding in Waco, Texas, and the main thing we were interested in was Ross Lyon and Grant Thomas!

Thommo didn't move the whole day. He was like the Godfather: people would come to him, but he didn't move. Cath and I had sent the invitation to the Thomas family. We thought Grant and Kerry would be there and maybe a couple of the kids. Guests had to fill in the blanks: 'How many are coming to the reception?' 'How many will be catching the bus to the reception?' 'How many are coming to the recovery barbecue?' And they'd answered, '9', '9', '9'. Claye, the oldest, had to work and couldn't come, but everyone else was there with bells on.

Thommo is still such a great mentor. Even now, I talk to him about footy, life, post-footy, relationships. Even Cath does. In 2015 when I was badly concussed in Adelaide, after she'd spoken to Mum and Dad, the first person she called was Grant.

Cath liked Thommo from the start; he and Kerry were just so welcoming. She loves going around there, being surrounded by kids. Their house is really close to where we live; I can ring up at four o'clock and say we'll be there in an hour for early dinner, and it's no problem. Most times I go over, he'll get me in the steam room for a pow-wow. We'll sit there and he'll talk about who's doing a good job and who needs to lift. He still gives me a lot of leadership advice, which has been great during periods when we've struggled. We'll come out of the steam room and run and jump in the pool, which is freezing.

Thommo bought a farm down at Johanna in the Otways in about 2011. Cath and I have been down there plenty of times—he just gives us the keys. It's a beautiful property, right up on the ridge overlooking the ocean. It's amazing: the bushwalks, nature. It's almost subtropical, very wet. The week before the 2014 season started, we went down. We were trying for a baby at that stage, and later we worked out that's where James was conceived. Thommo makes sure everyone knows that, which is nice of him.

I reckon everyone you ask would say I was his favourite. Or Lenny Hayes—Thommo loved Lenny. Perhaps BJ (Brendon Goddard). But he loved all of us. Goose (Matt Maguire), Bally (Luke Ball), Dal, Joey. But people would call me 'Soggy'—Son of Grant.

Thommo doesn't care what anyone else thinks. A lot of people say that, but he genuinely doesn't care, but not in the sense that he deliberately says things to upset others. He just gives his opinion and, if it's going to polarise others, he does not care. I wish I could live like that. He's extraordinarily smart:

he understands relationships, simplifies things other people make very complicated, boils them down to their core.

Thommo still loves the club. For a while there, being jilted hurt him, but he's a fan. He's been the main person who's held me accountable for making sure my life is in order once I finish playing. He's been really strong in that area, really challenging. Out of the blue: 'What have you done this week about life after footy?' I'll say 'nothing' and he'll say, 'Well what are you waiting for?' It's constant: he's constantly evaluating what you're up to.

•

I'd never met Ross Lyon before he replaced Thommo as coach at the end of 2006. I have to admit, I hadn't really even heard of him.

I was visiting Mum and Dad on the Gold Coast when he got the job. After I came back to Melbourne I arranged to meet Rossy at Houlihans, a cafe we went to regularly in Hampton Street. We ordered a sandwich each, and I had one of those old-style glass Coke bottles. We were sitting at a table out the front and as a car drove past a bloke hung his head out the window and screamed, 'You're a fuckhead, Riewoldt!' I grabbed the bottle, stood up and made out like I was going to throw it. Rossy almost fell out of his chair. 'Shit, how often does that happen?' he asked. 'I've been out of Melbourne too long!'

One of the early discussions we had was about captaincy. Ross had walked into a pretty difficult situation: over the previous three seasons, Lenny had been captain in 2004, I took the job in '05 and Bally was skipper in '06. Everyone was wondering what the new coach would do, and then he made us co-captains, the three of us. I could see what he was thinking. He needed to see more—we were all relatively young, around 23, 24, and he knew the next stand-alone captain would be a long-term prospect, someone who would do the job for at least five years. He wanted to make an informed decision.

I did my hamstring in the pre-season, then I did it again, which wasn't the best start under a new coach. Ross stepped in and really took control, pulled rank on the medicos, made a point of getting it sorted. I still ended up missing the first two games of the year. Round 1 we played Melbourne at the MCG, and before the first bounce I walked with Ross from the rooms up to the coach's box. I put my arm around him and said something like, 'We're with you mate, good luck.' He's brought it up a few times—how that gesture stayed with him, how much he appreciated it. It feels like that was the start of our really close friendship.

Ross's coaching style evolved. He'd probably say he got it wrong in his first season in 2007, whereas I'd say we just didn't play well. The whole year was a bit of a struggle and fairly uneventful, other than going to Perth midway through the year when West Coast had won something like 48 out of their last 49 games at Subiaco and we pulled off an upset in Robert Harvey's 350th game. We had a chance to sneak into the finals in the last round; we needed Collingwood to beat Adelaide, but the Crows won.

Things continued to go pear-shaped through 2008, until halfway through the season Ross made a call that enough was enough. I think he realised his job was probably on the line; he was a year and a half into a three-year deal, and we had the team to be playing better. After losing to Sydney at the SCG, Ross mapped out philosophically what we needed to stand for as a group. 'What do the great teams do? This is where we're at; this is what we need to do if we want to be great.'

Ross spoke constantly about forward pressure and defence, attributes that weren't ingrained in us. The review of that game, in the lecture theatre at Moorabbin, was the most excruciating I've ever sat through. Someone had taken a short step, and Ross would pause the video, hit the slow-mo, wind it on. 'Here's you. Here's the opposition player. Look at him charging at the ball. Look at your short steps . . .' At selection that week several players were dropped, including the high-profile and respected Nick Dal Santo and Stephen Milne.

We played Fremantle the next week and won. That was Ross's line in the sand—accountability, integrity of selection, not being held captive to talent. All the Ross Lyon lines that you've heard a million times. That was when he said, 'Enough's enough, this is going to be my style. It's gunna be uncompromising, it's gunna be high accountability. If you're a person who digs in and gives great effort, we're gunna have a great time. If you're not, you don't play.'

Most guys went into every review feeling uncomfortable. Ross would ask a question about the game plan or the structure, direct it at someone, and if you didn't know the answer he'd say, 'Nup? Okay, next. You won't play this week.' He'd mostly ask young players in a bid to ramp up their development. Fear can be a powerful motivator. He held everyone accountable to high standards and, if you fell short, you got chewed up and spat out.

Ross was just as hard on himself. We made the preliminary final in 2008 but got smacked by Hawthorn, which was another moment that influenced his coaching philosophy and style. We got manipulated by the Hawks structurally, and Ross was filthy on himself for letting that happen. We adapted to what they were doing rather than just playing to our structures: they pulled stoppage players away from stoppages, and we went with them. Ross was great at learning from mistakes; if he thought he hadn't got it right in the box on a certain day, he'd put his hand up and say so. He'd point it out if you'd got it wrong, but he pointed the finger at himself too.

After that, Ross said, 'How we play is how we play—we're not changing for anyone.' The pre-season leading into 2009 we trained how we were going to play really strongly, and that just became who we were. Thommo had set a really strong foundation about mental toughness and team ethos, and with the help of our sports psych Sean Richardson, Rossy just carried that on. We spoke a lot about taking the hard versus the easy path in our preparation. Effort and role was our catchcry: give great effort and play your role.

People said it was a really taxing game style to play, but I don't agree. When we were at our best, you didn't actually have to use that much energy on defence unless the ball was in your area. We were just so good at filling the space. It was more taxing mentally through that two- to-three-year period to prepare as fanatically and train as fanatically as we did every week. But that's what great teams do. If you want to be great, you can try to get there the other way—you might get lucky—but I only know one way.

The whole 'Ross role players' thing, the criticism from the outside for the supposedly clinical, dour way we played footy—when we were 19 and 0 in 2009, we didn't give a shit. No one got near us. We just won. The fans were pretty happy, we were pretty happy, and we were in the bubble. We didn't care what anyone said. We didn't listen to the noise. We were on top of the ladder. Ross doesn't get the credit he deserves for being a great motivator. Not a motivator in the 'rah-rah' sense, but in the way he created an environment where you just wanted to prepare as best you could and give great effort. Because he rewarded effort. Andrew McQualter and Robert Eddy—unheralded 'role players'—built careers on it.

Ross would never belittle people in a nasty way, never got personal. I think that's another misconception attached to Ross. He was never a berating coach—'prickly' is a good word. But gee there were some good sprays, some absolute beauties.

At half-time one day in 2009—we were going really well overall, undefeated that season, and on the day might have been a goal up or down—Ross walked around in front of the group reading the stats. 'Dal Santo: one tackle. Joey: zero tackles. Lenny: five tackles.' He looked up, found Lenny in the group and added, 'We love ya, Lenny.' Then me. 'Rooey: one tackle.' Pause. 'FOR THE FUCKING YEAR!'

I just put my head down. The boys were all bursting, trying not to piss themselves laughing. He gave some good ones, but that's the one that stands out for me. In hindsight most of it was just plain funny, stuff that we'll laugh about forever.

Ross used to get into Dal about the shimmy: the ball-out, reel-it-back-in, dodge-the-opponent stuff. Rossy has that funny walk, and he'd be up there in front of everyone mimicking Dal. 'Dal Santo . . . hot dog, hot dog, fucking hot dog.' He'd say stuff like that and you'd think, 'Where the hell has that come from? And what's he on about?' You couldn't help but laugh.

The Ross Lyon you see in a post-game media conference is must-watch TV; I never miss it. It makes me smile, makes me chuckle, makes me laugh. He used to say stuff like, 'That's it, kick it to Rooey down the line, one on three. He's handy. He might win one out of ten. But can we switch the ball? He's a handy player, Rooey, but can we switch the ball?'

I sent a clip of him to Lenny a couple of years ago; Ross was talking about Nat Fyfe being out of contract. 'I've worked with some great players before. Riewoldt and Hayes were pretty handy. They were all out of contract—Goddard, Dal Santo. They were pretty handy.'

The stuff Ross has trotted out at Freo, I've just loved watching it because I've heard it so many times. 'We haven't achieved anything, we're just a blue-collar team that works hard.' He's a Reservoir boy and it's never left him. He comes back to Melbourne and catches up with his old Fitzroy mates— that's the side of Rossy people don't get to see. He's a lad, just a normal bloke.

Ross is a foodie too, which would surprise some people. He loves good food. If we go out he might have a beer, but most of the time he'll order a Negroni—Campari, gin and vermouth. A smooth, crooner's sort of drink. It's my favourite cocktail as well.

My relationship with Ross is very different to my relationship with Thommo, but no less important to me. We're still incredibly close. I love his kids. Every time he comes home, he'll come around with Kirst and the kids for a barbecue. I know he's really grateful to all of us as a group; he feels to an extent that we dug in for him when he was a young coach, and he's been very successful on the back of some of that. He's an outstanding coach in his own right, but he's grateful for the role we played.

Ross's St Kilda coaching career was a really testing period of his life. He faced a lot of personal challenges, including losing his sister, but he just kept it really quiet. He was a strong voice for me when Maddie got sick—because he got it, he'd been through it.

Ross is a pretty private person; I wouldn't say he's got a big network of people. But once you're in with Rossy, you're in.

The fact that Ross came and saw me in hospital when he'd signed to go to Fremantle speaks to the strength of our relationship. I had no inkling at all that he was going to leave. There'd been a few whispers, but the playing group had met with him to map out the 2012 pre-season, and Rossy had presented the program.

We got knocked out in the first week of the 2011 finals, which was the end of a horror year for all of us. I went in to the Epworth for surgery on my knee, woke up and Rossy was in my room. I remember thinking, 'Gee, what a good bloke, coming in to check how his skipper is post-surgery.' I was coming out of the anaesthetic and right off the air.

Ross told me what had happened. I can't remember what I said, but I told him I understood. We both got pretty emotional; he had a cry. He felt like he needed to tell me in person, wanted to get in before I heard about it on the radio or TV. I didn't feel any sense of betrayal. I was privy to some of the stuff that had happened behind the scenes with Rossy and the hierarchy. When it got a bit complicated and there was the opportunity to go to another good gig, he took it. It was a stuff-up from St Kilda in my opinion. How can you let Ross Lyon as coach walk out? How can you let Fremantle come in at the eleventh hour and make that play? How can you let that happen as a club?

I've got no doubt Ross elevated my level of performance as a player, elevated my level of leadership, challenged me. The environment he created made me better. We had a lot of really frank discussions as friends through that challenging period of 2011. Outside that, the team really just played and performed. It was enjoyable. Rossy and I had a great working relationship that evolved as we got to know each other more, and when the shit hit the fan I really leaned on him as a mentor.

From a football perspective, Ross had an amazing ability to challenge me really strongly without crushing my spirit. As a person he was all about cutting out the bullshit, reaffirming your purpose in life, your priorities. He implored me to take care of my family, to maintain strong relationships. 'Support the person, challenge the behaviour' was his catchcry. He made me a better person.

Rossy is still a sounding board, but at times it has been tricky because he is no longer my coach. I didn't necessarily talk to him about what was going on at the club. It was sensitive, but our relationship then was based more on mutual support.

I made sure Ross knew I still saw Thommo. Rossy was fine. Richo knew; he had Thommo come in and speak before my 300th, which Thommo really appreciated, getting brought back into the fold. He still loves St Kilda, and he contributed a significant amount to the club. For Richo to reach out like that was pretty special.

7

MY BABY AND MY TEXAS

Before I met Catherine Heard my image of Texas was a cliché you could have thrown together from watching an old Western on TV. Desert, cactus, cowboys, big hats. Really, I didn't know a thing about the Lone Star state.

My experience of America had come from footy trips, doing the touristy things in New York, Los Angeles, Miami, San Diego, Las Vegas. In the past I'd spent a couple of months of two off-seasons in Los Angeles, so I got to know LA a bit better. It struck me as being like a country all of its own. Then I got to know Texas and saw people driving around with 'Secede' stickers on their big cars. It makes you realise they really wish they could go back to the days before the Alamo and be their own country. It's a completely different part of America.

THE THINGS THAT MAKE US

Cath absolutely hates that we met in Vegas. She's told me so many times, 'When people ask, say we met in Nevada. Don't say Vegas. It sounds so gross.' But it's part of our story and there's no point hiding it. And it's not that bad. To be honest, I'm quite looking forward to telling our kids one day when they get around to asking.

•

At St Kilda we'd spoken during the 2009 season about going away as a group, hoping it would be a celebration tour. In the end there were sixteen of us in Vegas, and pretty soon the grand final loss was a hazy memory.

We'd driven up together from LA armed with a single contact. Shane Warne had put me in touch with a guy who worked at a club called LAX, where one of the partners was Mick Doohan, the former 500 cc motorbike world champion. We hooked up with Warnie's contact and he gave us some advice: 'Whoever you meet on the first night, sling them a bit of cash, tell them you're here for a week and they'll look after you.' So we did that, and the next place we turned up to our names were on the list, we had table service—everything went beautifully.

We were staying in the Wynn Hotel, a famous Vegas spot. One of the first days we were there I saw this huge group of girls walk through the lobby, head for the pool and stay there all day. There were twenty-five or more of them, and we ended up intermingling for the rest of the week, bumping into each other around the hotel.

Towards the end of our stay in Vegas I was in the lobby. It was early, maybe 8 a.m., and I'd had a big night. Actually, by then I'd had about a week of big nights, and this time I don't think I'd been to bed. I was standing there wearing only a pair of board shorts that Cath later described as underwear. They were pretty small.

Cath spotted me, recognised me as one of the big group of Aussie blokes, and came up and asked if I'd seen her girl-friends wander through. We hadn't spoken before, and I've got to admit I hadn't even noticed her. But standing there in my almost-undies I was blown away. I remember thinking, 'Jeez, where's she been all week? How have I not seen her before?'

So I said to this tall, beautiful girl, 'They're out by the pool, I'll walk you out there.' Like she couldn't have found the pool by herself. Anyway, out we went, I invited myself to sit down next to her, and we didn't move for eight hours.

After a while the guys turned up and joined the party. Cath and her friends were from all over the place: Cath went to Southern Methodist University in Dallas, and her mates were from New Orleans, Chicago, California, all over the States. They were part of a sorority called Pi Beta Phi, which they explained was a kind of social group within a university or college. Of course at some stage they asked what we did and Zac Dawson said, 'We play Aussie Rules football.' They weren't having that. They could see we were athletic, but to them footballers were massive mountains of men. We didn't fit the bill.

Someone explained what the game looks like, how it's played, that it's the biggest sport in Australia, commonly known as Aussie Rules. They called us out straight away, saying, 'That's such a made-up sport. What are you gunna tell the next group of girls? That you train dolphins?'

Then Zac pointed at me and said to Cath, 'He's our captain. Here, I'll show you.'

The photo scandal hadn't happened yet (the photo was taken a week or so later in Miami), but I knew one of the first pictures that would come up if you googled my name was me sitting on the bench at the Gabba with a broken collarbone having a cry. I jumped in and said, 'Nah, don't do that, you don't have to google it.' I knew it was going to be embarrassing, and I also knew I was trying everything to impress Cath. I managed to get the phone and scroll through the photos pretty quickly, said something like, 'So that's what we do, we play football', and moved the conversation on.

By the end of the afternoon I was thinking, 'Gee, this girl's great. I really wanna hang out with her tonight, but we're on a footy trip—I can't break away from the group.' So I said to Cath, 'We're going to a club tonight, you should all come and meet us there.' We exchanged numbers, I said we were getting there around 10 p.m., and we went off to shower, change and have dinner.

We found enough energy to make it to the club, which was called Body English and located within the Hard Rock Hotel. Usually we would have been dancing on the tables, but everyone was so flat it wasn't funny. We were five days deep in Vegas by that stage and the boys were absolutely cooked. Vegas is a two-, three-night maximum proposition, and we'd been going hard, drinking solid for five days and nights. Then I got a text message: 'Hey, we're out the front, there's a huge line, don't worry about it.' I wrote back as fast as my fingers could move. 'No, stay there.'

I'd followed Warnie's guy's advice when we'd arrived at the club, collected 20 bucks off every bloke, given it to the bloke at the door and asked him to look after us for the night. He'd already put us in a good spot and now I grabbed him and said, 'Hey, we've got all these girls coming.' He asked how many and I said, 'Twenty or thirty.' He said, 'Perfect, we always love girls in here.'

I walked out and said to Cath, 'Hey, come up the front.' The bouncer unclipped the velvet rope and they just walked in. It was like this procession of beautiful girls all dressed up walking down the stairs. You should have seen the guys. We went from utterly hangdog, the most defeated group of men you've ever seen, to reinvigorated, charging, ready to go another five days. Cath didn't say anything to me, but she told me later on she was thinking to herself, 'Who the hell is this guy? They're Australians, they're in Vegas, and they've just managed to get thirty girls to the front of a massive line and into this club!'

We partied all night and had an absolute ball. We have photos where I've got my arms around her. We look at them now and are like, 'What is this? What were we thinking?'

Cath and I hung out the next morning and then the sorority girls all left Vegas to get on with their lives. The St Kilda boys continued on, had a couple more nights there, then six guys dropped off and the rest of us went to New York. We spent a week there and it was more of the same—drinking every night. Gosh, it's tiring just writing about it. Three more dropped off and we went down to Miami: me, Dal, Joey, Gilbo, Zac, Grammy (Jason Gram) and Kosi.

We stayed there for another week, needless to say another week of partying. There's plenty of stories about what AFL footballers get up to on end-of-season trips, and in my experience there certainly weren't any visits to the Grand Canyon or Statue of Liberty. All we did was drink and party. So that's what we kept doing. I certainly wasn't thinking at that stage that I was going to marry Cath, but I was still thinking about her.

Joey, Dal and I went back to LA and flew home from there. Cath and I spoke a couple of times while I was there; even then I was thinking, 'This isn't just a passing thing.' I really connected with her, perhaps because she saw me differently to girls I'd seen in Melbourne. The fact that she had no idea about footy meant she wasn't interested in me for anything other than me, and that was really attractive. I've always been a little bit conservative in the way I've lived my life. I could just sense that Cath was a very moral person, and that was really appealing.

Back in Melbourne we stayed in touch and by Christmas we were skyping—once a week, then twice, then three times. By the new year we were talking pretty much every day, and the conversation always went to the same place: 'What the hell are we doing?' What was becoming more and more apparent by the day was what a smart, well-rounded, caring soul she was. I could tell we were getting in deep.

Cath had a college break coming up, so I asked if she'd consider coming out to visit. It was a crazy idea and, now that I know how conservative her family is, I can't believe it actually happened, that we're here today. They aren't conservative compared to those around them—it's just the way people are in Texas. The South in general is a very conservative part of the States. Most of Cath's married friends didn't live with their husbands before the wedding. We were up against it to say the least. And I'm sure her family thought we were too young. I was 26, but Cath was only 21 when we met.

Her mum, Caroline, scoured the internet to see if there was anything unsavoury about me. Again, thank goodness the photo scandal hadn't blown up at that point. Caroline still says the fact that I was a one-club player impressed her. 'He must be a very loyal person. All right, go and visit him in Australia.' Cath's dad, Larry, wasn't such an easy sell. As far as he was concerned I was a footballer: strike one. His daughter had met me in Vegas: strike two. And I lived on the other side of the world: three strikes, you're out.

Caroline and Cath booked the ticket and then told Larry; that's how it went down. Caroline has a bit of an adventurous side, and she could tell we were serious about at least seeing if we were meant to be together. Larry is a great man, and once Cath had spoken to him he backed her judgement.

Cath came out for five days; Larry had said that was the limit as he didn't want her missing more than two days of college classes. Driving to the airport, I was so excited and nervous I was almost shaking. I wanted to walk in, carry her bags, do the chivalrous thing, but her flight landed early. When I pulled up in my car she was standing there on the footpath, waiting. I'd only seen her in person for 24 hours, and she looked different to how I'd remembered her. Better. Cath's memory of me picking her up is that I smelt weird, like cocoa butter. It was summer, I was tanned—she could be right.

She got in the car and it was so awkward, my mind was racing trying to think what to do. 'Do I give her a hug? A kiss on the cheek? What do I do?' We just started talking. Cath's always called the big, yellow sculpture that sticks out at an angle at the start of the Tullamarine Freeway 'the French fry'. She reckons that by the time we went past the French fry we'd run out of stuff to talk about. We were both so nervous.

I was living in South Melbourne but decided not to go straight home, that it would be good to go for a bit of a drive instead. I tried to give her a bit of perspective about where things were, show her a bit of Melbourne, of the city I called home. We went down to St Kilda, stopped at Elwood Beach and got some fresh air. Back in the car my phone rang and it was one of my mates, Westy, who has a farm up the road from my shack at Orford. He gave the all-time worst speech at our wedding rehearsal, but that's another story. I answered on speaker and Westy said, 'G'day, Ballbag, how ya goin'? So, do you use that hair cream to shave your legs? I wanna put some on my nuts.'

I just about died, and didn't even have time to say, 'Mate, I've got someone in the car . . .' Goodness knows what Cath was thinking, although you'd get pretty short odds on it being something like, 'What have I got myself into?'

•

I'd told Mum a few weeks earlier that I had this girl coming out to stay with me, that I hadn't known her long and obviously wasn't sure what would happen. 'She lives on the other side of the world, so who knows how it'll work out,' I said to Mum. But I told her I really liked Cath, and Mum and Dad were excited.

That second night Cath was in town we all went out to dinner in Port Melbourne, near Station Pier, the terminal for *The Spirit of Tasmania*: me, Cath, Mum, Dad, Alex and Maddie. Talk about being thrown into the lions' den. I was in a bit of a state, worrying about what they'd think of her. I spoke to Alex afterwards and he just said, 'I want one.' He used that line in his best man's speech at our wedding, which brought the house down.

Right from the start my family took to Cath, and that meant a lot. Maddie was always a tough nut to crack—she made Cath work like she'd made every girlfriend of Alex's or mine work—but pretty soon I could tell it was just for show and she really liked her. I was still learning so much about Cath as well, so it was good to sit back that night and listen to them question her about her life over dinner. Of course Dad couldn't help himself, and cracked an American-themed joke, something involving rhyming slang where 'Septic Tank' and 'Yank' featured. I'm not sure Cath knew how to take it. The rest of us just rolled our eyes like we always do.

In the short time Cath was visiting, we had an intra-club match and she came down to Moorabbin and watched. She didn't say anything, but thinking back it must have been bizarre. I was supposed to be a professional footballer, and there I was running around in front of barely 500 people at decrepit old

Moorabbin. At least I kicked a few, half a dozen from memory. That just adds to the corny scene, the boy turning it on in front of his girl.

It was a good time of year to be in Melbourne; we went to the St Kilda festival and had a wander around, and we celebrated Valentine's Day with a nice dinner while she was in town. When it came time for Cath to fly home, we knew it wasn't just a fling. I told her I felt invested, that we'd worked hard to keep in touch and that she'd come a long way to visit. I said I wanted to be with her and nobody else. We had that sort of conversation.

Cath was studying business and corporate communications and was due to finish college in May. Then in round 3, in early April, I did my hammy really badly, snapping the tendon. The prognosis was I'd miss the rest of the year, but in the end I was out for only twelve weeks, came back in round 15 and managed to play eight games before the 2010 finals. But the early stages after the injury were a real pain. I had full reattachment surgery and couldn't walk; luckily there was an elevator in the townhouse I was living in, because if I'd had to get up and down stairs, I would have been stuffed.

The silver lining came in Cath's reaction. She just said, 'Well, I'll come out and give you a hand around the house.' So we got to see each other again, which made the rehab so much better. And Cath and Maddie got to know each other too. Pretty much every day I'd drive out to Berwick and sit in a hyperbaric chamber, and most times Cath and Maddie would come along and just sit in the car for two hours talking. That's where their friendship was born, so that hamstring injury is actually something that's quite nice to look back on in a strange sort of way. Apart from the fact that Maddie would play Steph McIntosh songs in the car, I'm sure just to needle Cath. That's so Maddie.

We started talking about what Cath was going to do when she finished college in mid-year, and kept coming back to the idea of her investigating a move to Melbourne, staying for a few months and seeing if what we were both feeling was the real thing. I said I knew a few business people who might be able to help pull a few strings, but Cath was adamant she was going to find employment by herself. She organised the whole thing through Bob McNabb, a contact back in Houston, securing a working visa and a job with a huge executive recruitment company called Korn Ferry.

Every day she'd catch the tram into this big, foreign city and go to work. It was incredible what she did, and that was so attractive—her independence, her strength and courage to move to the other side of the world. I've come to appreciate what a magnificent home life she had: the opportunity, the closeness to her family, cousins, the ranches that are in the family and offer so many tangible adventures. To leave that all behind and come out here was so courageous, and it made me love her all the more.

My Baby and My Texas

•

Come grand final week of 2010 we had our flights booked to leave for Texas the following Tuesday; I was off to meet my future in-laws for the first time. Cath was watching the game with Mum, Dad, Alex and Maddie from Lindsay Fox's box. When the final siren sounded the room apparently groaned to the sound of everyone saying, 'Oh no!'

Except Cath, who jumped in, 'It's all right, we've got this, we've got the momentum, we're playing way better than they are, it's all good.' She thought we were about to play extra time, but Maddie—in her matter-of-fact, don't-suffer-fools way—set her straight. 'No, Cath, you don't understand—we've gotta come back and play the whole game again next weekend.'

Then Cath burst into tears and the scene flipped on its head, with everyone trying to comfort her by saying, 'It's okay, the boys will be fine, they had the momentum, they'll win it next week.' They didn't realise Cath was gutted because we were supposed to be flying home to Texas and our plans had just been thrown into a tailspin. She actually didn't give a stuff about the result. We'd only been dating a few months, and Cath had no idea how important winning a premiership was to me, my family and everyone in the stadium for that matter. Like anyone who's spent long enough in footy-mad Melbourne, she's certainly come to realise that now.

THE THINGS THAT MAKE US

That finals series was the first time Cath began to be recognised as my girlfriend, and straight away the potential downside of that profile became apparent. She came to the grand final parade with Maddie and some of the other players' partners, and at one stage Maddie—just mucking around and being Maddie—put a jumper over Cath's head when a newspaper photographer tried to take a snap of her. On the back of that tiny thing, a gossip columnist wrote a piece saying Cath clearly thought she was too good for everyone else, trying to hide like that, who does she think she is? It was a troubling window on the world she was entering.

Through the gloom of losing the replay, our thoughts eventually turned again to Texas. We had a few days in Hawaii to break up the trip and chill out with BJ, Rob Eddy, Zac Dawson, and David and Andrea Fox, then Cath and I flew on to Houston. Getting off the plane I was nervous, and had this overwhelming desire to find a bathroom, put on a fresh shirt and brush my teeth. We got through Customs and I saw there were bathrooms straight ahead—and right in between us and the bathroom door stood Cath's family. Her father Larry and mother Caroline were there, and Vivian, who's two years younger than Cath. Their brother John, who's four years younger than Viv, was still at school.

Cath ran up and they had a big group hug, then I sheepishly stepped forward and went to shake Larry's hand. And before I could extend my arm he grabbed me and gave me a hug too.

It was a symbolic moment, because from the very outset I've felt warmly embraced by Cath's family.

Larry is just such a good person. He's successful, he's modest, he lives a Christian life—although it may have different connotations in Australia. If you identify as a Christian here, people think you must be a zealot. Cath's family aren't in your face about it, rather they just live in a way that reflects their faith as good people. They attend church, bless the food at meal times, things like that. Over time that's become James's thing; as a toddler, he wouldn't let us start eating until we'd all joined hands so he could lead the prayers. Then he'd enjoy it so much that we'd have to do it six times.

The wealth in Houston is unlike anything I've seen: oil and gas money, old money, new money. The Heards aren't oil barons; Larry's a self-made man who started as a junior at a local real estate company called Transwestern more than 30 years ago. And he still looks young enough to be mistaken for Cath's older brother.

Their place in Houston is a big three-storey house on a small block in a typical, tree-lined street, but you've got to get out of town to see the real family gems. There are two ranches and they're very different. There's an old one out past San Antonio near the Mexican border, which has no TV, no phone reception, scorpions in the bedsheets and pipes that make a shocking, groaning noise every time you turn a tap on. There's a big, long porch with rocking chairs, just like in the movies, and a really cool swimming pool that's actually an old converted water tank with stairs leading up the side and a platform built around the top. Cath's aunt and uncle's ranch, which the family go to more often, is out past Austin in Llano. It's the Taj Mahal, like a resort.

Since I've known Cath, her family have bought a house in Waco, only a couple of hours away, which we visit all the time when we're in Texas. It's less humid there, much more comfortable, and their place is just stunning: 12 hectares of riverfront, horses, a pool, the lot. We go every weekend, and it's such a great place to be with the kids. Since visiting with James and now William too, I get emotional when it comes time to leave because it's just such a joy seeing how much they love it. When James was starting to talk, his vocabulary just about doubled on one trip, because he'd spend the whole day saying, 'Moo cows!', and all the horses' names and what he wanted to feed them: 'Copper, Tripp, Sterling, Honey . . . carrots!'

Larry and Caroline have been outstanding role models for Cath and me: as a married couple, as parents. I'll always be grateful for the way they've supported our relationship. Since becoming a parent, I've been able to appreciate how incredibly difficult it must have been for them to allow their daughter to move to the other side of the world. If they'd made that even a little bit difficult, it would never have happened; Cath's too much of a family person to want to put them offside. It would have been very easy for them to sabotage our relationship—not in a nasty way, but almost subconsciously. But they've been nothing but supportive all the way through and I'll always be so grateful for that. The life they're able to provide for us when we go back there, and for James and William—it's a world I never dreamed of but one I know I'm blessed to have.

•

Houston is a huge city and the state of Texas as a whole has 27 million residents, which makes it more populous than Australia. But even so it's far more urban than I thought it was going to be, full of commerce and industries and the big cities that sustain them. I expected barren deserts, red dust, tumbleweeds and cacti, but you have to head way out to West Texas to find that.

Some of the clichés are still there, which I like. On that very first trip we were walking through the airport and passed two guys wearing 10-gallon hats and huge belt buckles; I thought they must have been some sort of entertainment, like a welcoming committee. But they were just two regular guys unwittingly living the Texas stereotype.

The ability for me to be anonymous is a big part of why I love the place so much. Outside of the usual parenting ups and downs, there's no stress or responsibility; everyone back home knows we're away so the phone doesn't ring, and you just drop back a cog or two and enjoy being together as a family. We're used to the travelling; we get there, set up in our bedrooms, unpack our clothes, and just live. We don't need to pack as much anymore: we almost have a wardrobe in each country.

I'm a huge fan of American sport, and over there I quickly settle into having different conversations to when I'm in Melbourne. Over there I'm Catherine's husband, and I've made some wonderful mates through the family with whom I regularly play golf, go out to dinner, or just hang out. If I hadn't had post-season surgery, I'd be at a local Houston gym most mornings, which soon became somewhere I was known but felt comfortable. Because to them I wasn't 'Nick Riewoldt, St Kilda footballer', I was 'that Aussie bloke who's married to one of the Heards'.

Ricky and Cedric run the gym and have become really good friends. We go out to lunch with Ricky; he comes over and teaches James how to dribble a basketball. He knows what I do back home, but other than asking, 'How was your season?' each time we arrive back in Houston, my career is never discussed. I like that, and I'm sure it helped my football.

I take James and Will to the park. If a game of American football is on, I sit around and watch that, then we go out for dinner or stay in and eat with Cath's family. It's all pretty normal, simple stuff, but that's the beauty of it.

One year I played in a recreational softball league on Wednesday nights, and another time I played flag football but decided to give that up when I almost broke my leg. Flag football is a bit like touch rugby or gridiron without tackling, where you wear tags and it's your opponent's job to rip the tags off. One time a bloke came in to get my tag, overstrode, and hit me halfway up my shin with his cleat. The pain was excruciating and straight away I thought, 'I'm done here, I've fractured my tibia and fibula.' That wouldn't have gone down too well back at St Kilda, but I escaped with a scar down my shin. And just like that I became an ex-flag footballer.

The subtle differences you encounter are always amusing, and sometimes a bit embarrassing. The gym where I work out is pretty basic, and I go in there and do leg weights, upper body weights and get on the bike. One time it was so cold I put on a pair of tights, which we wore at footy training all the time without putting shorts over the top. I walked into the gym and there were a couple of huge, 130-kilogram ex-NFL players in there working out. They took one look at me and were like, 'Man, what you doin'? You've got ya junk hangin' out everywhere! Put some clothes on!' I went straight back out to the car and put some shorts on.

Over time Cath and I have acquired a bit of a Houston fan club who know our story and think it's a bit of a fairytale; they follow us when we're back in Australia through various social media channels. That's about the only context I get recognised in—someone hearing the accent and saying, 'You're not married to a Heard are you?' In all the years we've been going to the States I think I've been recognised by someone from Australia maybe twice, and that was only when we'd gone up to New York or LA. I have no inhibitions when I'm there: there's none of the whole cap-lowered-an-extra-centimetre that happens in Melbourne.

Cath has a cousin who plays college football for Baylor University, and from Waco we take a boat up to see him play. The stadium is on the Brazos River, so from the house at Waco we just walk out of the house, down to the river and onto the boat, drive it down to the game, park in the marina, climb out and walk to our seats. It's a bit surreal, but that's life in Texas. I have to remind myself that it's not real life. I've often thought, 'Gosh, it'll be great when I finish playing to come and live life like this.' But it wouldn't be the same; it's not a true reflection of what life would look like if we moved there. For a start, I'd have to get a job.

The first time I went to Texas we went hunting. Larry's got a younger brother and two younger sisters, one of whom, Susanna, is married to Gee Kane. His name is George, but to everyone he's just called Gee Kane. They have the ranch down at Llano, about 400 hectares, and I went hunting there with Gee and their son Harrison. You cruise around in the little four-wheel Mules with your rifles. There are hunting blinds where you can go and sit, feeders going off all over the ranch. You hunt white-tailed deer, either by stalking them or sitting in a blind and waiting.

On that first trip it was really late and we hadn't seen

anything, then a deer came wandering into sight right on dusk. I said to Harrison, 'Should I shoot it?' I'd been shooting in Tassie before; I knew what to do but, after he said 'Go for it', it was getting so dark I still didn't know if I'd hit it. We got down to where the deer was, about 200 metres away, and it was there, dead on the ground.

Gee Kane and Harrison showed me how to clean a deer. It's a messy deal—not like a roo, which is pretty straightforward. Also, when you kill your first deer they say it's customary to take a bite out of the heart. I was like, 'Shut up! No way!' But they said, 'No, you've gotta do it.' So I sucked in a big breath and went to take a bite, almost got it up to my mouth, and they stopped me. They were taking the piss, just wanted to see whether I'd do it. I'd passed the test.

I had the deer head mounted by a taxidermist in Houston, and all of the meat made into sausages: venison, garlic, jalapeno, all sorts. I know the whole thing probably sounds barbaric to some people, but there's a normality to it over there. People have ranches and they go hunting. Cath even gave me a .243 bolt-action rifle with a scope for my birthday a couple of years back. Before we had kids, it would lie under our bed in Houston like a pair of shoes. You have to spend time there to realise how different their gun laws are, and the mentality around them. You can buy a civilian machine-gun at the equivalent of Rebel Sport. That notion of something being 'my civil right' overrides everything. It's just so different.

THE THINGS THAT MAKE US

•

A man never forgets proposing to his wife, and I have more reason than most to remember that moment forever. Once I'd made up my mind to ask Cath, I was always going to do it in Texas. I just figured Cath's family had missed out on so much with their daughter moving away, and they were going to miss a lot more with us living in Melbourne, so it would be really nice for them to be part of it. And it would make it an even greater memory for us.

I'd asked David Fox's wife Andrea to help me buy a ring in Melbourne, and when we set off for Texas in October 2011, I had a nice wedding band in my backpack. I knew Cath was probably thinking, 'He'll do it this trip.' I just had a feeling she was expecting something to happen. We were in Sydney changing planes, catching a bus from the domestic to the international terminal, and Cath was on the phone to Andrea whom I'd already worded up to put her off the scent. So Andrea said, 'Nick spoke to David. I think he wants to wait one more year just to make sure you really love Melbourne and you're sure about it.'

Cath got off the phone and didn't say anything, but I could feel the ice. She was flat. There wasn't outward anger, just flatness. Meanwhile I've got the ring burning a hole in my backpack.

We had a couple of weeks in Houston then headed out to the ranch for Thanksgiving. I didn't know how I was going to do it, or when I was going to do it, didn't have a plan at all. But I knew the first thing I needed to do was speak to Larry. We went hunting the day before Thanksgiving and spent the afternoon sitting in a blind waiting for deer. You've got to be really quiet, so I'm sitting next to my future father-in-law, I've got my gun and he's got his, and I'm having this conversation in my head about asking for permission to marry his daughter. I realised it wasn't the sort of question you could ask in a whisper, 'Hey, Larry . . . I was just wondering . . .'

So I waited. We were kilometres away from the ranch house, it was pitch black, and then some headlights appeared. Someone had come to pick us up and the opportunity was gone. That night we went out to dinner in town; it was Thanksgiving the next day and no one wanted to cook. It's a 30-minute drive into town, there were fifteen or sixteen of us, and on the way back I deliberately went in a different car to Cath. I was sitting next to her sister Vivian and told her what I was planning, explaining that I desperately needed to get her father alone.

When we arrived back at the ranch Larry hung back and said Viv had told him I needed to see him. So I just cut to the chase and asked him. I was absolutely shitting myself, and he just looked up at the heavens and took this huge breath. I was thinking, 'What's that? Is that yes? Is it get stuffed?' And he just said, 'Mate, we're all in.' Then he gave me a hug. It was a beautiful moment.

Larry went back in and told Caroline. Everyone was sharing a bathroom and, when we were getting ready for bed a little while later, Caroline was standing next to me, brushing her teeth and just smiling. I spent most of the night staring at the ceiling unable to speak; I was so excited and nervous about what was going to happen the next day.

I still didn't have a plan: would I put Cath on a four-wheeler, drive up to the top of a hill and ask her, then come back and tell everyone? Thanksgiving lunch varies depending on where you are—if we'd been in town, everyone would have been dressed nicely but at the ranch it had a really low-key, summery feel. I sat down to lunch in board shorts, a singlet and no shoes. You could go and grab your lunch, help yourself, then head out and sit by the pool or stay inside at the table.

I gave Caroline a wink, went back to our room and got the ring, wrapped it up in a towel so it looked like I was going for a swim. Caroline called everyone in and there were cousins yelling back, 'No, we're out here having a good time!' I just said something like, 'Please come in—I want to thank G and Sue for having us all for lunch.' Cath was looking at me with this expression of 'What are you doing? Don't be an idiot, sit down and eat your lunch!'

Then I dropped down onto one knee and Cath lost it. There are photos, which is great. It was really special because everyone got to share it; it just felt right to do it in front of everyone because I knew how excited they would be. I had called Mum and Dad when I went to the room to get the ring, so they knew I was about to do it, and I called them again straight after. It was nice that they were kind of part of it too.

We wanted our wedding to be unique, an experience that we and everyone who was there would always reflect on with a smile. Weddings in Texas are generally church service and country club reception affairs; they can be huge, just incredible. With 97 travelling Australians among the guest list of 250, we thought it would be nice to do something different, so we got married at the Heards' river house in Waco a year later.

It was more like a festival than a wedding, and that meeting of cultures—even given the similarities between Australians and Americans—led to some funny moments. My bachelor party was a week out from the wedding. Brendon Goddard was there, my mate Jerome Batten from Queensland, Alex Thompson, my brother Alex, Cath's brother John, and a mixture of other mates from home and locals I had become mates with through Cath. We went to a bar for drinks during the day and watched college football, then a Mexican restaurant for dinner and on to a party bus around town.

Everyone was feeling each other out, didn't really know each other that well, so to kick things off Alex Thompson said, 'I just want to start by asking, when was the last time America won a war?' You could feel the oxygen disappearing from the room. I just put my head down on the table. Alex wasn't looking for an answer, he was just shit-stirring. It led to some butting of heads for a while, but by the end of the night everyone was getting on like a house on fire.

The wedding format was rehearsal dinner on Friday night, wedding Saturday and recovery party Sunday. Rehearsal dinner was a new concept to me. It was in a function space in a Waco hotel, and 100 people sat down to eat: friends, parents, siblings, grandparents. We made the mistake of making it open mic: Alex MC'ed, Dad said a few words, then pretty much anyone who wanted to could get up and propose a toast or say a few words. My mate Justin West from Tassie gave the all-time worst speech, which culminated in an inappropriate joke that featured Cath and me as the central characters. Cath's father Larry was sitting next to me. To say it didn't go down well is an understatement. Poor Westy, he was mortified for the rest of the weekend.

The wedding itself made up for any little hiccups. It was just beautiful in every way, right down to the weather: 30 degrees, still and sunny. The ceremony was really moving. We exchanged our vows in front of family and friends, under a grove of pecan trees, and committed to each other in God's name. We then moved around to the marquee on the back lawn that leads down to the river. The attention to detail was just extraordinary, little touches everywhere you looked that worked so well. Everything was branded with an insignia that combined the 'R' of Riewoldt with the 'H' of Heard: serviettes, menus, place settings. There were Team USA and Team Australia stubby holders, a see-through roof on the marquee so you could see the stars, a signpost in the middle of the party showing how many miles to Houston, Melbourne, Hawaii, Orford. It was just stunning. Cath wore cowboy boots under her wedding dress, which was so cool.

Everyone picked up the vibe and it was just on, one huge party. So many friendships that will endure came out of that night, which makes it all the more special for Cath and me. There was a cigar station, free-pour spirits, the band had been paid extra to learn 'Down Under', 'Khe Sanh' and 'You're the Voice', and when they came on the Australians took over the dance floor and went off. They had to bring in extra booze three times during the night. The caterers said they'd never seen people drink so much, and of course the Aussies got the blame. It was an amazing party.

Mum, Dad, Maddie and Alex flew over with Nanny Fay, the whole family together, and spent a week in Houston staying at the Heard house. Maddie was incredibly self-conscious about the weight she'd put on because of the medication, and I know she wasn't looking forward to the wedding because of that. But when I look back on the video of that day and night, and see the photos, I take great comfort in the fact that she had a wow of a time.

Maddie was a bridesmaid, and while she's not in many photos, that's probably because she was off down by the river smoking cigars with Cath's cousins, making smores (fire-toasted marshmallows between crackers) and doing god knows what. From all reports, despite all that was going on in her world, she had an incredible time and made some wonderful friends. That's a really comforting memory to take from the greatest day of our lives.

Cath and I headed to Mexico for our honeymoon, and my lot all went on a family trip to New York, up through Cape Cod and then to Boston. Maddie got really sick in Boston and had to be hospitalised for a few days. They didn't tell me and Cath for the first couple of days, and she eventually improved enough to get on a plane and fly home. I look back on that sort of stuff and there's guilt—there I was, enjoying my honeymoon, and Maddie was in hospital. I don't even know if I really appreciated at the time how serious her illness was.

•

At various times when we're in Houston, or at home in Melbourne, Cath and I have found ourselves looking at each other and asking, 'Who are you? How did we get here? Why were we so lucky to meet?' I know from my end I can't imagine sharing my life with anyone else; we make such an amazing team, and she's the best teammate I've ever had.

I have no doubt the entrée she gave me to Texas extended my career. It's made me a more worldly, balanced person, opened my eyes in so many different ways. It's just so different over there, and even though I know our stays with Cath's family aren't 'real life', the quality of the life we lead there is amazing.

My Baby and My Texas

It's also made me realise how expensive Australia is. We get sold a bit of a myth here—the lucky country, Melbourne the most liveable city, all of that hoopla. Melbourne's the most liveable city if you have a lot of money—there are people paying more than a million dollars for a block of land in an average suburb, for goodness' sake.

We'll do a year or two in Texas at some stage; I love the idea of our kids going to college there. Ideally I'll find something post-football that allows us to keep spending time there. If it turns out to be working in the media, which has the added attraction of staying involved in footy, we could be there every October for months. It's such a great time to be there too; the weather is beautiful, it's the start of the NFL season, the start of the college season. You're there for Thanksgiving and Christmas, then you come back here for January, February, March, probably the three best months in Australia.

There's still a lot I haven't done that I'm looking forward to. There's a song by the Josh Abbott Band called 'My Texas', which is essentially a list of things you have to do in Texas. 'If you haven't done this, this and this, you ain't met my Texas yet', that sort of thing. I've gone through and ticked ten or twelve. I've sung 'Carry On' at a Pat Green show. I've eaten Cooper's barbecue down in Llano. I've seen a Hill Country sunset. But I've never been to the Houston Rodeo. And I haven't taken my baby to the River Walk down in San Antonio.

One day. We have plenty of time.

8

LOVING AND LOSING MADDIE

For the first few days of her life Maddie was called Olivia. I was only six but I wasn't having that. There was a girl in my class at school called Olivia and I didn't like her at all. I cracked it, hard. My older cousin, Madeleine—who is now Will's godmother—used to babysit me and I looked up to her so much. Mum and Dad said, 'Well, what do you want to call her?' I said 'Madeleine', and I got my way.

And Olivia Caroline Riewoldt became Madeleine Olivia Caroline Riewoldt. She is the only person I've known with two middle names.

I guess having two older brothers helped to shape Maddie's early years. We called her 'Mooch', and she was just fearless. There's a story from a family holiday we had in Noosa that sums her up. She was two, and just wandered up to the pool at the place we were staying and dived in headfirst. A woman who was watching thought she was about to drown and went in after her in a panic. And there was Maddie, kicking her legs and flapping her arms—for all intents and purposes swimming—and having a ball. I've been in the pool at home with James and Will virtually every day since they were babies, wanting them to be able to swim like Maddie.

Mooch had tomboyish tendencies—she played footy, baseball and soccer—but right through her childhood water was her thing. The ocean especially—she was fearless in the ocean—but anything to do with the water, she was incredible. We moved to the Gold Coast when Maddie was four and I was ten, so the water became an even bigger part of her world and she loved it. She did Nippers, surf-lifesaving; Dad taught her to surf.

When she was eight, Maddie had a terrible accident that had a lasting effect on her. It was athletics carnival day at our school, All Saints Anglican. Another kid threw a shot-put when they shouldn't have and it hit Maddie in the head. It was an awful thing to happen and it was badly handled. Maddie actually walked to the sick bay; there was no ambulance called, and Mum had to come to school, pick her up and drive her to the GP. Straight away the doctor could see it was serious. He told Mum to put something over Maddie's head to stop her having an epileptic fit and they got her to the hospital immediately.

Loving and Losing Maddie

She had a concave, compressed skull fracture, was taken straight in for surgery and then stayed in hospital for a good while. We have photos of Maddie with half her head shaved, and this huge horseshoe scar. For the next eighteen years the scar was covered by her beautiful blonde hair, until she became sick and lost all her hair from the chemo, and there was her big scar again. The poor kid, how much can one person endure?

The accident really affected Maddie; it was like her whole personality changed. She still played footy and loved getting out in the ocean, and from the outside you probably wouldn't have known. But she went from being this fearless kid to sleeping with the light on. For years she slept in Mum and Dad's room on a mattress. She only moved to her own room when she was midway through primary school, when Mum and Dad bought her a TV; the comfort of the TV's background noise enabled her to fall asleep. She became a bit volatile, would just lose her temper and fly off the handle. She was never a very tactile person, which is weird for our family—we are always hugging and kissing—but from that moment on, trying to get a hug off Maddie was a challenge.

On reflection I guess I missed out on a lot of Maddie's life. She was only twelve when I was drafted and left home. There's no guilt, just regret that I wasn't around to see her go through high school. It's not something I ever would have thought about if things hadn't turned out like they did, because you just live your life. But I was off to Melbourne, and for eight years

I only saw her for a couple of weekends at the end of the footy season, or if they came down to Melbourne for a weekend here and there. That's what I missed out on.

Maddie and Alex were much closer in age, and argued and fought like siblings do. But once I had been drafted and had moved away from home, their relationship went to another level. As my profile grew, they both had to deal with some people seeing them as only my little brother and sister. Alex and I spoke about that after Maddie passed away: that his relationship with her was a lot different to mine, because for so many years I wasn't there. They had that in common—the idea, fed by media attention, that I was the golden child and they were left behind.

The shack at Orford gave us a substitute for all the times we missed out on. It provided us with the best memories we have of each other—of fishing, camping over at Maria, getting drunk together. That is why the beach where we scattered Maddie's ashes is so special. Maddie always described it as her happy place. When she was in hospital we'd speak about what she wanted to do when she got better. It was important to give her carrots, goals, a real want-to-get-out-of-hospital card. And she always said, 'I want to walk down that little path, put my feet in the sand and in the water.'

We would sit on the deck at Orford in summer and drink cider. Maddie was a funny drunk—she got loud. I would have loved to have seen more of her in that sort of mood. Sometimes when she drank, she'd smoke a cigarette, and I used to get so pissed off with her. That seems like such a small thing now.

At the shack Maddie would sleep on a mattress on the floor next to Nan. She refused to go out to the bunkhouse, even after I had it fixed up. When we were overloaded with people, Nan would sleep out there, take her jug to make a cup of tea in the morning, wander across at night to go to the bathroom. But not Maddie, no way.

There was a dripping tap in the shower and it drove Maddie mad. It could be the middle of the night and she'd say to Fay, 'Nan, get up and fix that f—ing tap!' She wouldn't get up and do it herself.

After Maddie passed away, we went down to Orford and three or four of Maddie's best girlfriends came too. We took them out fishing and they started telling us stories. Because Maddie was the youngest, the only girl, because she'd had that accident, a lot of the time we worried about her more than we should have. They had some great stories about Maddie doing silly stuff. It was really nice to hear that she had boyfriends, that she was naughty at times, that she did funny things. Because she never really spoke to me about those things, and I never really saw it.

Maddie was a great cook, incredibly adventurous with food. At the shack we would bring back crayfish we had caught and Maddie would tell us to keep the head, the legs, the whole lot, and she would boil it all down, extract the meat and make a lobster bisque. She would whip up crayfish ravioli and make the pasta herself. It was something she shared with Mum—she would get Mum's help, but it was such a passion that she could soon do it all herself.

As close as we were, Maddie's love life was a closed book; she never spoke to me about boys. But I did see firsthand one classic example of where her priorities lay. She brought this guy she was seeing out to dinner with the rest of us one night and we went to Nobu, which is renowned for its innovative take on Japanese food. We had a great meal and afterwards Maddie asked her date, 'So what did you think?' And he replied, 'To be honest, I'd probably rather a Big Mac.' That was it, he was done with. She wiped him straight away.

Because of the impact of the accident she'd had at school, I think Mum and Dad harboured fears about how Maddie would cope in a relationship, whether she would be able to settle down and give herself emotionally to another person, because she was so insular emotionally. The only person she opened up to was Mum. They were best friends and did everything together. But there was that volatility after the accident. I wondered how someone would put up with Maddie's mood swings. They were such a part of who she was that one of her mates started calling her Moody instead of Maddie.

All the way through, Maddie made life pretty tough on our girlfriends. She only really became friends with them after we broke up with them—and she only did that to make it hard for the new one. She put Cath through the wringer, but Cath knew how to take her. There was only about nine months difference in their ages and they became such close friends. That was such a difficult thing for Cath after Maddie passed away; she was grieving for me, but she had also lost her best friend in Australia.

Mooch loved her sport, and once she had picked a team she became obsessed. Liverpool in the English Premiership, the Yankees in baseball, then Houston and Baylor in American football after Cath came along. She was an encyclopaedia, could tell you anything about every player on the team. She was especially mad about soccer.

One night when she was in intensive care but not doing too badly, I was coming home from the airport after an interstate game with Leigh Montagna and Farren Ray in the car. We always went to the airport together. It must have been about 10 p.m. and I asked if they minded if we called into ICU so I could quickly run up and see Maddie. They came in with me, and Maddie was sitting there with her iPad watching a live Liverpool match. We might as well not have been there. She even told us to shush a few times because Liverpool looked like scoring. She was obsessed, just loved it.

She loved the Saints too, and especially my career. Maddie was my number-one fan—to a fault. If anyone said a bad word on social media or there was any negative commentary, she was a keyboard warrior. She wouldn't attempt to hide that I was her brother, would just leap to my defence and not mince her words. She was fiercely loyal. At times it was like she was going in search of the criticism so she could rebut it and get into an argument.

Maddie loved coming to the footy, loved all the boys. After she moved to Melbourne with Mum and Dad, if I was invited to go anywhere, Maddie would either come along or get really pissed off that I hadn't told her about it. Same with Alex. If I was invited to a lunch or something they would just come. I'm sure it was a bit weird for the people who asked me along to functions or events to see three Riewoldts walk through the door rather than one. But if Maddie wasn't included in something she took it really personally. I wonder if that wasn't another offshoot of the accident, that sensitivity about feeling left out.

Every St Kilda game in Melbourne, Maddie and I had a routine that we stuck to the night before. I would pick her up, we'd grab a Japanese takeaway on Bay Street in Port Melbourne, then she'd run in to Coles and get me two Gatorades and a KitKat, and we'd go and have dinner and watch a movie. That was every game of 2009. She would text me during the day, 'Are we doing the routine tonight?' She loved it, but she'd always go home because she loved her own bed so much. Even when she'd come over and watch Liverpool games that wouldn't start until midnight, she'd insist on driving home at three in the morning. It was only two minutes around the corner, but still.

Maddie was a big birthdays and Christmas person; she just loved big occasions where everyone was up for a celebration. I was an October baby and after meeting Cath I was in America every year on my birthday. Maddie was always the first to text me; she had worked out the time difference, and at 12.01 a.m. US Central Time I would get a text.

Maddie was a very loyal girl who loved her family and her close friends. She idolised her big brothers, both of us. There's comfort in that.

•

Maddie was 21 when she got sick, in July of 2010. She had been waiting tables at a friend's restaurant but for pretty much the whole year she hadn't been herself, found it hard to get off the couch. Mum would ask her to do something and she'd be like, 'I'm too tired!' We got a bit frustrated with her, told her to stop being so lazy. We had no idea she was operating off barely two cylinders the whole time.

Maddie complained of a sore throat and was clearly fatigued. She mustered enough energy to go to a music festival with some friends and came back covered in bruises, even across her shoulders from the strap of her handbag. A blood test indicated a serious abnormality, and she was referred to Professor Miles Prince at Cabrini Malvern. The fear was leukaemia.

I didn't go shouting from the rooftops, 'My sister's got cancer!' because we didn't know for sure. We kept it in-house and let it play out. It's such a strange time to look back on. It was the eve of the 2010 finals and I was pretty focused on the task at hand—making another grand final. Maddie was definitely on my mind, but I didn't let it derail me emotionally. Not in those initial weeks, anyway.

On 18 August Maddie was diagnosed with aplastic anaemia, a bone marrow failure syndrome. It was the first time any of us had heard of it. The initial prognosis was that a treatment approach would suffice and Maddie wouldn't need a bone marrow transplant. When Mum rang to say Maddie's condition had worsened and the search for a bone marrow donor had begun, I was on a beach in Hawaii with Cath, the week after the grand final replay. We were on the way to meet Cath's family for the first time, and Mum told me that as soon as we got to Houston I had to get a blood test done to see if I was a compatible donor. Alex was living in New York at the time and did the same.

I remember telling the woman who took my blood that I'd googled aplastic anaemia and done some reading, which of course is the worst thing you can do. Even if you have a cold you can come away thinking you're a goner. The nurse was drawing blood from my arm when I asked her, 'Is my sister going to be okay? Is she going to die?' She said Maddie was young, told me she dealt with this sort of thing all the time, gave me some reassurance that everything would be okay.

Initially there wasn't a mad panic or rush. There was an alternative treatment called ATGAM which Maddie had, along with a host of other drugs, but the side effects were horrible. She suffered chronic vomiting, had such a lack of energy she couldn't even get out of bed to take a shower. She basically became a prisoner because of the blood transfusions and other procedures she was submitted to almost daily. As a side effect, the medication made her put on weight, which she hated. In every way it was just so unfair.

Occasionally there were hints of success and glimpses of normality. She even did a fun run and a walk one year as a survivor. I thought she was going to be okay. I never entertained the thought that she wouldn't be.

Then she relapsed.

•

We were all on a steep aplastic anaemia learning curve. In essence, the end result of leukaemia is diminished cells, and the end result of aplastic anaemia is diminished cells—you just get there via different paths. Cancer kills the cells; with aplastic anaemia you don't produce the cells. Or you produce unhealthy ones.

You hear anaemia and think iron deficiency, which is something that frustrated Maddie the whole way through. At times it felt like people thought she should just eat some red meat and she'd be okay. She copped all those sorts of comments and it drove her mad. Even after she passed away, people thought she'd had cancer.

As much as we tried to comprehend the seriousness of Maddie's situation, we fell into a pattern of just dealing with with it rather than talking about it. Maddie was very much that way inclined; she wasn't someone to pour out her feelings and emotions. We knew it was potentially fatal, but when you're diagnosed at Maddie's age, at her level of health, there's every reason to put your faith in a full recovery.

I don't know if I subconsciously didn't want to acknowledge how bad she was, but it took a while to hit home. She had a really bad reaction in April 2011, after starting the ATGAM treatment. I played a game—I can't even remember who it was against—and came off the ground to a message saying Maddie wasn't good. I rushed in to hospital, took one look at her and almost fell over. It was the first time I thought, 'This is really, really serious.'

To say that Maddie was incredibly brave and strong through the whole ordeal doesn't even come close to doing her justice. She was basically a pin cushion for almost five years, had hundreds of blood transfusions—one a week for a long time—bone marrow biopsies, invasive procedures and endless medications. The effect was like pushing a pause button on her life, which was another layer to the tragedy—for her last five years, Maddie's quality of life was terrible. She couldn't work, couldn't travel, couldn't go to St Kilda or Melbourne Victory games, couldn't do any of the things she loved. She went from being a relatively healthy young woman to someone who struggled to have a shower or even get out of bed. We would go to Orford for Christmas, Maddie's special time and place, and she would have to go to Sorell every second day for a blood test to see what her levels were like. She somehow got herself to Texas for our wedding at the end of 2012, and still ended up in hospital in Boston.

Mentally it had a massive impact on her: the constant doctors' appointments, the blood transfusions, the physically intrusive procedures that came to dominate her life. We saw the strain that chronic illness places on a person, how it chips away at their mind. And still Maddie kept fighting. And smiling.

•

In ICU towards the end, Maddie asked Dad a couple of times, 'Am I going to die?' Dad found that really difficult; what do you say to your daughter when she asks you that? And for all that you love her, you can't be sure the answer you're giving is the right one. Now that I'm a father it breaks my heart to think of the situations Mum and Dad faced every day. As a family we just had to stay positive, and I think we can be proud of the fact that we did that. We had a significant role to play, and we did everything we possibly could to keep her spirits up.

Professor David Ritchie, an amazing man, ended up treating Maddie as her bone marrow specialist. When you ask him a question, he has a habit of going very quiet and closing his eyes while he thinks through the answer. By midway through 2014, with Maddie not getting any better, the whole family was sitting in his office asking him what could be done. He closed his eyes and went quiet. Alex looked at him, then turned to me with a 'what the hell is he doing?' expression on his face. I shot back what I hoped was a 'trust him, he's incredible' look in reply. It was quite surreal.

He said there were basically two options: more of the treatment Maddie had been receiving, which was less likely to have an impact. Or a bone marrow transplant. Maddie wanted her life back. With the options set out before her she was very pragmatic. 'I don't want to do another two, three years of this treatment and end up having to have a bone marrow transplant anyway. I want to get on with my life.'

Maddie was regarded as a very good candidate for a successful transplant. A sibling donor is considered ideal because the marrow is more compatible, but both Alex and I were deemed unsuitable. That's another thing that's hard to come to terms with—that we didn't even have the chance to try to save our little sister. It would have happened midway through the football season and meant three months on the sidelines, but

I would have done it in a heartbeat. Mooch always joked, 'If anyone can do it, can it be Alex? I don't want to cop all the abuse from Saints fans!' She had that sick sense of humour. And she loved the Saints. Double negative.

At the end of the meeting with David Ritchie, I stayed back after Alex left and hit him with the hard question straight up. 'Mate, please tell me—is she going to die?' He didn't guarantee anything, but he reiterated that she was a really good candidate. She was young, and they had a good donor.

Yet again I was naive about the process; I heard 'bone marrow transplant' and envisaged cutting open bones, sucking out the marrow and replacing it. But it was just a blood transfusion—marrow cells in a bag, fed into the bloodstream intravenously. It took barely a couple of hours, and then the waiting game began. Maddie had had all the chemo before then—they basically had to kill her sick marrow and then introduce the new marrow, which her body would either accept or reject.

Maddie wanted to have the transplant—by the time it came around she was excited, she'd had her hair coloured pink, was counting down the days and looking forward to beginning the journey to getting her life back. But she was nervous too. Before going in for the transfusion she wanted to go to church. We're not big church-goers, but as a family we have always had faith. Maddie took Mum and Fay—three generations of Millington women—to Brighton Baptist Church and met Pastor Sean. A short, rotund African man who moved to Australia from South Africa with his beautiful family, Pastor Sean had been through a similar illness to Maddie and they had an immediate connection. That has spread through our entire family, and he remains a constant in our lives.

Maddie's illness made us explore our faith. Cath and I prayed every night; it comes easily to her because she has worked on it all her life. They are her beliefs and she has grown up with them. It was harder for me, but I found myself drawing comfort from sharing a routine that was essentially about laying yourself bare and asking for help. Each night we knelt down next to the bed and prayed—for the nurses and doctors, for James when Cath was carrying him and then after he was born, and of course for Maddie. Always for Maddie. I went to the church a few times when Maddie was really sick and had prayer sessions with the elders. Pastor Sean became our family priest, someone who's been a rock for us through the worst time imaginable.

•

Initially Maddie responded well to the transplant, but while her bone marrow started to function and produce cells she was forced to take other drugs that caused separate issues elsewhere in her system. Mum called me not long after the transplant and said Maddie had had a bad reaction, that she had fluid on her lungs and her kidneys weren't functioning. Her kidneys were shot from all the chemo she had been given, and couldn't flush her system like they were supposed to. She was very jaundiced and, as I saw to my shock when I arrived at the hospital, swollen from all the fluid inside her.

It was late when I got there and Mum was still on her way in. I said, 'Hey!' And Maddie was like, 'Hey . . .' then started gasping for breath, heaving in and out. Without thinking I said, 'Oh fuck.' She heard me and panicked, started asking, 'What? What's wrong?' I don't think she realised until then. I said, 'Nothing Mooch,' then rushed out and got a nurse. They knew what was happening. Soon after the head of the ward came in and said, 'Righto Maddie, we're just going to take you down to ICU. We need to put you on dialysis for a couple of hours to get some of this fluid away.'

Mum and I were shitting ourselves. God knows what Maddie was thinking. I'd never been in an intensive care unit before. In the end we became immune to it, it was like home, but walking through there for the first time it was confronting and very, very scary. I remember thinking, 'This is it.' Over the ensuing seven months, the number of people we saw come through that place who never came out, the families whose grief we witnessed . . . You'd be walking in or out and have to pass the waiting room, and they would be in there, trying to come to terms with the loss of a loved one. We saw things that will be with us forever.

Maddie went into ICU in July, and stayed there for 227 days. No patient since the ward had opened at Royal Melbourne Hospital had been in there that long. Over the five years of her illness she spent roughly eighteen months in hospital, but nothing could prepare you for those last seven months. She had the best room in ICU, which isn't something to celebrate. It had a few windows and a little balcony, but for most of the time she was cytotoxic, or highly infectious, so anyone visiting had to wear the full gown, gloves and mask. You couldn't even touch her skin because she was secreting dangerous chemicals from all the drugs she was being given.

Maddie spent five of those seven months unable to eat or drink, on and off dialysis, and using a tracheostomy, which creates an airway through the neck to deliver more oxygen to the lungs. Sometimes we were allowed to take her out on the balcony; my memory is stuck in the last few months, over summer, when it seemed like every time we were out there it was a really hot day. The hardest thing about that time, which still breaks my heart, is how thirsty Maddie was. She was basically thirsty for six months. Occasionally she would be allowed to suck on an ice chip, then the nurses would say no more. Maddie's eyes would just sink; she'd point at her mouth and make a drinking motion. It's a bad feeling being thirsty, just shocking. We take for granted being able to just pick up a glass and have a drink. Maddie couldn't do that, and it was awful to watch. At times I just wanted to scream at the nurses to let her have some water. At other times I wanted to scream at Maddie, tell her it was a matter of life and death but she just couldn't have a drink. Ultimately we were just helpless spectators.

You question so much in a situation like that, have so many internal conversations. If you're going to lose someone, how would you prefer it to happen? Would you rather lose them suddenly? Or would it be better to have time to prepare yourself, but have to watch the deterioration of someone you love? Maddie spent from July until February in that room, and a lot of that time she was unable to even talk to us. Again, to say we admired her courage is such a ridiculous understatement. I can't articulate how strong she was and how proud of her we are. She became a shell of herself. She was unrecognisable from the beautiful blonde girl she'd been, but at the same time she was still our Maddie.

In November 2014 she underwent a second bone marrow procedure, from the same original donor. The sad irony is that it ultimately worked. The week before Christmas there was a glimmer of hope that Maddie might be allowed home for a few hours—in an ambulance and accompanied by ICU nurses. But a couple of days before Christmas we were told she wouldn't be allowed out, so we made a roster of family and friends to make sure Maddie would have someone with her throughout the day.

On Christmas morning Alex and I got up at 6 a.m. and put a big ham on the spit, got everything ready to have a lunch at my place while Maddie was sleeping at the hospital later in the day. At 7 a.m. Dad rang. He was in tears, couldn't really explain what was happening, was saying things like, 'They're trying to save her.' We went straight in and were told things had become very grim and we should prepare for the worst. By the middle of the day we were told nothing was going to happen straight away, and were sent home. So we went home and tried to sit down for lunch, as if anyone was in the mood to celebrate. It was almost as if Maddie had decided that if she couldn't have Christmas, none of us could.

On Boxing Day Maddie was even worse. Both of her lungs had filled with fluid to the point where the doctors could do nothing more. I called Brendon Goddard, who was at the MCG watching the Boxing Day Test, and he was at the hospital in less than fifteen minutes. I'll never forget that. My cousins Jack, Harry and Charlie flew in from Hobart, family and friends from Gold Coast, even Bali. The support we were shown, the love Maddie was shown, was incredibly moving. She was in a coma, but I'm sure she could feel everyone's presence.

And still Maddie wouldn't stop fighting. By 28 December her condition was improving, defying all expectation. The medical team and hospital staff couldn't believe it. Because she had been in ICU for so long, everyone there was incredibly invested in Maddie, they all loved her. Through all she endured she was so gracious, saying 'thank you' every time anyone did something for her. What speaks volumes is that the ICU offered counselling to their staff after Maddie passed. As big a bitch as she could be, she was hard not to love.

James had been born on 4 December 2014. By Christmas it didn't look like he would ever meet his Aunty Maddie, and even when her condition miraculously improved I didn't dare think it might happen. Then in January, with a new course of medication seemingly reaping results and Maddie even starting daily physiotherapy, I got a phone call to say she was no longer infectious. I was so excited, I just grabbed James and Cath and raced in there.

Maddie couldn't talk, but I could still hear her over the ventilator—which you're not supposed to be able to do—saying, 'I love you James, I love you James.' That's one of my favourite memories, hearing her say my son's name, telling him that she loved him. For a sliver of time, after so much darkness, everyone was happy. We have photos of James sitting on Maddie's lap on her bed. Photos of Mum with the biggest smile we had seen from her in years. That was the only time Maddie spent time with her nephew, but it was so special.

•

Maddie's improvement continued through January, and we started speaking to the doctors about the next step—primarily, what she had to do to get out of ICU. For starters she had to lose the trachy shield: they would take the tube away from her throat where the hole had been cut, Maddie would hold an oxygen mask there, and she would have to do the work to breathe instead of letting the respirator do it for her. It was really hard for her, but after so long on the machine she had to get some strength back into her lungs. We set up a wall chart like you would for a ten-year-old, and put stickers on it each day, marking her progress. Trachy shielding for two hours, sticker. Physio for another hour, sticker.

By the end of the month she was doing well, and I went to my old teammate Adam Schneider's wedding. It was a great celebration, but it made me realise how caught up we all get in our own world. A lot of the St Kilda players' wives and girlfriends were there, and they asked me how Maddie was doing. I told them it had been really tough, that she had been in ICU since July, that we had almost lost her at Christmas, that we had said our goodbyes. They all started crying—they'd had no idea. That was nobody's fault. It just showed that when someone is so sick for so long, the world keeps turning around them.

Even at the footy club I don't think most people realised how bad she was. I spoke to Alan Richardson in late 2014, when things were really grim, and told him I thought I should stand down as captain, that there was just too much going on outside football for me to do the job justice. Richo looked at me like I was speaking another language. Maddie had been so sick for so long that it had become the norm.

By February Maddie was in the best state she'd been in for a long time. Getting out of ICU and back onto the regular ward was regarded as a realistic and achievable goal. Then, within the space of days, she contracted a critical infection and went downhill. I was at training on the Monday when Mum called, saying there was a problem with her oesophagus. They thought there was a tear in the lining, and if that happens you're basically gone. Jack Newnes saw that I was crying as I grabbed my bag. I don't know what he thought—it probably looked like I'd cracked the shits about something and was just clearing off. If only.

At the hospital we met with Professor Ritchie, who told us it wasn't Maddie's oesophagus, which was good news. Then he gave us the worst news possible. 'She's been in here for seven months,' David said. 'And for seven months she's been the sickest person in ICU. We've done everything we can. She's too sick. She's not coming home.'

I was angry. They'd never said anything like that before; the conversation had always been about what could be done next, never that nothing more could be done. I couldn't stop thinking, 'But she's rallied before, why are you giving up this time?' It was denial, I can see that now, but at the time I just felt anger. For the second time in two months we were told nothing would happen straight away and were sent home, and at 5 a.m. the next morning Dad rang and said, 'Mate, you've gotta come in.' It was such a strange feeling, knowing the inevitability of what was about to happen. The drive to the hospital is something I often think about. I'm not even sure how I made it in there—I guess I must have been on autopilot.

We sat by the bed asking questions of the hospital staff: Is she in pain? Can we wake her up to say goodbye? That wouldn't have been fair on Maddie—she had been in a coma and would have been so disoriented; I'm sure she would have been scared. But how do you say goodbye to your daughter, to your sister, to someone you love?

I rang Cath and asked her to bring James in. I wanted him to be there, sitting on Maddie's lap. Alex's wife Roxy came in too; Nanny Fay was there, Pastor Sean too, with Mum and Dad and our close family friend Carlie Merenda. We all gathered around Maddie as they turned down the machines and removed some of the things that had been keeping her alive. I was holding her hand. We were all touching her. James's little hand was wrapped around Maddie's finger. And then she was gone.

9

GRIEVING AND GIVING BACK

I know things I wish I had never had to learn. Things about bone marrow failure, about treatments that offer hope and news that delivers only despair. About oxygen levels, how much the person lying before you is breathing independently, and how much a machine is breathing for them. I know how a hospital room smells when you're there every day, month after month. As a family we know what it's like to watch the light in someone precious and vibrant dim, no matter how hard they fight to keep it burning. We know what it's like to watch a loved one suffer for five years, never giving up, somehow still finding a way to smile.

We know what it's like to see the end approaching. We know how useless and worthless it makes you feel, to know there is nothing you can do to help. We know what it's like to lose someone you love more than words can say. We know because we lost our beautiful Maddie.

It doesn't matter how long you've had to prepare for it, when death arrives it's like nothing else. It's incomprehensible. One morning I was at training, running around kicking a ball with my mates. The next I was holding my sister's hand as she died. It was just so hard to take in. I was numb; we all were. Mum and Nan stayed with Maddie, helping the nurses remove the tubes that had been attached to her for so long, bathing her, making her seem like our Mooch again. I just don't know how Mum did that; she was incredible. Alex and I didn't want to go back in—I was worried about how she would look, whether she would be cold. But I'm so glad we did because she was so peaceful—free at last.

•

Eventually we went home to my place and people started flooding into the house, bringing food, flowers and love. Chairs were put out in the backyard, the crowd grew, and the sorry process of wondering what to say or do began. There were a lot of people there—family, footy people, really good friends. Lindsay and Paula Fox called in—they had lost a son, and it was touching that they reached out to us. Nothing seems funny at a time like that, but when Paula asked for some water Dad didn't pour it into one of the red plastic Solo cups everyone was drinking out of. He went to the cupboard and got one of our Waterford crystal tumblers. It was so Dad.

Weird things happened. I had a moment, sitting with Carlie Merenda, who has done so much for me as my manager but who was also close to Maddie, where I felt like I needed some sort of sign. If I knew in my soul that Maddie was in heaven, I felt like I'd be okay. If she could just send me a text or an email from heaven it would have comforted me. It was an overcast day, with a blanket of clouds above us. We were down the side of the house, and just as I told Carlie what I was thinking, there was a break in the clouds and a beam of light smashed me in the face.

I looked at Carlie and asked if she had seen it. She was speechless. It lasted barely five seconds and the clouds closed in again. We didn't see the sun for the rest of the day. I know how it sounds, because I hear that sort of thing and think, 'Yeah, right, coincidence.' Maybe I was just looking for something to cling to. But it's called faith, it's not called fact. It helped me in the moment.

A little while later, around dusk, we were sitting around the table out the back. Nick Dal Santo pointed over to the back corner of the garden and said, 'Whose dog is that?' It was hard to see in the shadows, but I assumed it must have been Maddie's dog Oscar. Dal pointed to a different part of the garden and said, 'Isn't that Maddie's dog over there?' And sure enough, there was Oscar.

We turned back to the corner, had a closer look, and there was a fox standing next to our big elm tree. It looked at us, then just walked as calm as can be down the side of the house, out the gate, and was gone. I'd never seen a fox in Victoria, let alone in Brighton. A couple of years later, pulling into the drive after attending a Maddie's Vision board meeting, there it was again, just standing there looking at me as I got out of the car. I don't know the significance of those moments in real terms, but I took them as signs from Maddie.

Thinking about what would happen to Maddie's body really troubled me. We were fortunate that Mum's family in Hobart owned Millingtons Funeral Homes; straight away they arranged for Maddie to be on the *Spirit of Tasmania* that night. She didn't have to spend a night in the hospital morgue, which was somehow a relief. From our backyard, when the conditions are right, you can hear the *Spirit* leaving Station Pier in Port Melbourne, the sound of its horn. Hearing it that night was pretty tough.

Our cousin Christopher Fuglsang met the boat the next morning and drove Maddie to the funeral home where his daughter Bridget—known to all as Biddy and one of my best friends—took over. They flew to Melbourne that day to talk about plans for the funeral: the flowers, songs, photos and readings. To have gone through that with people we didn't know, people who didn't know Maddie, would have added another layer of misery. Biddy and Maddie were tight; she had a job to do, but she was crying with the rest of us. It was such a difficult time, but it was comforting to have Biddy there leading the way.

The Foxes offered us their plane, which was another amazing gesture. It meant we didn't have to leave Melbourne on a domestic flight full of strangers, many of whom would have heard about Maddie's passing. There was Mum, Dad, myself, Alex and Fay. Maddie would have been so jealous that we were flying in a private jet without her.

Mum and Dad's friends, Lloyd and Jan Clarke, put us up in their hotel in Battery Point, another example of how caring people were. Cath and James followed us down, and people flew in from all over Australia to farewell Maddie. Lindsay Fox flew all the St Kilda boys down on his plane, which meant they could get in and out and back to training. Everyone made such an effort. For us. For Maddie.

I remember being really stressed about writing a eulogy, putting it off and putting it off because I wanted so badly to do Maddie justice. How do you sum up the life of your little sister in a ten-minute speech? What do you talk about? How much do you share? Eventually Alex and I did it together. I have spent all my adult life having to speak publicly as a footballer, and I worried that I went too much into work mode and didn't let the emotion wash over me enough. I'd hate to think it was a bit of a performance, the footballer doing his public-speaking thing. It was all filmed, but I haven't watched it. Maybe I'll sit down with James and Will one day and have a look with them.

THE THINGS THAT MAKE US

Because we had decided to scatter Maddie's ashes at Orford a couple of days later, there was no formal family farewell at the end of the funeral. I remember leaving the room, leaving Maddie behind, then feeling a need to be with her on my own. I just wanted a minute to sit with her, talk to her. When I walked back in the coffin was already gone, and I had to ask Chris and Biddy if they could please bring her back. I found myself saying 'I'm really sorry' a lot. Not that it was anyone's fault; I just found myself repeating it over and over and over to Maddie. I had a few minutes with her, then we went to the wake.

We went back to the hotel in Hobart, where I tried to have a drink but didn't feel like it. Eventually we went for a walk down to Salamanca and I had this sense that the world was already moving on. Maddie's friends were there with my friends, trying to drink their sorrow away, but I just wasn't feeling it. I guess it goes one of two ways: some people write themselves off, others withdraw. A couple of strangers who were drinking at the bar came over at one stage wanting to have a chat, and thankfully Maddie's friends saw the state I was in, cut them off at the pass and told them in pretty bold language to leave it.

Two days later we were at Orford when Biddy arrived from Hobart with the two containers holding Maddie's ashes. At one point I walked into the living room of the shack and they were sitting on the table. Essentially there she was, on the table where we had sat down to Christmas so many times. How do you comprehend that? I'm not sure my mind let me process it. On reflection I was just existing that whole time, putting one foot in front of the other.

Our Orford farewell to Maddie was really beautiful. A few of my mates—Justin Koschitzke, Brendon Goddard and Jerome Batten—stayed on. My brother's mates and a lot of Maddie's friends were there, all the family and our friends from Tassie. We all walked down to the beach with the stereo playing Maddie's favourite songs, plenty of Taylor Swift. It was blowing an absolute gale, but as we reached the beach it was like the wind just went up in the air. For twenty minutes it was beautiful. Mum, Dad, Alex and I waded out into the water and scattered her ashes. I can stand in the exact spot, lining up a house on the hill with the second peak of the range known as The Thumbs, then following a line through Maria Island. Dad sank a big bit of driftwood in a heap of concrete into the beach as a marker, but a year or so later it disappeared in a huge storm. It can't have gone too far; I'm sure it'll resurface one day. But I don't need it to know where Maddie is.

We had never spoken about what she wanted, her wishes if it came to this. But I'm sure she would have loved her final resting place. It was Maddie's special place, and now she'll be there forever.

•

I get upset with myself at times: how can I just go on living my life? How can I be okay? I'm sure everyone who loses someone knows that feeling. I shouldn't be okay, because Maddie's gone. But even in those weeks that we stayed on in Orford, I knew life would have to start again. Life would never be normal again. We would have to become accustomed to a new normal—a normal without Maddie.

Another football season was about to begin; I was captain, my team needed me. And more than ever I needed my team, the routine of a footballer's life, the distraction. I was coming from a long way back. During the weeks I spent in Orford, I didn't train at all. One day we went for a walk along Rebben Beach and I thought I had better do something, so I ran to the end of the beach with Oscar. That was the extent of my training in the weeks before the 2015 season. It wasn't high on the list of priorities at that stage.

I spoke to Alan Richardson and settled on a date that I would be back at the club. I can't remember going back, but I had told Richo to please tell the boys and staff at the club that I didn't need everyone to say sorry. For them, they would say it once, but I'd be hearing it 60 or 80 times. Everyone was really respectful and supportive. I had always been the leader, and now I was incredibly vulnerable. They wouldn't have seen that before, but their care was hugely appreciated.

I remember assistant coach Adam Kingsley saying to me

in the gym at one stage, 'You're allowed to smile again, you're allowed to laugh. It's okay. You're allowed to let something make you feel happy again.' It rocked me a bit—he meant it the right way and he was absolutely right, but it was so hard to think that it wouldn't always be like this. To imagine that I'd be happy again.

My first game back in round 1 we played GWS at Etihad, and in the last quarter I got smashed from behind by Tom Bugg. The physios and doctors stood over me saying, 'Don't move, don't move.' I just said to them, 'I am not going off this ground on a stretcher. Let me get up, help me get off, then do what you need to do.' They took me down to the rooms and Alex was already there. He had been in the rooms with me during the pre-game, sitting with me to help get me through. I was in a state. And there we were again, with the doctors saying I needed to go to hospital for scans.

Mum and Dad were still at Orford and we called them on the way. They didn't have Foxtel and didn't know what had happened. So I sat there in the doctor's car next to Alex, with a neck brace on and a phone to my ear, and told Mum, 'Don't freak out, but I'm on the way to hospital.' You can imagine Mum—she just lost the plot.

Then I was lying on a bed getting wheeled in for a scan, just as Maddie had, a million times. It was barely a month after she'd passed away. I was thinking, 'You've got to be kidding.' But almost straight away I could see it as Maddie just saying,

'Hey, don't be a sook, don't forget what I went through!' One second I had a smirk on my face, the next I was bawling my eyes out. The nurses must have been thinking, 'Gee, this bloke's a bit unstable!'

The next year we played Melbourne in the NAB Cup, and Tom Bugg had been traded there. He kept running past me saying, 'How's your neck? How's your neck?' The notion of crossing the line in footy is a funny thing. I just grabbed him at one stage and wanted to rip his head off. I didn't get aggro all that often on a footy field, but that was one time I really wanted to hurt someone.

I had a few games in 2015 where in hindsight I don't think I should have played. I wore a black armband for every game; I'd grab the tape in the rooms and find somewhere quiet to put it on. I didn't want people to see me getting emotional, but I cried most weeks. I'd be listening to my iPod—I listen to country music to try and chill out, Garth Brooks, a band called Florida Georgia Line. They've got a song called 'Dirt', about where we'll all ultimately end up. Every time that came on I'd wonder why it was still on my playlist, but it stayed there. If I was lying face-down on the massage table I'd have to stay there until I regained my composure.

Footy-wise that was a tough year. I did my calf in round 2, no doubt a result of lack of conditioning, missed three games, then missed a couple more later in the season. My body wasn't great, and emotionally I was barely holding it together. I was still trying to lead the team, and I think I dug in and did a good job. But below the surface there was a lot going on.

It isn't easy trying to grieve in the public eye, but the media on the whole were incredibly respectful. I'd expected to show up at the funeral and find cameras everywhere, but there was only one local news crew. I half-expected people to be camped out the front of the house when we got back to Melbourne; I guess I've just been conditioned to it. My relationship with the media since, through Maddie's Vision, has been tremendous. Not-for-profits don't survive without raising awareness and educating people, much of which the media have provided for us.

•

Maddie's Vision is just as it sounds—a way of honouring Maddie by trying to find a cure for aplastic anaemia, which was what she articulated to us all the way through her illness. She didn't want others to suffer the way she did. Mum's concern was that Maddie would be forgotten, but what better way to remember her than through a foundation bearing her name, one that is committed to making sure others won't have to suffer like she did? It's given us all a sense of purpose. It's part of our healing, but it's more than that. If Maddie's Vision can save lives, then Maddie's death won't have been for nothing.

Tony Shadforth—one of Mum and Dad's best friends and also Maddie's godfather—spoke at the funeral and planted the seed, saying plans were already afoot to start a foundation in Maddie's name. The response was immediate; people wrote cheques and gave them to us that day. I called John Gdanski, a lawyer who's also a family friend, and told him we wanted to start a not-for-profit. I contacted my accountant, Anthony Willis, and asked, 'What do we need to do?' We began to go through the process very simply, ask the questions about what it would be called, how it would look, that sort of thing. We started from zero.

An approach from the Snowdome Foundation was a massive part of turning an idea into a viable reality. Miles Prince, the doctor who had originally diagnosed Maddie, was on the Snowdome board. He came over one day with Nicky Long, another Snowdome director who would become CEO of Maddie's Vision, and Rob Tandy, also a Snowdome board member. Rob walked in looking like he knew exactly where he was going, sat down at the table and said, 'This is gunna sound really weird, but I sat at this very spot when we formed the Snowdome Foundation.' I'd bought the house from his parents a couple of years earlier. That was another little synergy in the whole thing, just weird.

They proposed that we come under their banner, effectively doing what we wanted, calling it what we wanted, running it how we wanted, but using all of their back-of-house corporate governance. Also using their DGR2 status, which makes any donation tax deductible. Those things take a lot of time and money to set up and we needed to get going fast. From a purely business point of view, we needed to act quickly. We had a captive audience; we needed to leverage the emotion that people were feeling around Maddie's passing. They gave us that capability, which was huge.

From there we went about setting up the board. Mum and Dad would be patrons, Alex and I would be on the board, Jarrod Nation would be our chairman. Jarrod's married to Madeleine Fuglsang—daughter of Christopher, sister of Bridget, and the Madeleine Maddie was named after. John Gdanski, Tony Shadforth, Jennifer Trethewey and Maddie's bone marrow professor David Ritchie were original board members. We thought it was ambitious asking David, because we'd seen through Maddie's fight just how busy he was. But he was there from the word go.

'Maddie's Match' was Mum's idea—to honour Maddie when St Kilda played our cousin Jack's Richmond, with a percentage of ticket sales going to Maddie's Vision as well as merchandise and the like around the event. It really put the brand of Maddie's Vision in the public consciousness—the logo that was a nod to Maddie's love of elephants, the purple that was her favourite colour. The 'Fight Like Maddie' catchcry, which simply came from how she refused to give in. It's amazing to think that it instantly became a hashtag and everyone knew what it meant. For Mum and Dad in particular, to be able to speak publicly so openly and honestly so soon after losing their daughter showed amazing strength. We were incredibly vulnerable, but Maddie's legacy drove us on. It's comforting to think that Maddie's courageous fight inspired so many people to invest their time and energy in the foundation.

A company called One Small Step Collective did all our marketing, storyboards and the like—a couple of hundred thousand dollars of pro-bono work. They're great people who came up with ideas to honour Maddie in ways she would have been comfortable with. I can't thank them enough. Jack and I did so much PR ahead of the first Maddie's Match, by the time the game came around we were just exhausted. I'd torn my calf the week before in the last quarter of the game against GWS. But I was always going to play—for a regular game you might miss a week, but you can strap a calf to take all the weight out of it and play if you have to. And I had to play. To walk out on the ground in front of 45,000-plus fans, an AFL record crowd for Etihad Stadium in 2015, and see the stadium lit up with purple, with Maddie's name everywhere in LED, it just blew me away. It was incredibly special. Maddie would have loved seeing her name in lights but would also have been embarrassed by all the attention.

My love for my immediate and extended 'footy family' grew exponentially from the support we received that day, as well as in the short build-up to it. As a family we met with

Grieving and Giving Back

St Kilda CEO Matt Finnis in March, only weeks after Maddie passed away, and floated the idea. He pretty much said yes on the spot, knowing full well that the time frame was incredibly tight for such a big and emotional undertaking. President Peter Summers also gave it his full endorsement. The support from the entire football club—that year and in the seasons that followed—was simply overwhelming.

•

Towards the end of 2015 it was clear Maddie's Vision had grown so quickly we needed a full-time CEO. Carlie Merenda did so much work in the beginning, taking charge of all our PR and effectively organising Maddie's Match single-handed. All of a sudden we had close to $400,000 in the bank; it was time to start thinking about long-term planning. We advertised for a CEO and Nicky Long got the job.

Money kept coming in. The generosity of people—from big business to individuals—still astounds me. In late 2016 we signed a deal with a commercial partner, Flavorite, who committed to giving us $100,000 a year just to put the Maddie's Vision logo on their tomatoes in Coles supermarkets. One hundred grand. The support from friends of the St Kilda Football Club—people like the Foxes and Gerry Ryan, who'd been great supporters of my career—was immense. I wish I could name everyone, whether they donated a dollar or a thousand, but there are just so many. A lot of them I'd never even heard of before. Mark Wizel, a lifelong Saints supporter I'd never met, wrote me a cheque for $30,000 one day. He was 33. And four-year-old Adrian Milicia donated his money box after seeing the coverage.

It became important to identify our purpose as an organisation. Were we in the business of support? If so, we could throw all the money towards, say, putting people up in accommodation when they have a loved one in the Royal Melbourne. Towards making them more comfortable. Moreover, towards making their loved one as comfortable as they could be. All Maddie wanted when she was in hospital was a shower, and there wasn't a swing or a pulley to allow her to do that.

We had to be strategic, almost ruthless, because anywhere you could send the money was worthy. In the end we went down the path of research—essentially, finding a cure and improving the outcomes for bone marrow failure patients. That aligned with Snowdome, because that's their MO: they want to find a cure for blood cancers. We had 26 applications for the first research grant, and every one of them was really impressive. In the end we awarded a fellowship to Dr Wayne Crismani, who identified a protein strand at a molecular level that doesn't work properly and can lead to aplastic anaemia. Here was the start of hopefully finding a cure.

•

Grieving and Giving Back

At times it's hard to get out of business mode around Maddie's Vision, which is something I've spoken to Alex about a lot. We have this conversation: 'Gosh, I can't believe we're doing this.' At times it feels like discussions about work, work, work, then you think, 'Shit, we're doing this because Maddie's not here anymore!' It's become so normal to be working on Maddie's Vision that at times it almost feels like she was never here.

I'm sure your mind protects you to some degree from going somewhere painful. You protect yourself. It's not always difficult, because it's not always front of mind. When I do the media around it I become so well rehearsed I flick into autopilot and can talk about it without the sadness. It is only when I let myself go back to some of the really dark stuff that it seeps in.

It's strange the triggers that bring Maddie back. When I was still playing, I could be driving to training and take a drink out of my water bottle, and that terrible time when Maddie wasn't able to drink would just pop into my head. Then I'd see how long I could go without having a drink. I knew it was stupid, that it would just make me sad all over again, but I'd do it anyway.

For a long time I couldn't listen to a song with the word 'she' or 'her' in the lyrics without thinking of Mooch. The word 'sibling' took on a new meaning. I would do school visits with the club, and when it came to question time invariably some innocent kid would ask if I had brothers or sisters. The first few times I just froze. I learnt to say, 'I've got a brother and a sister, but unfortunately my sister passed away.'

If I saw a scene in a movie or a TV show with a hospital, or someone who had been shot and was dying in someone's arms, I'd go straight back to the Royal Melbourne ICU. Anyone who has held someone's hand, been with someone when they have taken their last breath—I'm sure they've gone through the same sort of emotions. Even little things like watching the news and seeing a story about a twenty-something who had stolen a car or done something stupid, I'd just think, 'Fuck you. Maddie should still be here and you shouldn't.' I was angry.

The good memories have slowly become easier to locate. I can't remember Maddie really being in our house, because we bought it in June and in July she went in for her transplant. I don't have many happy memories of us here. We had one spa in the winter—I remember her jumping into the freezing cold pool, me jumping in after her, and Alex refusing to. That's the only real memory I have of her at our house. Maybe that's why it's difficult, because there aren't good reminders everywhere. A lot of the happy memories are about places, events, milestones. Maybe I'll always be glass half-empty.

At Maddie's Vision board meetings we'll be talking about governance, grant applications, very business-centric things. Then I'll look over and see the photo of Maddie next to a lit candle that Mum brings to every meeting. I look at it and can't believe we are sitting here doing this, but I know we're fortunate that we have the capacity to. A lot of families go through the same loss and that's it; they don't have the platform or the means to do what we've done. Maddie's Vision is a continual celebration of her life, of her fight, her courage. Of course you'd rather not be doing it—you'd rather she was still here, living her life. But even though Maddie has gone, she'll always be with us. And she's left me with the gift of perspective, which influences everything I do. The way I raise my kids, the appreciation I have for family and friends, the understanding that life is fragile and I shouldn't waste time on things that really don't matter.

•

Losing Maddie has heightened something that's always been part of who I am—anxiety. There's depression in my family. I'm not depressed but I've definitely known anxiety—particularly separation anxiety—and it's wrapped me up all the more in the years we've been left without Maddie.

I've always found it hard to say goodbye to people I care for, and that's become much more acute around my kids. But even growing up I had trouble saying goodbye. Our family have the most protracted, drawn-out goodbyes. If Mum and Dad pop over for dinner it can take us fifteen minutes to say goodbye—hugs, kisses, reaffirmation of the love we have for each other, the lot. And they live a couple of minutes away. I wasn't aware of it until Cath noticed it and said, 'Let's work on it. I don't want our kids having those anxious feelings.'

Even before Maddie got sick, when I was going to the States I'd really struggle in the lead-up because I knew there was a goodbye coming. As soon as I got there I'd be fine, but then it would kick into anxiety about leaving Cath's family and going home again. The attachment, then the separation. It's irrational, but mental health often is.

I've always had high anxiety around performance, but I don't think that's anything unusual in an athlete. But even taking sport out of the equation, I'm just wired for anxiety. As much as I wish I could, I can't sit and do nothing. Even having a beer with mates, I can't just sit there. I've got to be doing something: darts, pool, some sort of game.

After Maddie passed away I started having anxiety attacks. I could be in the shower, or driving the car, and it would come over me. I'd be able to pull off the road, and I'd be absolutely conscious and aware of what was happening around me. I have never passed out during an attack and, if I just sit quietly, put my head in my hands and compose myself, it will eventually pass. I might be in the shower and call out to Cath, and she's standing in the bathroom saying, 'It's okay, distract yourself.' I'm able to communicate while it's happening. James has seen me in this state and I've been able to talk to him and reassure him everything's okay. It's just so weird—for 30 seconds or so

I'll be rendered useless, like some sort of paralysis has come over me. It's just a fog.

These anxiety attacks were happening roughly once a month, then around the time of the second anniversary of Maddie's passing, in February 2017, they became more severe. About ten days before her anniversary I looked at my phone one morning, saw the date, and consciously started the countdown. That day I had five separate anxiety attacks: in the car on the way to the footy club, in the warm-up before training, during a running session, in the change rooms after training, then on the plane later that day when we were flying to Orford with the first-year players.

The doctors at the club and some of my closer teammates were aware of it for a good while. I told Joey Montagna about it, which was good, because he was running with me when it happened one time and would otherwise have wondered what the hell was going on. The frequency forced me to do something about it and I started speaking to a couple of people—one a mental health professional, the other Pastor Sean from the church. Seeing them about it has been incredibly helpful.

It was diagnosed as post-traumatic stress, which the doctors related to a bit of childhood stuff around the anxiety of my parents separating for a time, blended with the stress of losing someone close, of having children of my own around that time. I knew it was centred around the hospital and Maddie—that was pretty obvious.

Once James and Will came along I found it harder and harder to leave the house in the morning, knowing I'd be away from them all day. Again, I know that's irrational, and it wasn't that I necessarily thought something was going to happen to them. It just didn't feel right leaving them. It had an impact on my social life, not to mention my golf game, because any spare time I had I'd invariably spend at home. When Cath went home for her sister's wedding early in the 2017 season, and she and the boys were away for almost a month, I was a mess. I printed out the calendar pages for the period they were away and tried to fill every blank square—having people over, going out to dinner, whatever I could do to take my mind off the fact they weren't at home.

Talking about it helps. I've worked at the moments where I'm out and about and become anxious, where the feeling that I need to pick up the phone and check in becomes overwhelming. I've worked at not doing it, at not becoming reliant on that, and I've become better. I'm pretty open about it, even though Joey, the doctors, a physio and a couple of fitness staff were the only ones at the club who knew. It wasn't that I tried to hide it. When I sought professional help, the club had to write a referral, and they were concerned about sending the invoice through commercial operations or the AFL Players' Association because they wanted to protect my privacy. It didn't bother me. I had severe anxiety because my sister had died. I can imagine people feeling anxious about being anxious, for want of a better word, but I don't. I'm not embarrassed about this appearing in these pages. It's part of my story, and I'm sure a lot of people can relate to it, particularly those who have experienced loss.

Talking to Pastor Sean has been really helpful. As Cath is religious, we have decided we'll raise our kids to have faith and believe in God. If Maddie is in heaven I want to know about it: what it is, what it looks like, what it means. If anxiety is part of that journey to understanding, then so be it. If the upside is feeling a deeper connection to Mooch, I'll wear that.

Feelings are what we're left with, and as much as the good memories fight their way to the surface of your mind as time passes, the overwhelming feeling is hollowness. When I watched the video of Cath's father Larry walking her sister Vivian down the aisle, all I could think was that Dad will never get to do that with Maddie. It is deeper than sadness, more than just an emptiness at not being able to hang out with her and see her grow old. It's knowing that I'll never get to be an uncle to her kids, something I would have loved. It's knowing Mum and Dad will never be grandparents to her children.

I've lost my sister, so you lose everything that was normal about your life. All the best days—Christmas, birthdays—become the hardest days. None of us are the same. Everything we thought we knew when Maddie was in our lives, we've lost. But together, we're learning to live with what has become our new normal.

I saw a quote one day that resonated, a sentiment we can cling to as a family. 'Grief, I've learned, is really just love. It's all the love that you want to give but cannot. All of that unspent love gathers up in the corners of your eyes, the lump in your throat, and in that hollow part of your chest. Grief is just love with no place to go.'

10

LONGEVITY

I clutched my right leg around the shin, pulled my knee towards my chest and looked up at the big screen in search of the replay. There'd been a 'pop', perhaps even more of a 'bang', loud enough that a couple of Melbourne players nearby said they'd heard it too. It didn't look, sound or feel good at all. I screamed: 'Noooo! Nooooooo!'

I'd had grand designs on playing until who knows when, or at least the 2017 season and again the following year if all was well. I'd given myself the best chance to do that. I was playing good footy, and I was in really good shape. In the final pre-season game a fortnight earlier, against Sydney in Albury, my GPS reading was close to a career personal best: 16 kilometres covered in the game, with 2.1 kilometres of high-intensity running, or faster than 20 kilometres an hour. They're big numbers, especially in a shortened game. I was 34 and starting my seventeenth season, and I'd never been better prepared.

Now it was round 1 and I was sitting on the Etihad Stadium turf, surrounded by teammates, opponents and 36,000 fans but feeling horribly alone. And all I could think was, 'That's it.' Even before our doc Tim Barbour and physio Andrew Wallis got to me, in that short space of time, there was reflection. 'I've been doing this for more than half my life,' I thought, 'and this is the moment, this is the end. It's over.'

I thought I had hurt my right knee in a marking contest but could see from the replay that I'd hyper-extended as I went to push off after landing. I've got great relationships with 'Barbs' and 'Wal' and go back a long way with them. When they crouched down next to me I said, 'I think I've done my ACL.' And I could tell from their faces they thought I'd done it too. I remember saying to Wal, 'That's my career, isn't it?' He didn't really answer.

I disappeared into my own world. The things that went through my head were incredible. I thought about Bob Murphy, whom I'd become close to on an Ireland trip eighteen months earlier, and who cruelly missed the Western Bulldogs premiership after doing his knee early in 2016 not far from where I was sitting. I came to a fantastical acceptance: if this means I'm the sacrificial lamb and we're going to win the flag, so be it. As thoughts came in a rush I wondered whether the club would give me another year. If they wouldn't, I wondered if I could have LARS knee surgery and get back in 2017 and with luck play finals one last time.

The crowd got going when I was loaded onto the cart; I could hear and feel them cheering. I wondered if I should give them a thumbs-up to show that I was all right, but that seemed silly because I didn't know whether I was. In reality I feared I was anything but. I thought about waving, in case it really was the end. Chris Judd had waved after he had done his knee in 2015, knowing it was the last time he would leave the ground as a player. I almost followed his lead, but in the end I just sat there.

There's no back on those little carts, and the bloke who was driving it hit the brakes as we got to the ramp going down into the rooms and almost tipped me off. I slid along the cart, and someone said later they saw me shit myself. It's funny the things that stay with you.

At the door to the rooms, I climbed off and walked in. I heard later that people had seen that vision on Fox Footy and taken it as a good sign, but I knew walking meant nothing. Lenny Hayes played the week after doing his knee, then went down properly. Clay Smith from the Bulldogs went back on the ground after doing his for the second or third time. Walking doesn't mean a thing. You can walk with a ruptured ACL. You just can't play for a year. And when you're 34, that's forever.

I sat on the bed in the doctor's room and they did the test. It's called the Lachman test: you relax everything, and the doc grabs your thigh with one hand and your leg below the knee with the other and pulls it towards him. It's obvious if there's a solid end point, which means the ACL is lengthening and holding the knee in place. Doctor Ian Stone did the test, then he looked at me with a look of surprise. 'There's a solid end point.'

We all looked at each other, thinking the same thing. 'Shit, I haven't done it!'

They went on and checked my medial, lateral and PCL. If any of those is injured, you miss six to ten weeks, but an ACL is a year. I'd only missed a handful of games in the previous three years, and the season before I'd polled 19 Brownlow votes, the most I'd managed in my career. But the way my contract negotiations had gone over that time, the concern the club had over my body, I wouldn't have been confident they'd have taken the same approach the Bulldogs took with Murph and backed me to come back in 2018. Thankfully, we didn't have to find out.

I walked out of the doctor's room, grabbed my phone and tried to call Cath. It didn't even ring. Then I tried Alex, no answer. Mum and Dad, no answer. I didn't want them to stress for any longer than they had to, just to say, 'I haven't done my ACL, it's okay.' They all appeared in the rooms before I could get anyone on the phone, and I could see James was really upset. He wasn't crying, but he was rattled. He knew there was something wrong with Dad. Even a couple of days later, walking him around our neighbourhood, he was sitting in the stroller, saying, 'Daddy fell over. Daddy's knee. Daddy went on the little car.'

We went home, put the boys to bed, got some burgers delivered and sat on the couch. It was a strange feeling, having just looked my football mortality in the face. Cath was funny—her sister Vivian was getting married in Houston three weeks later, and Cath was very glass-half-full about the prospect of my knee being shot. I don't think I was even off the ground and she was online, looking up flights. Before I'd had the knee scanned there was apparently a buzz in her social circle back home, 'Nick might be coming to the wedding now!'

In 'sliding door' moments I've wondered what would have happened if the Lachman test had gone the way we'd feared: that there had been no end point when the doc tugged my leg, and the ACL was ruptured. It would have made for a crazy few days of conversations about the future and big, big decisions. If the club had said they didn't see a place for me in 2018, I might have had LARS surgery and tried to play again in 2017. Or I might have jumped on a plane and moved to Texas. Who knows. Again, thankfully, we didn't have to find out.

When I was back on the couch, Murph got in touch and sent me two photos—one of me going off on the cart, and one of him walking off after he'd done his knee—to show how tough he is and how soft I am. I called him and we had a chuckle. I don't think people really know what to say in those situations; it wasn't until Sunday, when it was confirmed I was okay, that I started getting a lot of messages.

I had gone on TV and said I felt like a bit of a goose when it turned out that it wasn't an ACL. I would have felt like a bigger goose if I'd waved to the crowd on the way off. Imagine that: the grand farewell, waving to the fans, throwing my boots into the crowd, asking the driver to do a lap of honour . . . and it turns out my knee is pretty much fine. The next morning I had a scan at 8 a.m. at Victoria House that confirmed there was no cartilage damage, no ligament damage and best of all no ACL damage. I'd split the capsule that surrounds the whole joint and stops the synovial fluid from leaking out. The capsule is quite thick, which is why I felt a pop. They put it at anywhere from two to six weeks. In the end I missed a week.

•

Every athlete knows it can't last forever, that you've got to retire sometime. The knee scare was an opportunity to peek over the edge, and it made me feel sick in the stomach. I'd had so many days watching the minutes tick by so slowly I could swear the clock had stopped, sitting in football purgatory full of nerves and anxiety as another game inched closer. I used to think, 'I'm actually looking forward to the day where I don't have to

Proposing to Cath with her whole family looking on. Thanksgiving 2011, at the ranch in Llano, Texas. (Author's collection)

Our wedding was a huge party, helped by 97 Australians making the journey to Waco, Texas. Cath looked incredibly beautiful, right down to the cowboy boots under her dress. (Nancy Aidee Photography)

Honeymooning in Mexico. (Author's collection)

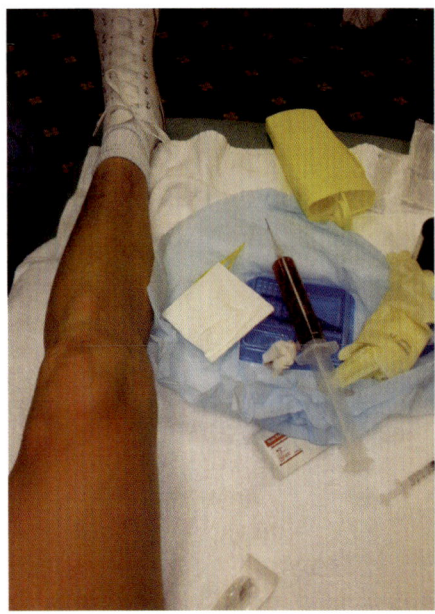 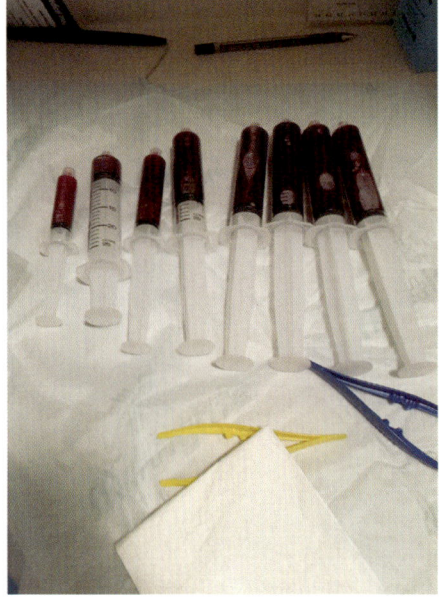

My knee became more and more grumbly throughout my career, to the point I had to have it drained every week during the 2013 season. (Author's collection)

Celebrating my 250th game, with the family. (Author's collection)

As much as preparing for games made me anxious, I thrived on playing. There's so much I'll miss about it, not least the feeling after you've kicked a big goal. (Wayne Ludbey/Newspix)

With big Saints fan Eric Bana after winning the 2014 best and fairest. (Author's collection)

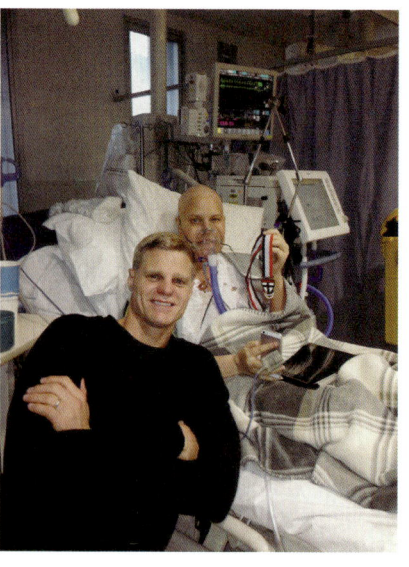

Delivering the medal to Maddie in the Royal Melbourne ICU the next morning. (Author's collection)

A big mark in Perth, International Rules v Ireland, 2014. (Paul Kane/Getty Images)

On the annual first-year players' camp at my shack in Orford, early 2015. From back left, Daniel McKenzie, Brenton Payne, Tim Membrey, myself, Alan Richardson, Paddy McCartin; front Jack Sinclair, Jack Lonie, Hugh Goddard. (Author's collection)

The best part of a footballer's week—singing 'Oh When the Saints' with Adam Schneider, Lenny Hayes and Leigh Montagna. (St Kilda FC)

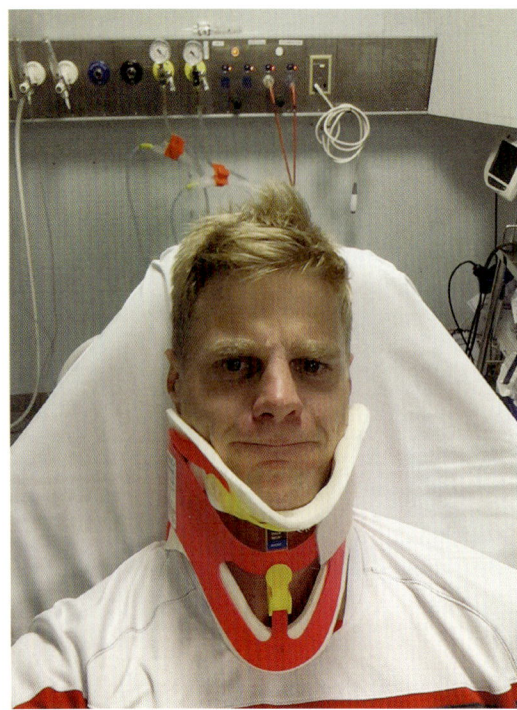

Back in hospital less than a month after Maddie's passing, having copped a big hit against GWS in round 1, 2015. (Author's collection)

With Dad, Mum, James, Cath and Alex ahead of my 300th game, which was dedicated to Maddie. Her fight inspired the creation of Maddie Riewoldt's Vision, an organisation that offers hope for a cure to bone marrow failure.
(Michael Willson/AFL Media)

With Bong Su and cousin Jack at the Melbourne Zoo, ahead of the first Maddie's Match. (Robert Cianflone/Getty Images)

I nicked my calf the week before the inaugural Maddie's Match, but I was always going to #FightlikeMaddie, boots and all. (Robert Cianflone/Getty Images)

Breaking my 300th game banner with James in 2016. I relished the chance late in my career to be a father and a footballer simultaneously. (Wayne Ludbey/Newspix)

Carried off by Sam Fisher and Sean Dempster after my 300th. (Michael Dodge/Getty Images)

I loved the closeness of the huddle, the shared sense of what was to come, as you delivered the final message to the boys before the first bounce. (Will Russell/AFL Media)

I'll always cherish the support I received from our fans over seventeen years. I can't thank them enough. (Darrian Traynor/Getty Images)

Me with James and Brendon Goddard with Billie, June 2016. BJ leaving the club was never going to affect our incredible friendship. (Author's collection)

Batman and Robin, August 2016. Still having Leigh Montagna by my side in my final years strengthened our bond all the more. (Scott Barbour/AFL Media)

Ranch life with the Llano longhorns. I love that Texas never disappoints in living up to the cliché, and I especially love that it's so much more. (Author's collection)

Cowboy James in his Stetson and boots, Rocksprings, Texas. (Author's collection)

At a Baylor football game in Texas with Cath, James and the Heards—Vivian, John, Larry (holding James) and Caroline. (Author's collection)

Christmas lunch at home with the Heans and Riewoldts, 2016. Will had been born ten days earlier. (Author's collection)

A peek over the cliff—the knee scare, round 1, 2017. I thought I was done, but in the end I only missed a week. (Quinn Rooney/AFL Media)

Promoting Maddie's Match, 2017. The support of my club and my teammates throughout the toughest period of my life is something I'll never forget. (Michael Dodge/AFL Media)

With Jack before Maddie's Match, 2017. I'll always love watching my cousin play. (Michael Willson/AFL Media)

As the sign says, For Maddie. (Michael Willson/AFL Media)

Keeping the Riewoldt name going—James, Alex with George, me with Will. (Author's collection)

With Will and James on Millingtons Beach, Orford—now known to us as Maddie's Beach. (Author's collection)

Post-game cuddles with Will. Taking after his Mum and Dad right from the outset, he was one long baby. (Andrew Knights/St Kilda FC).

Right to the end I loved training, which is probably what allowed me to play at a high level for so long. (Michael Dodge/Getty Images)

Announcing the end in front of teammates, media and family. (St Kilda FC)

I'm hugely excited about the future, and sharing whatever it holds with my beautiful family. (Michael Dodge/AFL Media)

Longevity

go through this.' Then you get hurt and think perhaps it really is over, and it changes everything. I couldn't believe I'd ever wanted it to end. I just wanted to keep playing.

Tom Brady, the great New England Patriots quarterback, has been a big inspiration to me. I had a picture of him in my locker at the club, staring out at me every time I opened the door. He was holding the Super Bowl they won in 2015 and the caption simply read 'Tom Brady, aged 37'. In 2017 they won it again, and I had to go searching for the updated 'Tom Brady, aged 39' poster. He was MVP in both games. It made me wonder, what's possible? If Tom Brady could be the best at 39, surely I could have a goal of still being a good player at 34, 35, even 36.

In the end I finished playing a month before my 35th birthday. I'd still played some really strong footy that year, although probably not with the consistency of the previous sixteen seasons. Knowing it was time dawned on me slowly. I still felt like I had plenty to offer, especially if I was played on a wing, where I'd performed so strongly in 2016. For whatever reason I hardly played there at all in my last season, which grated on me a bit. But somewhere deep inside an understanding grew, an acceptance that after seventeen years it was time for the next challenge.

I'm certain longevity added to my pedigree, to my reputation as a player. It gave me the opportunity to stay in the same environment with a completely different mindset, in a completely different headspace. If I had finished my career four or five years earlier, I wouldn't have had the opportunity to play footy and be a father at the same time. I'm glad I was able to do that, to take my kids to the footy and for James in particular to gain even a small understanding of what I did.

I feel like everyone goes through a phase where the cool thing to say is, 'I don't really love footy, it doesn't define me. I'll probably give it up in a couple of years anyway.' I went through a bit of that, around the time of the nude photo scandal, but by the last few years of my career that had totally flipped. I wanted to keep playing forever—not just for me, but because I knew we were getting better as a team and I wanted to be part of it.

For probably the last four or five seasons of my career, I'm sure people thought, 'This could be his last year.' My attitude was: what's possible? I always thought I could keep playing well, perhaps even get better. The 2016 season was vindication of that, when I finished in the top ten in the Brownlow while playing roughly half the season on a wing. I'd pushed up the ground at times the season before and I think it was good for everyone. There was a desire that Paddy McCartin and Josh Bruce not only play, but also be the main men in our forward line. They had to be given that opportunity, and it was good for me to add more flexibility to my game, to have another element that would have the opposition second-guessing themselves.

Longevity

Change reinvigorates. In the latter part of my career I changed my diet, dropped a lot of carbs like bread, pasta, rice and potatoes in favour of a higher protein intake. I concentrated more on strengthening my legs in the off-season, basically not running before Christmas, just doing leg weights and big sessions on the bike. It changed my body shape quite a lot; I was six kilos lighter than I'd been through the middle years, and 10 kilos short of the heaviest weight I'd played at. I'd argue that I looked stronger and more muscular, because basically all I'd done was drop some body fat. Playing up on a wing helped, but I couldn't have made those changes without losing something from my game if I hadn't been blessed with a good aerobic base to start from. I don't think many players would get away with that.

The running required up the ground was different to the running I'd done as a forward—still explosive, but not as explosive as it needs to be when you have a defender on you for the whole game. On the wing you start at a stoppage and have maybe five metres of separation between you and your opponent. You don't have to sprint as much to get the ball as you do playing forward. There's also the physical benefit of not having to stand under the high ball with people jumping into you, which makes a big difference to the toll the game takes on your body. My body shape was never especially conducive to being a power forward—physically, I wasn't Jonathan Brown or Tom Hawkins. I played that role, but I was never that well set up for it.

The challenge of learning a new position was fabulous, although at times it was a head-spin. When I first started going to midfield meetings I had no idea what they were talking about. I'd been playing footy for fifteen years and they were talking about 'cut-throughs', 'sweeper release to hit to three'—I had no idea. It would be like Tom Brady at 37 learning a new game plan, to throw to new receivers. But it's good to feel like you're still learning, still developing, even after so long in the game.

The evolution of the game helped, the fact that the wing felt like it had become an actual position rather than a spot where an extra on-baller would be sent to run and run. Like everywhere on a modern football ground, it's become a position where defence is as important as offence. The Hawthorn premiership teams of 2013–15 were emblematic of the wing's importance, with Isaac Smith and Bradley Hill holding their width, two running machines on the outside with Sam Mitchell and their in-and-under players winning the ball and getting it out to them. The wing is back in vogue as a position, and it was great to play there, albeit only for one season, so late in my career.

The day I thought I'd done my knee was an example of what a tricky balance it was between me playing forward and playing up the ground. I had started on the wing but after five minutes I ran a little flip with Jack Billings, took a strong contested mark, went back and kicked the goal. I felt dangerous

Longevity

and explosive, and kicked another a few minutes later. Then I tried to get back up on the wing and the runner came out and said, 'Nup, you're staying forward.' That happened a bit in the last couple of years—I'd go forward and kick one and Richo would be like, 'Who are we kidding? He's a forward! Get him away from the wing.'

But I was rapt to be given the chance to play there, to get a taste of the game from a different perspective. Waking up on a Tuesday morning in Texas and finding I'd polled 19 votes in the 2016 Brownlow was a blast. I'd played fifteen seasons as a key forward, been All Australian five times, and the most votes I'd polled was 17 to finish equal ninth in 2004, a season in which I kicked 67 goals and took 256 marks. I reckon that tells you what a midfielder's medal it is. That said, in 2016 I polled 19 votes (for equal ninth again) and didn't even make the All Australian squad of 40. Only two players that year averaged more than 20 disposals and two goals a game. Toby Greene was the other one, and he made the team on a half-forward flank. I quite liked the sound of 'Nick Riewoldt, All Australian wingman'. Clearly the selectors didn't.

•

After I found out my knee was just a split capsule and I wouldn't miss much footy at all, I had a conversation with Joey Montagna that made me realise how footballers learn to absorb pain to the point where, the longer you play, you almost don't notice it's there.

'Hopefully your limp will be evened out now,' Joey said. I asked him what he was talking about and he said, 'Mate, you don't even know anymore, but when you run the first lap at training you've got a limp. Every day.' I was like, 'No, I don't!' And Joey said, 'Mate, you've got a limp. Constantly.'

One of my strengths was my ability to recover; I'm a good healer, but I also gave myself the best chance to be a good healer because I was professional in my approach to my body. It helped that I had an ability to play through injury and pain, and I worked on that just like you do any gift. It's a major reason footballers retire—simply not being able to put their bodies through any more constant discomfort. I could have bowed to that five years before I finished, but I didn't. I'm proud of that.

I've had more than a dozen surgeries on my left knee—nothing major, but enough to reach 'bone on bone' stage long before I retired. I'll need a knee replacement one day—that's when, not if. I had two-thirds of my medial meniscus removed in my first season. Once you lose some of the medial the lateral ligament over-compensates, wearing occurs under the kneecap in the trochlea, and that's where I've been left with the most damage. I'm pretty well educated on physiology after half a lifetime listening to doctors; you get to the point where you become pretty good at self-diagnosis.

The left knee was at its worst in 2013, when I had it drained every week throughout the season. I'd play, ice it, be as professional as I could, but by the middle of the week the swelling would have accumulated. On the way home from Seaford I'd call into Olympic Park Medical Centre where I had a standing reservation. They'd do it under ultrasound—a little bit of local anaesthetic to begin with, then they'd stick the syringe into the joint at the side and aspirate it, or suck it out. Most of the time it looked like a yellow, really viscous fluid—essentially what weeps when you have a graze or a cut. The fluid is trapped in a joint, so it can't go anywhere.

They'd take anywhere between 40 and 100 millilitres at a time, which doesn't sound like a lot until you see it come out. The worst I had was in 2016 when I went knee on knee going third up in a ruck contest against Adelaide. They drained 140 millilitres the next week, and it was pretty much just blood. As much as that injury hurt, I was sad to see the end of the third-man-up in the ruck.

You play for a long time, you get injured, that's a simple reality. I missed fourteen weeks with a hamstring in 2010 that could have ended my career. I had broken collarbones, concussions, ankle surgery, facial surgery and a chronic knee. I'd get the knee jabbed before games occasionally, but not often. It was just always there, sore and grumbly. But I'm glad I pushed on, because if I'd finished a few years earlier, I don't think I would have been held in the same regard.

Professionalism is a prerequisite to having longevity in the game. You need to go above and beyond in every respect: preparation, recovery, treatment, exploring new techniques, and crucially having a really strong relationship with those who are charged with keeping you on the field. Two constants throughout my career were club doctor Ian Stone and my chiropractor Azim Hosseini. Stoney has been my doctor, my family's doctor, a mentor, a sounding board and a friend. I wouldn't have played for nearly as long without him. The same can be said of another club doctor, Tim Barbour, and physio Andrew Wallis. They ride the bumps and bruises with you from a friendship point of view, but of course have to maintain a high level of professionalism and duty of care, which must have been a difficult balancing act given the strong relationships we've shared.

In May 2015, I was knocked out playing against the Crows in Adelaide and suffered concussion that was bad enough to force me out of the next week's game. I was out for three or four minutes on the ground, and when I came to I was highly agitated, telling everyone to get away from me, leave me alone, almost to the point of being violent. In the ambulance on the way to the hospital I had no idea I was in South Australia. I'd seen a good mate—Luke Townsend, who lives in Adelaide—for breakfast that morning. He was in the ambulance and I kept asking him what he was doing there. I had no recollection of having seen him for brekkie.

I had an overwhelming sense that something bad had happened, but I didn't know what. Maddie had passed away a few months earlier but I couldn't remember it. The club doctors were all there and I kept asking them, 'Is Alex okay? Is Maddie okay? What's happened?' They didn't know how to answer my questions. All of a sudden it dawned on me that Maddie had died. It was like finding out all over again. I was hysterical, and the docs were the ones who had to hold my hand and get me through that. They'd ridden that whole journey with me, and I only realised later how difficult it was for them to see me reliving it all over again with basically short-term amnesia caused by concussion. That's the depth of the relationship you share with your doctors over a long football career. At various stages Stoney and I have discussed relationships, family illness, marriage, the future. He was a crucial sounding board in my eventual retirement from the game. Stoney, Tim and Andrew Wallis have been really important people in my world, and I can't thank them enough.

Azim Hosseini was my chiropractor for the last fourteen years of my career. During that time, without fail, I saw him at least twice a week: the day before every game, and then in the rooms before every game, when he would come in and treat me. He'd go through a range of stretches, back and neck manipulation, loosening of my knee joints, basically a full head-to-toe, 20-minute tune-up. He'd place his hands on me and have me meditate for a few minutes. He's big on the transfer of energy, and it was as much a mental work-out as a physical. He became such a huge part of my preparation. I never had any issues with my back or hips, and I attribute that to Azim. There were weeks when I thought I'd struggle to get up and play, but we found a way. I know I wouldn't have done that without Azim. He's also been such a great friend, another significant person whom I would never have met if it wasn't for footy. His positivity is infectious, which is why my sons already gravitate towards him and love it when he pops over for a visit.

When I had the knee scare in the opening round of 2017, there were still people who had a crack on social media—'surprised he didn't cry' and 'jeez, he carried on, he's such a sook', that sort of thing. You'll always get that, but I think on the whole I was seen in a more positive light in the last few years of my career. Maybe people simply had more time to get to know me. Maybe I'd become more likeable. That's what having a family gives you—you're less consumed by things that might rub people up the wrong way. Things about you that could be seen as selfish.

A lot happened after that time when I could have walked away from football, and I think it helped change the way people saw me. Perhaps they admired the fact that I didn't leave St Kilda when I had an opportunity to. Or they related to the personal grief that we've experienced as a family. And perhaps they admired the fact that I played at a high level as an older player.

Whatever the reason, the longer I played the more people would say to me, 'I used to hate you, but now I don't mind you.' That was a nice thing to hear.

11

FRIENDSHIP

I've improved as a friend, but I needed to.

Early on, about the time my career really took off in 2004, I was selfish in everything I did: towards my family, towards my friends. Being an athlete makes you that way if you let it, and I fell into that trap. Everything was on my terms: 'I'm too busy to catch up, sorry.' I could have done so much better. I don't want to give any excuses for that—I won't use what I was doing as a cop-out.

If I've lost touch with people it's been my fault. I haven't always been the best at maintaining relationships, getting back to people, being proactive in my friendships. Particularly that time in my early twenties, I wouldn't say I was a great friend to a lot of people who had been really good friends to me. Not in a nasty way, but you just get busy, you start losing touch, and then it snowballs.

I was so time poor, it became difficult to maintain friendships that already existed—getting back home and spending time with people became harder. I'd get carried away, didn't invest as much time in those friendships because of what I was doing. The here and now of playing AFL footy is all I could think about. I don't think that's unique to professional sportspeople.

For a young player I made a lot of sacrifices and I was pretty dedicated, almost to the detriment of my friendships with my teammates. We were incredibly close yet within the group, while I'd say I was respected, I don't think—early on at least—that I was necessarily well liked by a lot of my teammates. It wasn't so much the older blokes, because they saw the benefit of a young bloke who was so focused. More my peers, the guys drafted around the same time as me. I was a bit isolated in the way I went about things. I was just very serious too often, and that affected my friendships.

I'm sure that during the 2005–06 period there were boys at the club who thought that I was a big-head. I veered off the tracks, became obsessed with image. I think they still respected the way I trained and prepared and went about it on game day, but as a teammate and as a friend I lost myself a little bit. That's where you rely on the friendships to drag you back in.

Friendship

That was also the period when I went on *The Footy Show*, tried too hard, wanted to be something I wasn't. Having ridiculous haircuts, trying to force a persona and create an identity that wasn't me. On reflection it was so obvious. There was a men's salon and grooming place in the city called Man What A Fuss—a few of the boys used to go there. I went in there for a haircut and they said, 'We could tint your eyelashes too.' And I was like, 'Yeah, why not?' So round 1 against Brisbane, the night I broke my collarbone, I've got the Lions boys getting into me about wearing make-up! What was I thinking?

The fact that it didn't really openly cause friction—cause a mate or a family member to call me out—is what makes it so embarrassing. Everyone was just so supportive when it would have been easy not to be. I didn't necessarily pitch tantrums, but I made sure everything was done on my terms. I look back on it now, and I'm embarrassed that I made life for those around me more difficult than it needed to be, just to suit me.

But my teammates and friends saw through it. It came to a bit of a head on our end-of-season trip to Hawaii in 2005. I could feel that I was a bit ostracised, then one day when we were all sitting around having a beer, Matty Maguire called me out, told me I'd been arrogant all year. Everyone else chipped in—it went around the group with people speaking their minds about each other, not just me. It resonated; I didn't stray for too long.

It's naive to think every player at a football club is going to be best mates—a workplace of 45 people, everyone getting on like a house on fire. You're working with such a diverse group of people, it's just not going to happen. Late in my career we had welcome drinks for our new players. Jade Gresham was there at 18, I was 33, and Jade's old man was there aged 38. I was closer in age to his dad, and I had much more in common with him too. That sort of age difference makes it impossible for everyone to be best friends.

I'd come home from the club and I'd be on nappy duty, doing baths, having dinner at 5.30 p.m. The young blokes were going home, going out for dinner or to the movies, getting on Tinder or whatever they did. Everyone at a footy club has a common purpose, but that doesn't mean you have much else in common.

There's always a few in the group working at cross-purposes, who don't invest the same amount as others. Depending on what the temperature's like in the group at the time, what the culture's like, they tend to find a way of exiting. The culture determines how quickly that happens—or they change their behaviour and attitude.

There's a big difference between respecting the players at your club and liking them. I've played with people I don't necessarily like—I wouldn't choose to live my life the way they did. But I've respected them for the way they've gone about their football. You have to be able to get past your differences, or reaching that common goal is going to be even harder.

Friendship

•

Alex Thompson was my first best friend, even if we're cousins. Alex had the shack next door at Orford, and he was a big part of my childhood when pretty much every weekend was spent fishing, building forts, riding bikes, just disappearing all day and doing stuff.

We still have a relationship that's more like brothers—he loves to needle me. He's a Hawthorn supporter, so there have been some painful years. He used to needle me so much about losing the 2009 and 2010 grand finals that it just wore me down. We could be playing darts, someone would lose, and Alex would chime in with, 'That's just like the Saints in '09!' It's brother-type behaviour—to get a rise and to piss you off.

It came to a head one night in Triabunna, outside the Spring Bay Hotel. I finally snapped. 'I know you think it's funny, but to pour your heart into something and fall short, I don't think you understand how much that hurts,' I said to Alex. 'Just stop, because the next time you do it I'm gunna punch you straight in the face.' I still love Alex, Hawthorn and all. We just know each other so well.

We left Tassie when I was in Grade 4, just before my tenth birthday. I found changing schools difficult and got picked on a little bit. My brother Alex and I had gone up a grade because the year levels are different in Queensland—me to Grade 5, Alex to Grade 2—and it was tough to start with. I was small, and I remember at one stage getting put in the wheelie bin and the fire hose coming in. Alex and I used to find each other in the playground a bit, because we didn't have anyone else.

As I grew and matured, most of my friends came from playing footy and cricket at Broadbeach. Luke Presley is one of my oldest friends; he's a Gold Coast guy. We lived in each other's pockets from the ages of thirteen to eighteen, stayed at each other's places, and are still great mates today. I think the fact that I ended up really good mates with guys on the Gold Coast who were into sport meant I avoided a lot of the teenage traps. It was so easy to go down the wrong path living there. A lot of my friends from school would go into Surfers on Friday night at fourteen, fifteen, sniff around, court trouble. I was staying at Luke's house because we'd have footy or cricket the next day.

I've always been a big foodie, and one of my oldest friendships was born of a shared appreciation of quality school lunches. I remember gravitating towards Jerome Batten during lunch break one day, as I was eating my chicken, avocado and sundried tomato roll that Mum had made. I think Jerome might have been tucking into a smoked salmon sandwich, which caught my eye. We have no sporting connection at all—Jerome was never into footy or cricket. When we catch up it's all about trying new restaurants, new foods. He's a beautiful soul, was groomsman at my wedding and remains one of my best friends.

Friendship

Drinking was never a big part of my friendship group. Sure in Year 12 and at Schoolies you experiment a bit, but having a friendship group built around sport meant I didn't fall into those traps as readily. And I think you carry those traits through. The thought of James and Will experiencing places like Orford and the ranch, and building friendships around those situations when they get older, is very appealing.

My brother Alex and I crossed over friendship groups a fair amount in our teens, even with the three years' difference in age. As you get older that gap becomes less of an issue, and really, my brother has always been my best friend.

One of the most unusual friendships I've had is one of the few that wasn't founded in sport. Most of my friendships have been with teammates, or classmates who were good at sport. Nathan Bartlett lived down the road and was one of the smartest guys I've ever come across—he got the equivalent of 99.9 something in his final year of school. We spent a lot of time hanging out, me getting him more involved in sport, and him helping me academically. I'm not sure if I subconsciously sought that bond, from about Year 9, because I was interested in academia, in politics, in learning basically. But it was a really nice friendship to have in those high school years. We even had our first job together, setting up the chairs for the choir at the local church. We got 30 bucks each per week, which wasn't bad.

Once footy becomes your job, you have lots of new people coming into your life, and there's always a seed of doubt about their motives. That was always in the back of your mind when you met girls. I think becoming a footballer affected my female friendships more than it did my male ones; I didn't end up with too many girls who were my friends. That's swung back—you mature, you figure out how to handle that. But for a time it became difficult for me to meet people outside the footy club.

I was conscious, even at nineteen or twenty, that people wanted to be your friend not necessarily for the right reasons. That's why young footballers in particular become so close—you've got commonality, you're living the same lifestyle. Maddie was always the best filter for any of that stuff: she'd see through people straight away. Mind you, Maddie was harsh in the extreme. But she'd still see through them.

On one hand I think I was naive at times. But the fact that I don't have too many friends outside footy, that my friendship group hasn't expanded that much with the exception of footy—I'm not sure whether that's because I could see through bullshit, or whether I was a bit of a closed book. I don't think it was down to being great at reading people.

One of my flaws as a captain was being a bit elitist—my friendships tended to be with the guys who were the biggest contributors, and at times I struggled dealing with those who weren't. Some people would call gravitating to the hardest worker smart management. I don't know about that, but I invested more in the guys I thought could really add to our group.

Friendship

I've played more than a decade of footy with blokes I have nothing in common with, haven't seen much at all outside the club. Despite being a huge part of what we've done, sharing the runs to the grand finals with them, we've never really got past the surface of anything. The key is accepting that it's fine—you don't have to be best mates.

There were times I was worried about teammates, had conversations with them about how they were living their lives. Not just in my capacity as a leader, but also as a friend. I was on the other side of that as well—with everything that happened with Maddie, I've never felt more embraced as a friend. I know guys were worried about me, where I was at emotionally, the toll it was taking. I'll never forget their love and support. Friendship isn't just about individuals. You hear people talk about being 'a friend of the football club'. I've never known friendship like that shown to me, Cath and my family in Maddie's last few months, when things were so raw and difficult. Almost daily, meals would arrive at our house, so that cooking became one less thing we had to worry about. They were sent by St Kilda, my football club. That was so touching, and real friendship.

In our close group a lot of us have been through some significant challenges. Supporting Stephen Milne as a friend in court, getting called out in the media for it—it was important that I did that as a friend, and looking back it was a positive sign that I'd matured from the days of doing everything on my terms. And it comes back to you, through guys supporting me and Dal through the photo stuff, the incredible support I received after losing my sister. There's so much that happens in the lives of your long-term teammates: guys having sick babies, suffering serious injuries, having their careers finished. You go through the absolute extremes of highs and lows together, both professionally and personally.

Milney and I are very different people. Now that we're not teammates we can go three months without catching up, but we always have a way of finding each other. When we do get together it's the same stuff: he knows everything about me, I know everything about him, nothing's sacred. And it's fun. But without footy we would never have had a friendship, we're just totally different people.

Because we don't have premiership reunions, the real core of the 2009–10 grand final teams have made a point of catching up every three to six months. We jokingly refer to our get-togethers as 'runners-up reunions'. We'll go out to dinner and tell the same old stories we always have, reflecting on footy trips, good times, missed opportunities. Cath got sick of me coming home and not being able to tell her what any of them were doing with their lives now, so at one catch-up I threw it open to the table for everyone to give a 30-second update on what they were up to. Milney thought it was a great laugh. 'This is good, let's get the tape recorders out,' he said, egging Nick Dal Santo on 'because you're in the media now, Dal'. They're people I

Friendship

shared a lot with, grew up with in a way. We didn't get the thing we all wanted in our football careers—a St Kilda flag—but I love that we still celebrate our time together as well as what we mean to each other.

Some of the really strong connections in that group would floor people, like the fact that Lenny Hayes is best mates with Stephen Milne and Steven Baker. I mean, gosh—Milney and Bakes being mates people can understand, given what extroverts and characters they are. But throw in straitlaced Saint Lenny? Really? Lenny probably wins the title of best footballer I've ever played with, and he also wins the award for best bloke. One of the old-school rules in football was don't let your daughter or sister near the football club. Lenny flies in the face of this; he's the one bloke I'd have been happy for Maddie to have dated.

The great thing about sporting friendships is they develop over such a long time through having common goals, through so much shared adversity. You develop amazing relationships. Some are formed with unlikely people, but Brendon Goddard and I fit in the peas-in-a-pod category of friends—we're cut from the same cloth. I've mellowed, but we're both on the serious side with similar morals, similar interests. We were always regarded as the cops of the group, the ones who'd pull blokes up for getting on the piss or doing the wrong thing. For a while BJ's nickname was Sergeant Goddard.

BJ has been a great friend not only to me but to my family, to Alex, to Maddie. For a couple of years we had a trivia gang who'd go to a pub in South Melbourne every Tuesday night. It was in that period through 2009–10 when life was great: footy was good; Mum and Dad and Maddie had moved to Melbourne. We'd seen the sign out the front of The George and decided to give it a go. So me, Alex, Maddie, BJ, Carlie Merenda and a few others would have Japanese for dinner in Port Melbourne then head across to the pub to play trivia.

BJ was good at the sport questions, golf in particular, and the paper plane-making part of the competition. Alex was really strong in pop culture, especially movies. Maddie was great at the gossip and music stuff. We were okay too, we won a few times. The winners got to nominate a number and spin the wheel, and if your number came up you got something like 50 slabs. Otherwise it was a meat tray, the usual pub prize. It was a lot of fun, really normal; people just left us alone. The only thing that stopped us going was when I lost my mind after the photo stuff and didn't leave the house. But it's a fond memory of a good time in my life.

What I love about BJ is that he knows who he is and doesn't bend, regardless of circumstance. At times I feel like I bend my personality to suit the situation, the crowd. If I'm in Texas I won't wear what I wear in Melbourne, because I prefer to fit in. BJ just knows who he is and doesn't care what people think. In my best man's speech at his wedding I said he has a really rare quality as a friend, because he knows himself so well and has such strong morals, he's a moral compass for everyone else.

Friendship

He challenges his friends to be the best version of themselves possible. If I'm doing something that he thinks I might regret, he won't stand back and let it happen. He'll just stamp on it. That's what I admire most about him.

The outfit for the guys at his wedding was so BJ. He usually only wears black, but for the wedding it was black pants above the ankles, slip-on loafers with tassels, a grey suit jacket with a feather in the pocket instead of a flower, a shirt and tie. I was extremely dubious, but it actually looked okay in the end. That said, the shoes were horrific, and I took them off straight after the service. I was getting around the reception asking girls for adhesive bandages. My feet took two weeks to recover.

We were in Dallas on the footy trip in 2012 when BJ told me he was leaving for Essendon. We were outside a bar and he just said, 'This is what I'm gunna do. The Bombers have offered me four years, the Saints only offered me three. I just feel like it's time.' I just said no worries, we'll be friends regardless. Rossy had left; things probably weren't looking great—we were probably heading more the other way. BJ got the feeling the club was probably happy for him to move if it meant getting some picks through the door. But our friendship transcended our relationship as teammates.

A week later, a fortnight before my wedding, we met in Cancun in Mexico. Nick Dal Santo was getting married too, so we made it kind of a footy trip–cum–unofficial bucks' get-together. BJ was tossing up whether he should come or not, because he was leaving. I said, 'Mate, if you don't come it will be really tough with you from then on with the boys.' On the first night we spoke about it for fifteen minutes, got it out of the way right from the off. Milney started with: 'So what the fuck's goin' on?' BJ told the truth, teared up a bit, then for the next five days no one even spoke about it.

The same thing happened with Luke Ball at the end of 2009 when he was leaving for Collingwood; Bally decided against meeting up with the boys in New York when we were all there at the same time. That was a tough time for Bally and for a lot of our relationships. I reckon BJ had learnt that lesson.

Bally and I are very close, which isn't the way the media wanted to see it when he left the Saints. In a press conference around that time I said something like, 'Bally wasn't delisted, he was offered a contract.' There had been criticism of the club and I was trying to clear up a perception that St Kilda had pretty much let him go, but it snowballed into this me-against-Luke thing. But we were always great mates, roommates on every footy trip.

Clearly it was harder on Bally than us when he went to Collingwood because he was unavoidably isolated from his mates. I've never experienced it, but it's got to be harder on the person who's leaving than on those you leave behind. I think Bally took a lot of St Kilda IP with him; Collingwood clearly started playing like us. I'm told on day one Mick Malthouse basically got him through the door and dissected our game

Friendship

plan. They took it to a new level, and good luck to them, that's the nature of the industry.

The way Bally handled himself when they beat us in the 2010 grand final replay pretty much sums up the sort of person he is. I'm not sure how I would have reacted in that situation, but he handled it with absolute class. The way he was almost apologetic for beating us, didn't rub our faces in it when he got up to accept his medal, I remember thinking, 'Good on you Bally.' It's such a small thing, but I reckon if he'd gotten up and given it the big fist pump, carried on, it would have made our friendship a bit trickier. But the bond between us has never changed.

Bally and his wife Amy live around the corner; we've got kids the same age. I see Luke as much as I see anyone. We're pretty similar; we share a lot of the same views, the same family values. He's an intellect, a conservative. But when the time is right he's got a bit of scallywag in him, which I enjoy. I've just got a lot of respect for him.

Matt 'Goose' Maguire married Luke's sister, Sophie, another link that's kept us all incredibly close, despite the fact that Matt played almost the last half of his career in Brisbane. Goose is just a beautiful man, both inside and out. The first time Cath met Goose, she thought he was the best-looking man on earth. He's always got a kick out of that, and the fact that she was prepared to say it.

One of the most interesting teammates I had was Michael Gardiner. When he arrived at St Kilda from West Coast in

2007 his reputation preceded him—for having a proclivity for mischief, to put it mildly. That might seem at odds with my image, and make us unlikely mates. But now I see Gardy almost more than any other teammate: our wives get along really well, our kids are the same age, which obviously helps, but we have a genuine care and respect for each other. Gardy's said to me on more than one occasion that he truly believes the opportunity he had to come to St Kilda, the friendships he made there, almost saved his life. Maybe not in a literal sense, but looking at the path some of his ex-teammates went down, you get the picture. Today, Gardy is a successful player in the real estate game, a wonderful husband and a father to three beautiful girls. I'm proud to call him a great mate.

Leigh Montagna and I were the last two standing, so our friendship grew every year. Every year we continued to be the last of the originals it became stronger and stronger and stronger. I really love our friendship. It's a bit different, because Joey's a Melbourne boy and his schoolmates are all here. Same with Bally; they've relied less on the footy friendship group. But Kosi, Goose, Dal and I, who didn't go to school in Melbourne, have all fallen back on football for our core group.

My friendship with Joey really blossomed over the journey. To have gone through the whole transition with him, plus everything else that went on in our lives, is really nice. As a friend, he challenges me, which I value. That's a quality I find endearing in a friendship. The last few years we were almost seen as

Friendship

a Batman-and-Robin combination at the club; whenever one was mentioned, especially in relation to contract extensions or retirement, we were always lumped together. As a sounding board, at times a calming influence, at others a cheerleader, he got me through so much. We got each other through some big situations, on and off field, and I treasure that. I'm very fortunate to share that type of bond with a number of guys I played with for a long time. Dal, Kosi, Blakey, James Gwilt, Adam Schneider—we all have kids around the same age, and a lifetime of stories to rehash while we watch them play together.

My cousin Jack Riewoldt, his wife Carly and my sister Maddie were all the same age. When Jack was drafted at eighteen we weren't as close as we are now, simply because of the age difference and the fact that I'd been living on the Gold Coast and he was in Tassie. But our friendship—and it's weird saying that because we're first cousins—has really grown. Maddie's sickness has made us even tighter, and I'll never forget all he did for the first 'Maddie's Match' when my Saints took on his Tigers.

We're similar in a lot of ways, not least because we're both very emotional people, but Jack's definitely a bit more excitable than me, gets a bit more up and about than I do. He's more of a character too, the bloke who'll leap into the Santa suit at Christmas every year. I've absolutely loved watching him play footy, hearing the commentators cry, 'Riewoldt!' when he takes a mark or kicks a goal. I don't really get a kick out of watching footy, but if Richmond are playing that's really the only time I'll sit down and have a look—to watch Jack. It's as close as I'll come to watching a brother play. He's blood, and I love him.

From the beginning to the end of my time at St Kilda there was only one person who was there right through—our club doctor, Ian Stone. He's been an incredible sounding board to me, and an amazing friend to our whole family. Through all the time Maddie was unwell, Stoney was a constant comfort, visiting in the hospital, explaining things to us that we didn't understand. He's just a wonderful man. He's effectively the family doctor: when Alex and Roxy were honeymooning in Bali and Roxy wasn't feeling well, Alex rang Stoney for guidance. He's always there for us.

Which makes the story Mum tells about the aftermath to my collarbone injury that night at the Gabba all the more embarrassing. I'd flown back to Melbourne and gone under the knife at Vimy House, and was coming out of the anaesthetic. I've always been a shocker with anaesthetic: it turns me into a rude, argumentative smart-arse. It was Easter when I did my shoulder, and all the nurses were wearing rabbit ears. Apparently when I came around after surgery I thought I was in the Playboy mansion, and started saying things like, 'Come here, darling' to the nurses. Stoney came to see me and I could hear him out in the corridor talking to the nurses. I started calling out, 'Stoney, ya fuck! Get in here!' That's not me, and it's so embarrassing. When I had surgery later in my career,

Friendship

I'd apologise in advance before they put me under so they knew what was coming.

Someone who doesn't need any warning about what I might do or say is Carlie Merenda. She knows me inside out, and our relationship is one I treasure as much as any I've made in footy.

We met when Carlie started working for Flying Start in 2004 and, when the whole thing with Ricky Nixon exploded and I got out of there, Carlie effectively became my manager. I was at a point in my career where I didn't think I needed a manager in the traditional sense, so I engaged Tom Petroro to do my contracts with Carlie being the go-to for everything else. She's managed my appearances, organised my diary, liaised and nurtured relationships within the AFL, the footy club, everything. A lot goes into it all, and Carlie has steered the ship for me.

Carlie has also been virtually family, which has been a beautiful thing. Carlie and Maddie became great friends; she's also great friends with Cath, a virtual aunty to James and Will. She's been in my life for such a long time—Carlie was friends with Steph McIntosh when we were dating, so she's known me as a single person, as someone else's partner, as a husband, a father, a brother, a son. She takes James and Will to the park, comes over and hangs out with the kids to give Cath a bit of a break when I'm out. When Cath flew home for her sister's wedding with James and a four-month-old Will in 2017, Carlie flew with them to New Zealand for the day, just to help on the first part of the flight, then turned around and flew home.

At times it's been tricky because the lines in our relationship are so blurred, but we've managed to navigate it and always had really honest conversations. Carlie played a similar role with Ben Cousins through his career, and rode every bump and pothole with him. She tried to manage that as best she could—she's a stayer, someone who'd never walk away from something because it became too hard. By comparison I've probably been a pretty easy client. She drives a fairly hard line, holds me accountable, doesn't let me get away with any bullshit. If I haven't replied to an email or a phone call, she'll let me know about it. She can give me a serve and get away with it, just like family.

•

Footy's opened doors to other friendships I would never have had without the game. Like my relationship with the trucking magnate and former St Kilda president, Lindsay Fox and his family. Of everyone they've been the most, for want of a better term, hands-on friends. Lindsay, Paula, their son David and his wife Andrea and their kids were at our place within hours of Maddie's passing, which was amazing. Paula had come back from Italy a few months earlier with rosary beads she'd had blessed by the Pope. They hung on Maddie's bed.

Friendship

Gerry Ryan, the 'caravan king', has been another extraordinary supporter of the club, and a very good friend and mentor to me at various stages. They're just really good people.

It says a lot about Lindsay that he only ever came into the rooms when we lost; he wasn't a back-slapper who was only there in the good times. After the 2009 grand final in particular I was devastated, just about inconsolable. Lindsay took me into the boot room and gave me a hug, said something like, 'Your family's here, they don't want to see you upset like this, the sun will come up tomorrow.' It snapped me out of a funk.

From the outside it often surprises people that footballers can have strong friendships with players from other clubs. You don't have many opportunities to get to know your opponents, and the only way you can forge those friendships is when you spend a period of concentrated time together. For me the first time that happened was the 2004 International Rules series in Ireland, which is when I became friends with the former Bulldog and Tiger Nathan Brown.

Coincidentally, as a seventeen- and eighteen-year-old on the Gold Coast I used to do a bit of visualisation work with Browny's uncle, who lived up there. All that positive affirmation stuff—'I am the best player because . . .'—that I used to write in my diary. I hadn't met Browny, but I had that connection. On the 2004 Ireland trip a friendship blossomed, and we're still great mates.

I looked up to Browny: he was the fashion plate with the clothing label, the cool haircut. The tinted eyelashes were his fault for sure—I only went to that place in the city because Browny did. But we did some good things together too, like going into partnership in the Waterside Hotel on Flinders Street with a group of other footballers: Wayne Campbell, Nick Daffy, Brendon Gale, Michael Gale, Sean Wellman, Stuart Wigney. I was 21 and it was my first big footy investment. Ricky Nixon advised me against it, but it ended up being one of the best investments I've made.

At the end of 2015 I went on another Ireland trip and came back with two more great mates: Browny's old teammate Bob Murphy and Hawk Jarryd Roughead. When you're on those trips at 21 or 22, if you get along, you get along and everyone else can go and get stuffed. But when you're all over 30 and your wives have come with you, if the girls don't get along, you're doomed. We were just fortunate that everyone clicked.

It started in New York where we stopped for a camp on the way there. We had a couple of nights out and BJ—almost out of character for the serious head that he is—led the charge. Then in Dublin, on the first night we were there, we all went out to dinner: the Riewoldts, Murphys, Rougheads and Montagnas. That was it, that was the introduction. The girls sat up one end and drank red wine, we sat up the other and did the same. When we got a day off, Cath and I caught a train to a little village about half an hour away with Bob and his wife Justine, a place called Howth that's virtually an outer suburb at the top of Dublin Bay. We had fish and chips at a pub, walked up to the lookout, just hung out and spent some time together. Roughy and Sarah came along when we all went to the Guinness factory.

You just get to know each other on a different level and realise that, even though you might be different, you can still be mates. Murph's the classic example of that—he's got an Elvis tattoo for goodness' sake, try and get more pop culture than that! We're so different—politically, he's to the left and I'm to the right, for starters—but we just get along. It's funny, we just seem to have the same opinion about a lot of things.

Leaving Ireland, we all said, 'We've gotta make sure we catch up when we get back.' You always say that and it never happens, but we made the effort. The next season we had everyone around home for a 4th of July Sunday lunch. Cath put together an American-themed quiz, which was funny. Murph prides himself on being up with things, but he'll never live down answering 'New Caledonia' to the question 'Name three of the five states in America that start with the word "New"'. Murph, Roughy and I have a message thread, and that constantly bobs up.

I didn't really know how to handle Roughy's illness, I guess because Maddie was still so raw and fresh at the time. I just threw a text that said, 'Mate I'm thinking about you, stay positive.' But I sent Sarah one as well, saying I was there if she needed someone to talk to. It can be harder for those who are watching; you've got no control. It was worrying. A lot of what you were reading was a positive outlook, but I felt a bit more pessimistic because that's how I'd been pre-conditioned. I'd heard 'positive outlook' before.

That 4th of July Roughy wasn't well. Cath was pregnant, Sarah wasn't drinking because Jarryd wasn't, Justine took a hit and joined them. Murph and I both said, 'One in, all in?' Then we went, 'Nah, we'll open a bottle of red.'

I guess it's a bit strange to end up sharing an opponent's highs and lows, riding them with him. Obviously your health is a different matter, but even when the Bulldogs broke through to win the flag in 2016 and Murph missed out because of a knee injury, I was gutted for him. We were in Texas and I'd sent him a message before the game, then when I got up and saw they'd won I felt physically ill.

Bally winning was tough, but that was more about us *not* winning. I wished it was us, but I'm sure Bally wished it was him with St Kilda too. With Murph I felt like I was one of very few people who could really relate to how he was feeling. We've had a lot of those conversations. It ripped my heart out on two levels. One, it was the blueprint of what a St Kilda premiership would look like, with the drought breaking, the history of struggle. But it was compounded by the fact that Murph wasn't part of that. Because you're thinking, 'Well if the Bulldogs get to do it at least Murph gets to . . . oh no, he didn't.'

Friendship

I've let Murph and Roughy know that I've got one regret about our friendship—that I would finally have had a couple of mates to hang out with at the annual captains' day in the pre-season, except I wasn't captain anymore! I went every year for eleven years: you'd see Browny, Pav, Hodgey, you'd develop a bit of a relationship and get below the surface a bit. But otherwise it was, 'Who do I know that's gone to Adelaide? Oh yeah, our old assistant coach.' 'So, how's so-and-so going?' It can be so paper thin and superficial.

I did say to them when Roughy was announced as captain in 2017, 'I've been going to these fucking captains' days for eleven years, making small talk with people I don't really know. Finally there's some blokes there I can have some fun with—they'll probably bring out beers at the commission lunch for the first time ever—and I'm not there!'

•

My career has effectively given me a connection with four footy generations. Guys like Robert Harvey, Nathan Burke, Stewart Loewe when I started; Aaron Hamill and Fraser Gehrig after them; then the crew who started out with me, or around the same time as me. And in the end I was with Jack Steven, Jarryn Geary, Josh Bruce. Longevity afforded me that, and despite our difference in age and life experience, my friendship with the guys who were around me when I finished is something I'm so grateful for. They were my teammates through the hardest years of my life. They'll always be special to me.

A lot of the friendships that have changed or influenced me over the journey have been with such a diverse range of people. People who've challenged and inspired me on so many different levels, friends who've taught me so much along the way. About how to be a good friend, how to be a good father.

You meet a lot of people and it can be overwhelming, in the sense of, 'how do I maintain all these relationships?' There's only so many days in a year to have a barbecue, to do the things you need to service a friendship properly. That's forced me to really drill down on those people who are important to me and invest more time in keeping them close. I've learnt to be much better at it, and that's made me a better person.

12

BEING A SAINT

During grand final week of 2013 Eddie McGuire invited me over to his house to talk about my future, essentially (at least to my thinking) where I saw myself going in the media. I'd done *The Footy Show* sporadically for a long time, and with the Saints finishing way short of the finals I was spending that September doing special comments for Channel Seven. Working in the media post-footy is an avenue I'd thought about pursuing for a long time, and there are few better people to have that conversation with than Eddie.

I lobbed at his house in Toorak, and it was just me and him. We opened a beer and Eddie said, 'Look, I want to talk about you coming to Collingwood.' Just bang, straight out with it. Gosh, Eddie's good. I can't believe Collingwood people when they bag him. To have someone in your corner like Eddie McGuire, who likes nothing more than getting out and slamming the desk for your club, is pretty special.

So Eddie played his hand. 'You've done the right thing by St Kilda, they've already said you're going down a path of rebuilding. Goddard's left, Dal Santo's leaving, Montagna's talking to clubs.' He knew things weren't great at the club and he was right; a couple of weeks later Scott Watters was sacked as coach. Lenny, Milney, Kosi and Blakey (Jason Blake) had all finished up. Throw in the names Eddie was using as bait and there was a chance all of the old guard would be gone except me.

We had a conversation, which was largely Eddie selling what Collingwood had to offer. 'Instead of playing in front of 20,000 on a Sunday afternoon at Etihad you'll be playing in front of 100,000 on Anzac Day at the 'G, that sort of stuff. Almost as a sweetener he threw in that, with Emirates as the club's major sponsor, Cath and I would virtually have our own personal travel agent at our disposal for those annual trips to the States. Never mind that Emirates don't even fly direct to the States, it was part of the sell.

Cath was already in Houston, and a few days later I got on a plane to join her. It was the day after the grand final. I'd worked with Seven on the coverage the day before, seen Hawthorn beat Fremantle for the first of its hat-trick of premierships, and I was glad to be getting out of there. We were sitting on the runway waiting for clearance to take off, I had a champagne in front of me, and my phone buzzed with a text message. It was Eddie.

'Hey mate, before you take off . . .' It was almost spooky—I had to sneak a look over my shoulder to check he wasn't on the plane! 'Before you take off, I just want to leave you with two words: Brian Lake.'

The message went on about how Lake had left the Bulldogs, a similar club to St Kilda on a similar downward trajectory, and the very next year he'd played in a flag and won the Norm Smith Medal. 'This is what you deserve,' Eddie's text said. He's so good; he knew I was going to be on a plane for the next fourteen hours, and that was all I'd be thinking about. It was an incredible sell.

I didn't even know if he'd spoken to Collingwood's recruiting boss Derek Hine or more importantly coach Nathan Buckley—I presume he had. He was talking three years, on decent money for a soon-to-be 31-year-old.

In thirteen years at St Kilda I hadn't come close to leaving. There had been discussions between my then-manager Ricky Nixon ahead of Gold Coast coming into the competition. I heard some figures—$1 million-plus a year over five, which would have been the biggest contract ever signed in the AFL—but I never saw a formal offer. Staying at St Kilda was a pretty easy decision. It was eight or nine games into the 2009 season, we were undefeated, and it looked like we were on the path to having sustained success.

Mum, Dad and Maddie had moved down to Melbourne at the start of 2009, which would have made for an ironic turn of events if I'd packed up and headed the other way. In the short time I was mulling over a move, Mum and Dad gave me some terrific advice: 'You're always going to have money. The difference isn't life-changing money, but the decision to leave is.' It hit home that big decisions should be made first and foremost on the direction they'll take your life, not on what they'll inject into your bank account.

So now Collingwood—or at least its president—was making a play and I had to consider another big move, against a backdrop of a team that was seemingly going in the opposite direction to the one I was leading when Gold Coast came knocking. Once I got to the States I spoke to Tom Petroro, who looks after my contractual stuff, and then with the club. I told them the Magpies were keen, said I was thinking about it, and asked what was going on with Joey, who'd been in talks with Essendon. The waters became even more muddied when Scott was sacked and, in reply to a voicemail I'd left him, he sent me a text that essentially said the club wouldn't think twice about doing the same to me.

If Joey had left, who knows what I would have done. But I stayed, played another five seasons, and finished as that person Cath's mother Caroline liked before she'd even met me: a one-club player. And I'll always be incredibly proud of having been a Saint my entire football life, proud that when my kids grow up there's only one place I'll ever take them.

I'm drawn to St Kilda for all its warts, its eccentricities, its rich history and the bits that haven't been nearly as glittering. I'm a St Kilda person. And I love that I'll always be able to say that.

•

Dad was a Saints supporter when I was growing up, but I followed Mum into the Hawks. To a child of the 1980s, St Kilda had never won anything and Hawthorn was winning everything. That said, I wasn't a huge footyhead as a kid, if only because you couldn't be in Queensland unless your footy of choice was rugby league.

I arrived at the club knowing virtually nothing of its history, other than the sorry fact I'd heard Dad lament many times: they'd won just one premiership. Other than that I went in cold on the legend of 1966.

In my first year, St Kilda had a team-of-the-century dinner, which everyone was doing at the start of the 2000s. They unveiled the big Jamie Cooper painting, and all of the living legends were there. All night, Kosi and I worked the room together as star-struck eighteen-year-olds. We left with a greater sense of how almost mythical the 1966 grand final was, because everyone you met said they were there. Over the years

THE THINGS THAT MAKE US

I've wondered if the MCG used to have a capacity of 300,000, because that's how many people I've met who reckon they were at the game.

That night in 2001 was the first exposure Kosi and I had to a longing we'd hear from St Kilda people—fans and ex-players alike—a million times during our careers. 'I wanna see another premiership before I die.' 'We've only won one, please give us another.' 'It's your turn.' 'It's up to you.' That was the first time I felt like being a Saint was to be part of something truly special and unique.

It was also the first time I met Tony Lockett, the great full-forward who's such a reclusive, shy person that I could count on one hand the number of times I saw him in nearly twenty years at the club. I respect the way he's chosen to live his post-footy life, and the lasting impression he left each time we met was just how extraordinarily humble he is. You wouldn't know he was the game's greatest goalkicker from meeting him, far from it. When our much-loved old trainer Kenny Whiffin died a few years ago, Plugger drove down from his property near Bowral in New South Wales for the funeral, was there for an hour, said a quiet g'day, paid his respects, got in his car and drove home. That says a lot about him.

I've seen a lot of the actual premiership players over the years, guys like Brian Gleeson, Verdun Howell, Ian Stewart. Cowboy Neale was working at the club in my early years, and Barry Breen is a regular at functions—I see a lot of Breeny. To a man they've all been great about the mixed blessing of being the players who won St Kilda's only flag. They're fed up with being 'the ones'; they're extremely proud of it all, but they're just so keen for someone else to have a go. They know they've been the poster boys for way too long.

St Kilda is all I know, but it's always seemed to be a club like no other. The star-crossed history has a lot to do with that, and the tendency to celebrate its stars in lieu of ultimate team success. Then there's the old chestnut of 'culture'. Did a supposed party culture in the 1970s and '80s set the tone for a lack of team success, or did St Kilda celebrate its stars because there was so little team success? I'm not sure which perpetuated the other.

I've heard some of the players of the 1980s address the issue of culture. Geoff Cunningham hated the term, and the 'party boys' tag that invariably followed it. He and his old teammate Greg Burns reckoned the club was no better or worse on that front than any at the time; when the game was still only semi-professional, Saturday night was a time to let your hair down. Maybe the difference at St Kilda, and what shone a brighter light in the club's direction, was that the Saints had Trevor Barker.

I never met Barks, who died far too young of cancer four years before I was drafted. But I heard a lot of stories—about his playing exploits, about his extraordinary sense of club, and of course about his off-field exploits. But as much as you hear of Barks the ladies' man, within the club the stories are legendary of how hard he trained, the work he did to promote the club through a time when St Kilda was at a low ebb, the massive reduction in pay he took to stop the club from going to the wall.

Even when we were based at Seaford, we'd go back to Moorabbin the day before games and do our weights session in the Trevor Barker Room. There wasn't much left of the club's old home then, but it was fitting that the last building to be knocked down ahead of the rebuild that took us back to our heartland housed one of the most famous rooms in footy: the old Saints disco, which fittingly took the name of its most celebrated patron.

When I arrived at the club, the disco's last days were long gone, but it still had the big velvet curtains, mirrors on the ceiling and a huge silver disco ball over the sunken dance floor, about a five-metre diameter circle a couple of steps down from the main floor. When it became our gym, they had to cover it over and shore it up to support the weights, but if you'd taken a crowbar and lifted the boards it would have been like stepping back in time.

The old Huggins Stand was still there at the start of my career, and we basically migrated from one end to the other and eventually all the way out the door to Seaford. The change rooms below the grandstand could have told some stories too, not to mention the sauna and spa that were apparently often put to use during nights at the Saints disco. It was all fairly dilapidated, but I didn't have anything to compare it with. I hadn't been to the States and seen the quality facilities professional clubs were blessed with; there was no Lexus Centre then, Hawthorn was still based at Glenferrie, Essendon at Windy Hill—AFL football was clinging to its suburban roots. Moorabbin was pretty much on a par with everyone else.

Moorabbin was a bit like the club itself—you had to love it, warts and all. One day, not long before we moved to Seaford, we were out on the ground doing a warm-up drill in the centre square. The stand was falling apart by that stage—literally. It was blowing a gale this day and all of a sudden there was this massive CRACK! Everyone looked up and saw that a sheet of corrugated iron about the size of a couple of big bay windows had snapped off the top of the stand and just taken off.

It was like the feather at the start of *Forrest Gump*, floating at the mercy of the breeze, travelling incredibly fast but at the same time almost in slow motion. It could have gone anywhere, but it flew over the middle of the oval towards us. It must have travelled 60 or more metres, and then it speared into the ground like a two-metre wide javelin, about 30 metres from where we were training. It was like Rolf Harris's wobble board, just wedged in the turf quivering. It could have cut someone in half.

Then everyone was like, 'Well, it's probably not gunna

happen again, we'd better get on with training.' That's a St Kilda story.

The move to Seaford was an absolute disaster. I'm not sure who drove the decision and I don't especially care, but for a dispute at council level over pokie machines or whatever it was to affect a football club that had been around 100 years so dramatically—because for those who lived it every day it was dramatic—was just wrong. What it did to the morale of the playing group and the staff, and our ability to interact with the community, was just really disappointing.

We had probably assembled the best list in the club's history, made the grand final in 2009, again in 2010. Then, for the 2011 pre-season, everyone gets shipped 40 minutes down the coast to a satellite training venue. The day we walked through the doors we were expecting to move into a world-class, elite training facility for professional athletes. I'm going to sound like a spoilt brat, but it was no better than what we'd had at Moorabbin, except new. It was just so poorly designed.

Above the door where we ran out onto the ground at Seaford there was a graphic of the team breaking through the banner before the 2010 grand final. After Brendon Goddard and Zac Dawson moved to Essendon and Fremantle, respectively, the numbers on their backs in that picture were changed. It was ridiculous, unnecessary and disrespectful, and raised more than a few eyebrows among the remaining grand final players.

Being a Saint

One of the great things about being based at Moorabbin was that when you had an hour off, a group of you could jump in a couple of cars and go down the street for a sandwich or a coffee. You got away from the club, spent time with your teammates, interacted with the community, and you had a bit of a presence on the streets in a really strong St Kilda area. All of a sudden that all disappeared.

At Seaford, you scoffed down your lunch in twenty minutes and were onto your next session. You didn't sit down with your teammates; it was a clock-in, clock-out environment. And there was nowhere close by where you could get away from the club. We had probably five places we'd go to regularly near Moorabbin. I'd hate to think what us moving did for some of those businesses—between all the Saints players there was probably 500 bucks a week getting tipped into some of those cafes.

From day one it was only a matter of time before they made the call to get out of Seaford. I understand the club was in an awkward position, but gee, the amount of times we got asked about it. It was well known that everyone hated it. I was asked about it in an interview once and called it 'geographically challenging'. I got my arse kicked for being negative.

It was like we were homeless but, worse than that, we were soulless. There was even a council edict that the club couldn't fly a St Kilda flag. When I heard the news that we were going back to Moorabbin, where a new facility that would cater for every footy level from Auskick up to the AFL team was being built, I was doing handstands. Our ability to become a destination club for free agents, attract sponsors, engage with our supporters and, most importantly, win games of footy, means we will all benefit as a result. I would have dearly loved to be reunited with Moorabbin for one last year before I retired.

•

In the way of sporting clubs with plenty of space in their trophy cabinet, St Kilda has the most loyal supporters. I love that it's also got so many visible high-profile fans. It's pretty cool for an eighteen-, nineteen-year-old coming into the game to meet Molly Meldrum, Michael Gudinski, Shane Warne, Eric Bana. It felt like St Kilda had this rock-star following, from all different walks of life. It was pretty cool at the start, but over time it just evolves into proper relationships.

From time to time, really close friendships develop with these famous people, such as the one between Molly and my family.

Even before Maddie was unwell, Molly would call Mum once a month, just to check in. He'd phone my Nan too, which they both loved. It started through Ricky Nixon having dealings with Michael Gudinski, and soon my whole family were watching games from Michael's box at Etihad Stadium.

Being a Saint

Molly would be there, Daryl Somers if it was a Geelong game, and they all got on like a house on fire.

We'd go around to Molly's place for dinner; the Gudinskis would be there, and we'd just sit in this extraordinary Egyptian-themed house, gaping at everything in sight. Letters from the Beatles on the walls, stuff from Madonna, Elton John, you name it. My generation doesn't have a clue how significant a player he was in the entertainment industry. We don't say much when we're at Molly's, but to be a fly on the wall, to hear the stories, is amazing.

He operates on a different wave length to most of us, but he's got a beautiful soul. When Maddie passed away Molly had an angel painted on the wall out the front of his house in her memory. She got special mentions in Molly's book, *The Never, Um, Ending Story*; it came out when she was in hospital and Maddie was so pumped there was a little tribute to her in the back.

I'm very fond of Molly, and of Michael and Sue Gudinski, who is a lovely woman. They're big Saints supporters, but I feel like our friendship went to a level where it transcended footy. Michael is very giving and through his generosity I've been to some really cool shows. Springsteen at Hanging Rock was the absolute pick; Cath and I were in a little VIP area off to the side with Michael and Sue, Molly and the actor Ewan McGregor.

We said 'g'day', but when you're in that sort of place you

can't harass people. Cath was desperate to get a photo with Ewan McGregor, and she wouldn't stop talking about how good looking he was. I pretty much had to restrain her. We were at this incredible three-hour show, and every time I looked at Cath she was looking at Ewan McGregor. I was like, 'He's playing "Born in the USA", babe, this is your song!' Nup, not interested.

The first time I remember meeting Warnie was at a team barbecue at president Rod Butterss' house in Brighton. It's developed into just a normal friendship. I'll get a text once a month, 'Hey, I'm in London, I'm on this number', or 'I'm in the States.' Or, 'Hey, I'm back, I'm playing cards, come around.' The card nights have become more difficult since we had kids, but they were always fun if only because they were so ordinary. I can imagine what people might think of a poker night at Warnie's—strippers, topless waitresses, everyone on the booze. Most of the time everyone's wearing trackies and thongs and a T-shirt and we're drinking water.

Warnie is mates with a lot of the Saints boys, so it might be me, BJ, Joey, Steven Baker. And Joe and Tony Hachem, a world champion and a bloke who's come top ten in the Aussie Millions about five times. And Warnie, who's sponsored by 888 Poker. I end up sitting there watching the pot get bigger and bigger—and these serious card players engaging in a battle of patience—and wonder what the hell I'm doing there. Essentially I'm just there to make a donation.

I admire Warnie. It would be incredibly difficult to live your life in such a public forum, but he seems pretty happy to do so and doesn't care what anyone thinks. I've used him as a bit of a sounding board at times—he's been incredibly resilient over the years. As a leader of the footy club it was interesting for me to explore how he'd handle certain situations. Being able to tap into his gamesmanship, his will to win, has also been a huge benefit of our friendship. As a friend he'd bend over backwards to help you in any way. His kids are beautiful kids, he's a great dad. He's just a really good guy.

For such a big-time Hollywood superstar, Eric Bana keeps an incredibly low profile and is so unaffected. He walks his dogs around the neighbourhood, goes to the coffee shop, is the sort of person who has people doing double-takes thinking, 'Wasn't that . . . nah, couldn't have been.'

I'd seen him do 'Poida' on *Fast Forward*, his impersonations of Ray Martin—I was old enough to remember those characters and thought they were hilarious. By the time I met him he'd done *The Castle, Chopper, Black Hawk Down*, some pretty significant stuff.

Bana is just a cool dude. He rides motorbikes, does up cars. He doesn't try to be cool, he just is. Unless he's away working he's in Melbourne and, if it's footy season, he's at our games. He'll occasionally pop into the rooms, but he's very much in the background. He's a real footy fan—in the outer, headphones in, listening to the call on the radio. I like talking footy to him, it's something I can speak about that he finds interesting. But he's just such a normal guy, that's what's great about him.

When the nude photo scandal was at its height, I sought Eric out to talk about how he copes with life in the spotlight, and he told me a story about Brad Pitt and Angelina Jolie. It was bizarre enough sitting there at the time, let alone looking back on it. Eric said, 'When I was working on the set of *Troy* I was talking to Brad . . .' And I was sitting there thinking, 'What the hell's going on here?'

Anyway, Eric said he asked Brad how he deals with the paparazzi all the time. And Brad told him, 'We're just vanilla. Every time they photograph me or Ange, we pull the exact same face—no expression at all, vanilla. That's all they get, which makes them less inclined to publish it because they're always getting the same thing.'

Rossy Lyon was the one who suggested I ask Eric for advice, so the next day at the club he was all over it, asking me how it had gone. Next thing Rossy's standing in front of the whole playing group during some session about footy and media, and he goes, 'Rooey—what does Brad Pitt do?' All the boys are looking at me, clearly thinking, 'Who do you think you are, mate, name-dropping Brad Pitt?' It was embarrassing, but looking back it was at least a funny moment in a dark time.

The golfer Geoff Ogilvy is another big Saints fan. Geoff's wife Juli is from Paris, Texas, so our friendship became stronger than just the St Kilda connection when I married a girl from Texas. We've had 4th of Julys at our place with them, with Cath decking the place out and conducting an American quiz. I played golf with Geoff once, which was awesome except for BJ beating Geoff off the stick. I play off about 15, BJ plays off one. He was painful enough when it comes to golf without beating a US Open winner.

It's what I've learnt from these encounters that's been important. For Eric Bana and his wife Rebecca to invite me into their home and talk to me when I was in a really dark place was an extraordinary comfort through a very difficult period. To see the way he's remained unaffected, despite all his fame, all his success, to see what a great family man he is, has had a profound effect on me.

You've got to be careful not to abuse those friendships, and that's been a juggling act at times with Maddie's Vision. I've invited those guys to everything, but there's never an obligation. I'd never go around to Eric's and ask him to sign a photo. Warnie's always said, 'I'm happy to help you out in any way.' But you don't want to overstep a line, because you know yourself what that's like.

In times of real struggle, support from people like that is no different to support from someone down the street who's been a lifelong friend. But for my family—and particularly for Maddie—to know she was getting messages from Molly Meldrum when she was extraordinarily sick in hospital, that was really nice. Those things give you a bit of a boost. That's why people ask footballers to visit hospitals I guess—it's fleeting, but if it provides a bit of happiness in that moment, then that's great.

I was at St Kilda for more than half my life, so it's only natural that a lot of people who will be my lifelong friends have come from that association. In the beginning, that's all it is—an association. Your personalities, fate, the effort you put in dictate whether you have a relationship moving forward. All that's provided at the start is an introduction, an opportunity to meet. Then you do with that what you will. But without St Kilda I wouldn't have all these friendships.

I'm proud of my club, and protective too. The longer I spent there the more I felt that something could happen at one club and not get any traction or attention, but if the exact same thing happened at St Kilda it would be a completely different story—the way it would be reported, how it would be assessed, the way it would be handled. The two events would go on entirely different paths.

In some sort of spiritual way I feel like part of St Kilda has rubbed off on me. Someone wrote something about my life and my football story being intertwined with St Kilda's, the whole Greek tragedy. When Maddie was sick, a lot of the time I was thinking, 'This is our grand final.' Maddie's fight was the one we were going to win, and everything else would seem so insignificant. I said after 2009 that losing the grand final felt like someone had died. It's all relative at the time, but how stupid and shallow does that sound now?

I played in a premiership every year I played footy bar one—until I got to St Kilda. Under 12s, two in under 13s, a win and a loss in under 15s, another flag in under 16s, then Southport reserves, Southport seniors, drafted. In some cosmic sort of way, it feels like the winning magic has worn off. Maybe I wasn't always like this; maybe St Kilda has seeped into me.

Late in my career I'd find myself thinking about our 42,000 members, wondering who they were and how many I'd actually met. I wish I'd met every one of them, if only to ask, 'Why St Kilda?' Not to question their choice, rather that I'm interested in what aspect of the Saints drew them in the most. I know footy is entertainment, so in a sense buying a membership is a fee for service. But committing to the Saints as emotionally as our fans do is about so much more than that. The passion I've witnessed over seventeen years has been extraordinary—in times of jubilation or disappointment, that passion has never wavered.

I've loved getting to know a fan like Georgie Day, and offloading pieces of memorabilia for her to display in her pride and joy, the St Kilda Heritage Museum. I've loved hearing Bruce Eva and Steve Fisher telling stories of their wild days in the Moorabbin 'animal enclosure'. I've loved walking along the street, passing someone wearing a Saints shirt or cap, and simply nodding to each other and sharing a smile. I've loved driving to games seeing a Saints sticker on a car or a red, white and black scarf flapping out the window. There's a shared pride and sense of belonging. It's amazing how much I identify with our colours now. It's like they're part of my DNA.

I'm a St Kilda person, and I love what that represents. But in a lot of ways it's a bit of a cross to bear. A flag changes the narrative. I can't believe how close we got—the bounce of a ball, a toe poke, Tom Hawkins hitting the post and it being called a goal. Getting so close feels like it should change the narrative, but all it does is add to it. I wanted so desperately to be a part of the group that delivered what St Kilda fans wanted so badly. They deserve a flag, and it will always burn that I couldn't give them the ultimate thank you for their support. Especially given the way they thanked me for my service. The support and best wishes I received over the last month of my career will stay with me forever.

St Kilda has been my home for more than half my life and Saints people have become my extended family. To me, that's what being a Saint is—being part of a family. In my last few years, with Matt Finnis as CEO, the club adopted the slogan 'How I want to be'—a line from our club song 'Oh when the Saints . . .' It aligned so perfectly with our identity as a club, and it's inclusive nature. Regardless of who you are, you're welcome at the Saints. And the path we go down together transcends football. I will be forever grateful to John Beveridge for recruiting a skinny seventeen-year-old from the Gold Coast and sending me on that path.

13

WINNING AND LOSING

The urge to win does strange things to people, as anyone would have discovered if they'd looked up at our balcony early one spring morning in 2009. It's not every day you see an AFL captain pointing a gun at a tree in an inner suburban street.

In footy-obsessed Melbourne, September means finals. For me, the first spring I spent living in a three-storey South Melbourne terrace meant being woken at 5 a.m. every day by the non-stop warbling of a bird. I don't even know what sort of bird it was, but if I close my eyes I can still hear it.

My bedroom was on the second floor, and at the first bloom of spring the bird took up residence in the beautiful gum tree outside my window. Game day is a time of ritual and routine for a footballer, and if I was woken early on the day we were playing I could never get back to sleep. Back then, pre-kids, I'd try to sleep for as long as I could on the day of a game.

It was driving me mad, so I said to my teammate Justin Koschitzke, the good country boy from Brocklesby, 'Have you still got that gun?'

So there I was, standing on my balcony with Kosi's air rifle trained on this bloody bird. I had my finger on the trigger ready to squeeze when a thought entered my head: karma. As much as the bird was driving me around the bend, I convinced myself that killing it would come back to bite me. Something would go wrong. We wouldn't win the premiership.

So I didn't shoot it, and for the whole of September the bird kept chirping away. I moved into the spare bedroom at the back of the house, and on the last Saturday of the month we went within a whisker of winning the grand final, but lost to Geelong. That's the sort of unhinged, mad person the drive to win can turn you into. You can convince yourself that your fortunes will turn on the craziest little things. You can lose your balance.

I'd do it differently now. The bird would be gone. Because I know there's no such thing as karma.

•

Winning is everything. As an athlete in a team sport, it's what you're measured on. It really is all that matters.

Winning and Losing

Football provided me with so much more than a premiership alone could have. There are many, many blokes who've played in flags and it hasn't stopped their lives from ending up a mess. A premiership medal isn't the golden ticket to a lifetime of happiness, satisfaction and pride. But I know the fact that I didn't win one will always count against me. I know there's only one thing that could change that, and now it's too late.

The reality is that, in a lot of people's eyes, my record will never stack up against someone like Jonathan Brown's, because Browny won three flags and I didn't win any. It's hard to articulate this without sounding like I'm denigrating Browny, which I'm not. He was a great player. And he was a great player with three premiership medals. End of story.

Plenty of blokes have won a lot of club best and fairests, but these awards are window dressing compared to a premiership medal. You need a flag to rubber stamp them. I'm honoured to have won six Trevor Barker medals, but they're in a box in the garage. I'm not sure a premiership medal would be.

I'm proud of what I achieved in the game: the best and fairests, five All-Australians, being St Kilda's longest-serving captain. But there's a gap, and it's a big one. Robert Harvey was All-Australian eight times, won four best and fairests and two Brownlow medals to boot. He's an absolute champion of the game, but it still feels like his CV is missing the thing that I dearly hoped mine wouldn't. It doesn't get much better than two Brownlows, four b&fs and eight All-Australians. Only one thing can improve a record like that. One little medal. Chris Judd won five club champion awards and was All-Australian six times. And he played in a grand final that West Coast won by a point. That solitary point puts an exclamation mark on his greatness.

I'm not greedy. You just need one. For a long time, I beat myself up about the fact that I didn't have a premiership. Then I took inventory of what I could have done differently. Could I have worked harder? Could I have trained more? Could I have wanted it more? No. Mistakes, wins, losses are all part of a career. I was always accountable for those, I continued to be brave and took the chance to be great. My tank is empty.

The reality is, I gave it my best shot and it didn't happen. It is what it is.

•

Losing always hurts; no one likes losing. But there are degrees of losing. Losing when you're a developing side is different to losing when you're contending. You can lose and go forward when you're developing. You can lose and win.

When you're a young player, it's about winning, but it's also about forging a career and establishing yourself. With age and experience comes a greater desperation to win. Winning becomes what you play for. You start to understand that you become defined individually by how successful the teams

Winning and Losing

you've played in have been. That's the same in any sport. Scottie Pippin is virtually an NBA all-time great, but his status has been elevated by the happy fact that he played with a bloke named Michael Jordan.

The longer you play without winning a flag the more you feel the clock ticking. We made back-to-back preliminary finals in 2004 and '05, my fourth and fifth seasons. We lost by a goal to Port Adelaide in 2004, and to Sydney the next year after being seven points up at three-quarter time. Port and the Swans went on and won those two premierships. Hawthorn in 2008 got one against the odds. The Bulldogs did the same in 2016. Maybe we could have pinched one in 2004 or '05. It was gut-wrenching, but it still felt like we were building something under Thommo. It felt like our time would come.

By the time we made the 2009 and 2010 grand finals I had more of an understanding that my personal legacy was going to hinge on winning a premiership. That I could be a very good player over a long period of time, but if I didn't win a flag that would be a black mark against my name. Not just an asterisk, a black mark. 'Yeah, good player, but . . .'

I feel like it's a black mark against my leadership. That's a simplistic way of looking at things, but it's how I feel. What hurts as much as anything is that I honestly believe we couldn't have worked any harder or prepared any better in either of those years. I don't think Geelong prepared any better than us in 2009. I know Collingwood didn't prepare any better than us in 2010. We couldn't have done any more. But on the biggest day, we simply didn't finish the job.

Gosh, if people could have seen what we invested in it. The way we played under Ross Lyon was a brutal, incredibly taxing game style, with such a strong emphasis on everyone being accountable defensively. Even when we won the first nineteen games of the 2009 season it never felt easy, because we were investing so much from a preparation point of view. But once the momentum kicked in, it was like a tidal wave that couldn't be stopped.

The mental preparation that went into conditioning every player—knowing where on the ground he should be in every scenario, how he should approach each contest, where to take the ball and how to move it up the ground—was incredibly time-consuming, but it brought results.

But at the same time, because everyone was doing it, everyone was all in, it was easier. It was such a well-oiled machine that even though every player felt the responsibility to contribute individually, you didn't feel you had to win it by yourself. That made it easier for everyone, from the top down.

When you know you're in a position to win a flag you're prepared to invest more. You think about it more, you live and breathe it more, it's more all-consuming because you know there's more on the line. It was the hardest footy in my career, but it was the best footy ever too. I was single, I didn't have

Winning and Losing

anything else I needed to attend to. We just did everything we could to be the best we could. Every night after training we'd go to the St Kilda sea baths and jump in the ocean. It might have been mid-winter, teeming with rain, waves breaking on St Kilda beach, but we'd still be out there. We did it as part of the team recovery at the start of the week, but then we were back there Tuesday nights, Wednesday nights, standing in the ocean in the dark. We were all in.

We had played in the preliminary final the year before and got smashed by Hawthorn. Our last pre-season game of 2009 we went to Port Adelaide and lost by 80-odd points. Then we came out and did what we did. Even in round 1, we were playing Sydney at Docklands and they were five goals to one in front at quarter-time. Then they didn't kick another goal until halfway through the last quarter and that was it, we were away.

We started the season with a quiet confidence—hopefully, we'll make the finals, and then we'll see if we're good enough to go all the way. By the time we beat Geelong on a Sunday afternoon in round 14 in front of a full house at Docklands, we were starting to believe we had a real chance of winning the premiership.

My first grand final week was mayhem, and being me and being St Kilda, of course there was drama. We had our main training session on the Thursday in front of a huge crowd at Moorabbin, and towards the end I strained my hip flexor, the group of muscles that allow you to bend your knee upwards—or effectively, the muscles that allow you to run. I was running in a simple training drill, then all of a sudden I couldn't accelerate. I hadn't been training full-on anyway—no one was by that stage—so I left the ground without showing any obvious discomfort. But I walked into the rooms thinking, 'Oh no, what have I done?'

Normally, for any muscle strain that required scans, you'd go to Victoria House in Prahran. But in grand final week you couldn't have the captain of one of the teams rocking up for scans—that would have been all over the news in a flash. We had to find somewhere secret to test it, so that night our team doctor Tim Barbour, head physio Andrew Wallis and I were out at Box Hill Hospital so I could be injected in the groin under ultrasound to see if we could numb it. It was a bizarre scene—late at night, almost midnight, the St Kilda captain running up and down the hospital corridors. Welcome to grand final week.

There were whispers going around that something was wrong, but with the help of some more jabbing before the game I was right to go. The whole day was very strange—they didn't have the ten-minute window for teams to have a run on the ground, so we did our warm-up in the car park underneath the Ponsford Stand. They say grand final day is different, and it sure felt it.

I remember virtually nothing of the game—not Matthew Scarlett's celebrated toe poke in the middle of the ground, nor

Winning and Losing

Paul Chapman's goal over his shoulder that won it for them. I landed on my head halfway through the first quarter—came out and flew for a mark on the member's side of the ground, got up over Sean Dempster and his opponent, flipped in the air and landed upside down. That probably contributed to the game being a blur.

It's funny the things that do stay with you. I remember we got 'stepped' twice in the last quarter out on the wing, which was a huge no-no. If the opposition was bringing the ball into attack from deep on the boundary, the player approaching the ball carrier was instructed above all else to not let the opponent baulk—or 'step' inside—otherwise all of our defenders would be out of position. I can't remember who did it, and I wouldn't drop them in it anyway, but we got 'stepped' twice in the last quarter and at least one of them resulted in a Geelong goal.

It was a miserable, cold and squally Melbourne day. The conditions played their part in making it a brutal contest. The game set a record for tackles: we laid 118 and they had 96. Harry Taylor was my direct opponent and he had 15 spoils for the day, which was a record in finals. And he broke his hand in the first quarter when it was punched from behind; he didn't even know until he couldn't shake hands after the siren.

I took five marks, and nobody on the ground took more than that. I had 13 possessions and kicked a goal. I laid half a dozen tackles. Despite my giving a great effort, my output was average, and in a grand final you're expected to be better than that.

People ask, 'What would you do differently?' I don't really have any regrets, because our effort was so strong, but I clearly wish the game had panned out differently. We just didn't execute well enough on the day. We missed shots at goal that we should have kicked: snaps from the top of the square, straightforward conversions from dead in front. Really, the grand final should have been over at half-time, when we had 37 inside 50s to 14 or something outrageous. We just didn't finish. It is what it is.

Sitting on the ground, waiting for Geelong to get their premiership medals, that is the beaten grand final team's little window on hell. You have never felt more like being somewhere else in your whole life. Rossy was standing behind me, reading the stats. He wasn't sad, he was just angry—not at anyone in particular, just at all of us. 'Thirty-seven fucking inside 50s to 14, 58–42 for the game. How the fuck did we lose?'

Collingwood were by far the best team all year in 2010, and for us to come from four goals down at half-time and draw the grand final was an unbelievable effort. I'm proud that I suffered what I was told was a potentially career-ending injury in round 3 that year, when my hamstring tendon snapped halfway along, and I made it back to play the last twelve games of the season. A hamstring that tears off the bone is different;

you can plug it straight back on to the bone. Ruptured halfway down is worse.

At least it provided a running gag with Jarryn Geary for the rest of my career. I led out from half-forward and Gears kicked it, but the pass was going over my head so I had to prop, and 'bang!' I joke with Gears that he cost me a Brownlow and a Coleman Medal. I was leading both after two rounds: 6 Brownlow votes and 11 goals. Chances are I wouldn't have won either, but that doesn't stop me throwing it up at Gears every time 2010 comes up.

It could be paranoia, but I feel like people point to those three grand finals in two years to mark me down. I didn't play great games—I'm the first to admit that. In the grand final replay against Collingwood I played poorly, but we all did. We were cooked. But I thought I played pretty well in the draw. I averaged 16 possessions, 8 marks and 2 goals over my career, and that's exactly what I had that day. I kicked two goals three, and two of the behinds were touched on the line. One of them was bouncing through, popped up on its last bounce and was touched by Nick Maxwell. That is one of those little *Sliding Doors* moments.

There were other famous ones. When Brendon Goddard soared above a pack twenty minutes into the last quarter, clunked a mark and went back and put us a goal in front, I was amazed. I just thought, 'Incredible. To do that in the dying minutes of a grand final. Surely we win now.' But they rushed a behind, then Travis Cloke put them a point in front. Cue the most famous—or for us, infamous—bounce ever.

We were kicking out of defence and I pushed up the ground because I knew we needed to win the ball. I knew there couldn't have been more than a minute or two left. I took a big mark at half-back, on the member's flank. We had a play that threw caution to the wind if you needed to score late in a game. Whoever had the ball would pull the kick in to the point of the square at half-forward, rather than take the percentage route along the boundary line. It was termed an 'attacking three-quarter kick'.

I kicked it there, Kosi competed, Lenny Hayes was there at the fall of the ball. It was the epitome of a team that was so well drilled it knew where to be and what to do without thinking. Lenny snapped it forward into Stephen Milne's path, and there was nothing between Milney and the goals. And it bounced at right angles through for a point.

You talk about things becoming symptomatic. It feels like that's Milney's little cross to bear. How did that not just land in his lap? Milney kicked 574 goals in his career, many of them in situations just like that. But when it mattered most, the ball wasn't there for him.

The hour or so after the game was just bizarre. You knew you were part of history, that you'd just played in only the third drawn AFL grand final ever. But there was just an eerie numbness about the whole thing. It didn't help that we'd been relocated to the old change rooms under the Great Southern Stand because the toilets had overflowed and flooded the Ponsford Stand rooms. It was just all so strange.

Physically I really struggled through the week between the draw and the replay. I'm sure all 44 players would have felt the same; the mental toughness it took to get up the following Saturday was enormous. We ticked every box, did everything we were expected to do. We had a couple of team meetings, tried to get into action a bit quicker than we might normally have. We were upbeat, positive and saying the right things.

The replay felt like one of those games where if one team kicked they'd have it won, and that's how it panned out. The last quarter was just miserable. We were done, and it was one of the only times I felt so gutted that I wanted the siren to sound and get us out of there.

What would I do differently? I couldn't have prepared any better. I feel like I couldn't have led the team with any more of my being, any more of my soul. If all it got us was close twice, well so be it. If I felt like I could point the finger at myself, or at teammates who didn't try hard enough, that would be a different story. But I don't have any of those emotions.

I know others were happy to point the finger at me, at my performance in that game, and that is something I have to wear. The moment late in the first quarter, when Collingwood had kicked three goals and we still hadn't got our first, doesn't help.

Adam Schneider kicked it to me from out on the flank, and when I marked it all alone in the goal square I thought I had the entire 50-metre arc to myself. I turned around, took two steps and went to kick it. And along came Heath Shaw, 'like a librarian' was Dennis Cometti's call. It was an unbelievable piece of play—talk about not taking anything for granted, about playing to the last second.

It's grand final folklore now, and my paranoia is such that it feels like it has been used as much to show my ineptitude on that day as it has to highlight Heath's amazing fight to the death. There is nothing I can do to change that.

I'm proud of the way I played in the two preliminary final wins over the Western Bulldogs that took us into those 2009 and 2010 grand finals. We shouldn't have won in 2009 and we probably shouldn't have won in 2010 either. But I understand how these things are marked. Win the grand final and it doesn't really matter how you play. The most Wayne Carey kicked in a grand final was two goals. The year 'Buddy' Franklin won the Coleman and kicked the ton he managed one in the granny. But Carey's North teams still won. Buddy's Hawthorn team won. Winning is everything.

In the miserable hours after the 2010 grand final loss, I sat next to Zac Dawson on the bus from the MCG to our function at the Melbourne Convention Centre. Zac was looking at his phone, and then he started shaking his head and swore under his breath. I asked him what was up and he just said, 'Don't worry

Winning and Losing

about what anyone says.' I asked what he was talking about, and he said, 'It's just a text from my mate saying you blokes are shit, and it starts with the captain.' That has stuck with me.

At the dinner I got up to speak, looked around the room, and didn't know what to say. In the end I said something like, 'Here we go again, hey?' Not surprisingly it fell flat. Those are the nights when you see the former players, bump into the big fans like Eric Bana or club stalwarts like Georgie Day, and you're embarrassed. You think they're looking at you thinking, 'You weak prick.' That's what I thought. That's what it does to you.

This shouldn't sound disrespectful to Geelong, but I feel like we should have won in 2009. In 2010 we could have pinched the drawn grand final. Against Geelong we effectively got beaten by a kick: Max Rooke rolled one through after the siren when everyone was slumped on the ground. Tom Hawkins hit the post and it was called a goal, which wouldn't have happened a couple of years later when the score review came in. In 2010 we had all the momentum when the siren sounded with the scores level. Soon after we would have played extra time, not come back the next week. How very St Kilda.

There's no solace in the fact that there are fourteen of us who played in all three of those grand finals, who have come closer than any person in the history of the game without winning a premiership. That doesn't help at all.

In one respect we had a decent stretch: 2004 prelim final,

2005 prelim, 2006 finals, 2007 miss, 2008 prelim, 2009 granny, 2010 granny, 2011 finals. We won a lot of games through that period, and winning made it fun. There was no better feeling than walking arm-in-arm from the field with your teammates, high-fiving fans, belting out the team song. The next 24 hours were filled with the satisfaction of a job well done, and then we moved on to the next challenge together.

In reality, we had two mini-runs through that period. In round 1 of 2011 we played Geelong at the MCG, they came back and kicked one late to beat us in a low-scoring game. Round 2, Richmond at the MCG, we played a draw and Lenny did his ACL. We were one-and-a-half and five and still made the finals, which was a good effort. But the wheels had fallen off. Rossy left, we hit rebuild and went through three coaches in four years.

Those missed opportunities come back to me every time I see a team win a title—not just the AFL premiership, but the Super Bowl, the World Series, the English Premier League, anything. That doesn't disappear. I don't know if it ever will. When you're on the wrong end and the stakes are so high, it can meddle with your view of what winning actually means. You almost subconsciously adopt a winning-isn't-everything mentality to let yourself off the hook. You search for examples—kid yourself perhaps that given the way people see the Eagles 2006 premiership against a backdrop of what has happened to some of the key players, that there is more to life than winning. Of course if we had won those grand finals, if I had been a premiership player, I wouldn't feel like that. It's amazing how you turn things around in your head to make yourself feel better.

When the stakes are so high the degrees of emotion are just as vast in their difference. Those grand finals were potentially the greatest day and feeling of my life to that point. But they ended up feeling like someone had died. I know how stupid that seems now, but at the time it's the worst thing imaginable.

14

LEADERSHIP

I don't know if leaders are born, but I do think circumstances conspire to make them. You can work at leadership, give people more responsibility and hope they'll develop into leaders. In my case, my parents separating when we were still living in Hobart was the first time I was called on to lead. When people talk about leaders being born, I guess that was my birth as a leader.

I was only eight, but I became really conscious of making sure everyone was okay—Mum, Alex and Maddie. As a child there's not much you can do in terms of being a provider, but I could lead in making sure my brother and sister were toeing the line, making life as easy as we could for Mum.

After Mum and Dad got back together and we moved to

Queensland, primary school was initially a bit of a struggle. But by Year 7 I was school vice-captain. You'd think this would point to some early signs of leadership potential, but I'm not sure. I don't think it was necessarily a popularity vote, more an appointment of someone the teachers thought was a good student, who worked hard and got along well with people. And was probably already showing himself to be a bit of a nerd.

When I was captain of Broadbeach under 13s that side of me definitely came through. Like all junior sporting teams there were guys who were only there to muck around at training and it used to drive me insane. I was definitely a goody-goody. I've mentioned that the first best and fairest award I won was at St Kilda, which says a bit about how up and down my junior footy was. I was captain of the state under 18s in my top-age year of the national championships.

A bit like school when I was made vice-captain, there wasn't really a vote on who would captain the Queensland under 18s, just an announcement from the coaches when we came together in Coorparoo before the championships that I'd been the best performed player that year so I'd be the captain. That goes to being in a leadership role because you're one of the best players, but I think there have been other times when I got there because people saw me as a leader. Cases where you have one without the other are rare—Dane Swan was Collingwood's best player for a long time, but he knew he wasn't a leader and nobody at the club tried to force him to become one. And that's fine.

What is leadership? For me it's facilitating, guiding, helping people to achieve breakthrough performance. Not just high achievement, but achieving better than their natural gifts say they should. There's a lot goes into that—the showing, the telling, creating a culture, holding people accountable to that culture; leadership occurs within all of that. The leaders I encountered in my earliest days at St Kilda covered this spectrum, and so did the young group I was part of who were quickly ordained our club's next generation of leaders.

We all shared a common view that we were that core group who would hopefully stick together and win a premiership, which we were almost able to do. There was definitely competition within the group as to who the ultimate leader was. I certainly saw myself that way. Justin Koschitzke did too, albeit Kosi saw himself a bit more in the Stephen Kernahan mould—the bloke's bloke, whereas I was more heading down the Nathan Buckley sort of path, not quite so much room for humour, just head down and get on with it.

I had to win everything. We went to the Grampians for a camp in an early pre-season. It was two teams, and of course Kosi was on one and I was on the other. I had BJ and Leigh Fisher that I can remember; in Kosi's were Nick Dal Santo, Luke Ball and 'Goose' Maguire. Using maps and clues that were dropped in at appropriate times by the guides who accompanied each group ('there's a such-and-such somewhere around here'), we trekked through the Grampians National Park, finding things that would lead to the next clue.

It didn't mean anything, there weren't any prizes, but I was desperate to win. That's just who I was. The group I was in put ourselves out there; while the others spent the two nights bedding down at the campsite, we hiked to the top of the ridge, set up our tents, built a fire and camped up there. The other camp leader complained about how terrible it was, that they were basically camping in a toilet block. We knew we had a small but significant leadership edge on that occasion.

•

I walked into a football club where ultimate success was thin on the ground but there were leaders everywhere you looked. Robert Harvey was my first captain, a revered figure who I knew coming in was a fairly quiet person and a lovely bloke. Harves didn't need to make a noise. His method of leading, the way he trained and prepared, was immense. You saw him push himself until he had nothing left to give. You knew that's what it took without him having to verbalise it.

Stewart Loewe had such a big presence it almost made you cower. He was the sort of bloke you wanted to follow. He'd thrust out his arm and you'd see those enormous buckets, and his handshake would just swallow you. I remember the first

Leadership

time he shook my hand I just thought, 'Wow!' His fingers came halfway up my forearm!

I have never forgotten a conversation Loewey had with Kosi and me one night in our first season, over a beer at Wild Bill's nightclub at Southland. He spoke to us about how fast a footballer's life goes. We thought he was talking like an old bloke, had no idea what he was on about. He was telling us to make the most of it. Later that night we ended up in the back seat of Spida Everitt's Kingswood with Spider and Barry Hall, parked outside some other nightspot, with them urging us to come in and kick on. We looked at each other, said thanks anyway, got out and walked home. Maybe Loewey's words hit a mark after all.

Justin Peckett was someone who was very strong on holding the young guys up to the light. He had a crack at me one day after we had done a one-off one-kilometre time trial, a departure from the usual three one-kilometre runs where you'd have to conserve a bit of energy in the first two. I said something like, 'I can't believe I beat my time by that much!' And 'Frankie' Peckett told me, 'You should be doing that on every one.' He thought I was a bit too comfortable, that I had a lot more to give. I would have been in the top ten runners in our group at that stage, but I didn't really know how to work hard. I thought I did, but in reality I wasn't even close.

Frankie knew I could be better, but the person who really helped take me there was Aaron Hamill. 'Sammy' crossed to

St Kilda from Carlton at the end of 2000 on big dough and with a big reputation, still aged only 23. I rate him as the teammate who had the biggest influence on my career.

Dad had encouraged me to identify a role model and latch onto him like a sponge. I could just tell from the way Sammy went about it that he was that role model: he was fanatical, he was ferocious, his appetite for work was huge. I must have driven him crazy. We would be out on the track an hour after people had gone in, kicking goals, testing our hands, always inventing games. In the old, long-demolished gym at Moorabbin we'd put up a bit of rope, mark out a rudimentary court with cones or whatever we could find, and play footy tennis. We would do anything as long as it involved a ball.

Through the countless extra hours I put in with Aaron, my hands became so good that I could run absolutely flat out at someone kicking the ball at me as hard as they could, stick my arms out dead straight, run through the ball at a million miles an hour and it would stick every time. I couldn't have done the amount of work we put in later in my career, because I wouldn't have been able to get up and play at the end of it. I had to manage my body so much more as I got older, as everyone does. But in those early years I felt invincible, and that was Sammy Hamill's doing.

Towards the end of my career he was an assistant coach at the club. Our relationship was different—we'd use each other as a sounding board all the time. We were still peers in a way,

Leadership

because I was nearing the end and he was retired, but there was always a respect born of knowing he'd had such a huge, huge impact in helping me to understand what it took. I was like any young player—you come in, you feel like you're working hard, but you don't know the level you can go to. You haven't discovered how deep your reserves are. Some players never learn. But Sammy taught me that pretty quickly. To open a player's eyes to that, that's leadership.

•

Thommo's decision to rotate the captaincy was controversial from the outside, but from where I stood it was very smart. He was so big on empowerment—'you blokes run the club'—that it made sense to give the potential captains he had at his disposal the chance to prove themselves. His philosophy around it was that he had never seen anyone perform worse after they had been given more responsibility. Pretty simple really.

Lenny Hayes had the gig in 2004, taking over from Aaron Hamill. Lenny was in the Harves' mould—just follow me. He was the hardest trainer, fearless on game day, with his only shortcoming being that he perhaps wasn't as comfortable with the challenging-your-teammates part of the gig that captaincy demands. But if you talk about a spiritual leader, Lenny was all you could hope for.

Bally had the job in 2006 and he brought a similar

combination of admirable traits that make strong leaders. He was intelligent, measured, utterly fearless on the field. He was a good captain.

In between, in 2005, I had my turn. As a dress rehearsal it couldn't have got off to a worse start. My first press conference as captain I tried to articulate Thommo's empowerment ethos: his 'whatever you blokes want to do, that's what we're going to do' mentality. Talk about naivety—I could see people thinking, 'Who does this bloke think he is? He's barely 22, and the first time he speaks as captain he's talking about how the players run the club!' It was incredibly silly in retrospect, but I wasn't doing it unsolicited—that's what we were told. I probably didn't need to say that, just keep it in-house. But that's how Thommo wanted us to feel and behave.

Then in my very first game as captain I broke my collarbone against Brisbane at the Gabba. I felt like I'd lost my identity. Tim Watson wrote a column in *The Age* that was headlined 'The boy who blinked', basically saying I'd come out talking a really tough game as captain and stumbled at the very first hurdle. We were premiership favourites, I was Brownlow favourite, the new captain, talking up this player-led charge, and then there I was sitting on the bench having a cry on national TV. It felt like the whole thing came crashing down on top of me.

I never spoke to Tim about it; I wasn't angry, more embarrassed about the way I went down, how I had shown emotion and been criticised for it. It was a lesson learnt.

Leadership

Not being able to finish my first game as captain, then missing the next six, was tough. Thommo appointed Bally as my stand-in and I remember feeling put out, thinking he should have at least consulted me. I felt like I should have been involved in the decision, but the disappointment lasted only a few days. Later in the year I hurt my shoulder again and missed three weeks. That time Thommo took me to see Kosi about taking on the captaincy. I had gone down early in the round 14 game against the Bulldogs and Kosi had polled two Brownlow votes in that game. In the next three weeks, filling in as captain, he polled nine votes. Best on ground every week, 11 votes in four weeks. That was the purple patch of his career, which internally gave even more credence to Thommo's philosophy.

•

I had been the No. 1 draft pick, but I didn't walk into St Kilda fantasising about the day I'd be captain. There's too much doubt in your mind—over whether you're good enough to be a player first and foremost, let alone a leader. I was in a team that was on a clear rebuilding path, where the emphasis placed on winning isn't as great as it is when you're contending. That's normal. It's a growth mindset—go forward, even when we lose. That changes over time, but I certainly didn't walk in on day one and think, 'I'm going to captain this club.'

Through the three years of the rotation, then in 2007 when Ross Lyon made Lenny, Bally and myself co-captains in his first season as coach, we knew we were auditioning. I think I was the most comfortable leading in a confrontational manner—having those sort of conversations, holding the group accountable. I think that's what appealed to Ross the most. The external qualities people would have expected Ross to want in his leader were pretty close to how it was.

In 2007 I won the best and fairest and was made stand-alone captain for 2008. Halfway through the season I'd kicked 21 goals from twelve games and wasn't performing well at all. It was the first and only time in my career I was questioned about my standing as an elite player. Mike Sheahan wrote an article about it at about the halfway mark of the year, questioning my leadership, my standing as a player. I finished the year with 65 goals, won the best and fairest and was All-Australian centre half-forward.

Mike had a bit of a thing about my goalkicking and would go back to it every time I was a guest of *On The Couch*. 'What about your goalkicking, Nick?' And I'd say, yes, I had a bad year in front of goal in 2005 (when I kicked 33 goals 36 behinds), but I was reasonably consistent thereafter.

As my own performance in 2008 lifted to the standard I expected—and the sort of football a captain should be playing—Lenny initiated a chat that meant a lot to me. He just sat down next to me one day and said, 'It was the right choice for you to be captain.' Competition for the position never made things uneasy between Lenny and me, never. But to hear him say that, to have his backing and endorsement, made me feel so much more comfortable in the role.

If it was my preparedness to be confrontational that got me the nod as captain, it was probably also the thing that at times worked against me. I know there was a perception that I was hard on blokes internally, at training and in games. I'll wear that, but that is who I am. I know that my greatest strength at times as a leader was also my greatest weakness. My ability to challenge and hold people accountable sometimes yielded really positive results. And depending on the player, depending on my delivery—which in the heat of battle I know could be demonstrative—sometimes the results weren't what I was looking for.

Josh Bruce came to St Kilda in 2014 after two seasons, fourteen games and three goals for Greater Western Sydney. I rode him pretty hard at the start, because I could see what he was capable of but didn't think he was working hard enough to make it happen. Josh was in that phase of his career I had been helped through by Aaron Hamill—where you think you're doing all you can, but you haven't discovered yet how deep your well really is. After working that out, he kicked 50 goals for us in 2015, another 38 the next year and was a big part of allowing me to play up the ground and let a new St Kilda forward structure develop.

Through our successful period under Ross Lyon you knew you would be having hard conversations, that was just part of being a St Kilda player. Rhys Stanley came to the club during that time and I invested heavily in him, particularly in the 2011 pre-season. Physically Rhys is a machine: 200 centimetres, nearly 100 kilograms, and probably the best athlete I've ever encountered in footy. I tried bashing him verbally, I tried putting my arm around him and cuddling him, and for one reason or another I just didn't get anywhere. But it doesn't work for everyone.

•

Captaincy is full of rituals and routines, such as addressing the players in the huddle on the ground after the coin has been tossed. Generally you'd have a theme—how we play when we're at our best, perhaps reiterating something that had been spoken about during the week as being vital to bring to the contest from the start. But it was pretty generic and easy to see how it could become tiresome, not least for the listeners.

Through ten seasons as captain and one as co-captain, I often spoke in the meeting before the 'captain's run' at the end of the week, which was the traditional last training session before game day. Then I took training, which, although a light session, still involved more talk, and on game day there were more addresses and more words. By the time you gave another

Leadership

address out on the ground before the start of the second half, it would be the fourth or fifth time your teammates had heard from you in just over 24 hours. It was too much.

They didn't need to see and hear any more of me, which is where the pre-game routine I developed over the years helped, because at least I was out of their sight for a while. My game-day ritual was borderline obsessive-compulsive. I'd arrive at the ground two-and-a-half hours before the start, always in the first handful of players to turn up, and start with the process of unpacking my bag into my locker. Mouthguard out of its case then on top of the case; towel in the middle on the bottom shelf; diary on top of that; headphones on top of that; drinks to the right; deodorant and cologne up the top; wallet, keys and watch in the middle. Then I'd go to the toilet, come back, put on bike pants, shorts, top, and carry my boots in to get my ankles strapped. Then I'd have my wrists strapped, have a chat with the physios while I put my boots on, and feel a little more ready to go out and do my thing.

I'd pick up a footy, walk out on the ground, and there would still be nobody there. There's something eerie about an empty stadium, especially when you know that in a couple of hours it's going to be heaving. I'd kick the footy to myself while I was walking, get to the point of the centre square, then run a lap of the square fairly briskly, bouncing the footy as I went—left, right, left, right. Then I'd spend some time racing off in random directions around the oval, kicking the footy up in the air, letting it land and trying to get it to spin back to me.

From there I'd do maybe four hard strides with a bit of a stretch in between, and by then a few more of the boys would have made it out onto the ground so I'd have a kick with a partner, start leading all over the ground and getting on the end of the footy. When the other team walked out, I hoped they would see that and know what was coming. I probably only ran a kilometre and a half, but I guess there was a certain amount of intimidation factor in it. Really, I did it to get myself out of my comfort zone and feel like I was challenging myself. The more I could do that in the lead-up, the easier it would be when the game started. The routine wasn't something I performed consciously as a leader, but I guess it showed leadership.

It actually started much earlier in my career, when nobody knew about it because I'd do it at home before leaving for the ground. When Cath first moved over I'd drag her out the back of our South Melbourne house and have her kicking the footy at me. She didn't even know what a footy was. Earlier, in 2009 when I was living with Alex in Brighton, I'd have my nap, wake up and go over to Dendy Park and go for a run. Again, it was that need to take myself somewhere out of my comfort zone. I got so worked up on game day that the easiest thing to do would have been to pull the doona up and hide, or go and lie on the couch. So I'd take myself into this strange 'get on with

Leadership

it' space, jog over to the park and start doing strides. It must have raised a few eyebrows with the Saturday afternoon dog-walkers, but it worked for me.

I was happy to see the captaincy go to someone else while I was still playing—the fact that I was still playing was the main thing. Jarryn Geary was a good choice: the most rounded leader, a great preparer and trainer whose leadership style was a really good balance of challenging and supporting. Some had wondered if he was a good enough player, but he finished top five in our best and fairest in 2014 and 2015, and was runner-up in 2016. 'Gears' was certainly good enough.

I hope it helped him that Joey Montagna and I were removed from the major leadership roles we had had, but were still there to guide and play a role, still able to have those challenging conversations where needed. I hope it helped us as a club. I viewed it as similar to when I was a young captain and had great sounding boards like Robert Harvey, Aaron Hamill and Andrew Thompson.

During the 2017 pre-season, after I'd stepped down as captain, the second of our three practice games was against Carlton at their old Princes Park ground. I played the first and third games but spent that one in the coach's box. We had a trademark at the club: 'Saints Man'. You'd come in on Monday morning, walk up to the whiteboard, pick up the magnet with your name on it and place it in one of two columns on the board. You were either a Saints Man, or you weren't.

It was really just a mirror test: were you happy with your effort? Were you aggressive at the ball, aggressive at the man? Did you give 100 per cent effort 100 per cent of the time? It didn't mean you thought you had had a great game. People criticised my performance in the grand final against Geelong, and the draw against Collingwood the next year. But was I a Saints Man? Bloody oath I was. I had a crack, I was desperate, I played Saints Man footy. Did I have a great day? No, but it wasn't because of my effort.

Anyway, in this pre-season game against Carlton one of our younger players didn't bodyline the ball—basically he jumped out of the way of an opponent. It was a bad look, and he knew about it because the coach got him off straight away, gave him a dressing down, and told him if he wanted to wear the Saints jumper that wasn't acceptable. On the Monday we did the review of the game, and I took a look at the 'No' column on the Saints Man board on the way in, and his name wasn't there. I sat back and waited. I'd worded up Seb Ross, who was conducting the review, to ask the player in question. He mumbled some meek answer, 'Oh yeah . . . I tried to take the ball, I went one-handed because I was trying to get around the bloke.' It was spin, the sort you hear from someone who knows they've done the wrong thing.

It looked like that was going to be it, so I piped up. 'Are we happy with that? Are we just going to move on? If we had twenty players who all did the same thing, but all of them still

Leadership

said they'd lived Saints Man values, would we be happy with that? Would we be happy with the direction we're going?'

I didn't want it to sound like I was sitting there in my ivory tower, so I told the young player it wasn't about him, that I'd had efforts in games where I hadn't gone hard enough, or hadn't gone back with the flight or put my head over it strongly enough. Anyone who plays for long enough is going to have those moments in footy. It's not about that as much as it's about being hard on yourself—don't give yourself a pass and tell yourself it's okay. Because if you do it today and we all say it's okay, we're not going where we want to.

Leadership is a tricky business. In 2016 we beat Essendon, who were famously without the players who'd been suspended for a year over the drugs scandal. We hadn't won for a few weeks, and we didn't play very well this day either, but we got over the line in the end. After the siren it felt like we were behaving as if we'd just won the flag. There were club staffers on the ground handing out cameras to the players, telling everyone to get over to the fence and have selfies taken with our fans. I understand how important that sort of engagement is, but in the heat of a moment that wasn't nearly as joyous as it was being made out to be, it didn't feel right. As a captain I drove high expectations.

I was trying to get all the boys together, get them down into the rooms to bring some reality back to the moment. I said something like, 'Can we act like we've actually won a game before? Get off the fucking ground—we haven't just won the grand final!' Apparently it came across like I was barrelling a specific staff member, which was never my intention. It wasn't meant to be directed at anyone in particular—I had my leadership hat on, and was trying to drive the high standard our group needed. In the following days there was a big deal made out of it, and the upshot was the next week I was encouraged by the club hierarchy to stand in front of the entire playing group and say that I hadn't been a 'Saints man' because of the way I'd spoken to a staff member. I'd just played my heart out. As a competitor, to stand in front of the group and say I hadn't lived our values hurt.

Looking back on my career, one of the things I'll be most proud of is the fact that I've given great effort every week, for every minute. To be pressured into not ticking off our trademark, to saying, 'No, I wasn't a Saints man this week', that didn't sit well with me.

•

I didn't always enjoy the annual captains' day, where the eighteen club leaders gather at Etihad Stadium, pose for photos as a group and in pairs to showcase rivalries and the like, and front the biggest media scrum you see all season. But looking back I'll miss the privilege of standing alongside my contemporaries, men I greatly admire, like Matthew Pavlich, Jonathan Brown, Jobe Watson.

Leadership

Leadership gave me that experience, and I'm forever grateful. It also gave me a confidence that my professional life would be okay, no matter what comes next. I can't overstate how much I think being a leader set me up for the next phase of my life. A lot of what I've learnt in football—in a leadership capacity, and in a team environment—will be directly transferable to life as a former athlete, be that in the corporate and business world, the media, wherever life takes me. A lot of athletes get towards the end of their career and are very apprehensive about what's next, but I know those qualities I've developed as a footballer and as a captain stand me in good stead for my next chapter.

There's a bond between the captains, even if it's only pushing that brotherhood on one day in pre-season aside and trying to rip each other's heads off. My fellow captains were incredibly kind in reaching out after Maddie died, even if at the time I was in such a state I might not have shown them how much I appreciated it. What they said in *The Chosen Few*, a video shot by Peter Dickson, was very moving—Travis Boak on losing his dad, Jarrad McVeigh and his wife on losing their baby daughter—I'll never forget it. I spoke to Jobe Watson a lot about what he went through with the Essendon scandal, how he almost walked away from the game. At the captain's day in 2015 he just looked so miserable, so I sent him a text saying I felt for him. I think it might have jolted him a bit: 'Shit, Rooey's just lost his sister.'

THE THINGS THAT MAKE US

To have been an AFL captain is very humbling. To do it for eleven seasons was a rare privilege. To be St Kilda's longest-serving captain is an honour. Throughout my time in the role I felt a connection to those who'd gone before me—Darrel Baldock, Trevor Barker, Danny Frawley, Robert Harvey. But it's still missing something, and that will never happen now. I'm glad I didn't become the longest-serving AFL captain in the history of the game. To be that, I think you need to have won a flag.

15

SCANDAL

The AFL captains' day, which is held every year at Etihad Stadium in the second-last week before round 1, involves a cocktail-style breakfast with the league's sponsors, followed by a photo session, signing of various merchandise and memorabilia, a media session out on the ground where the eighteen captains spread out along the boundary line and are surrounded by TV, print and digital journalists, then a sit-down lunch with the AFL. In the eleven years I attended as St Kilda captain there would be an update on the game given by the commission chairman, Mike Fitzpatrick, and then the chief executive—in my time, Andrew Demetriou and later Gill McLachlan—would facilitate an open discussion. This was an opportunity for the game's on-field leaders to raise what they thought was working well, what wasn't, and generally air their opinions on the state of the game.

At the 2012 captains' day, on the back of a year in which the 'St Kilda Schoolgirl' saga had spiralled out of control, I put my hand up and said something that had the gathering spluttering in their soup.

'I hate footy. The way the media has covered this story, the impact it's had on me and my family, it's reached the point where I don't want to play anymore.'

I probably gave myself up a bit—you're about to start a new season, where just beneath the friendly façade of eighteen captains breaking bread together lies a desperation to get an edge on your opposition, and one bloke is saying he hates the game and wants to give it away. But that's how bad it had got. I felt like I'd been put through the absolute wringer, where reporting of the naked photo saga had chosen to ignore key facts. I asked the AFL bosses why they didn't hold the media more accountable. The media is a key stakeholder in the game, and I didn't think it was right they should be allowed to get away with irresponsible and incorrect reporting, particularly at the expense of other key stakeholders—the players. The story that I'd had something to do with that girl was perpetuated for months, when a little basic research would have shown that I hadn't even met her.

It struck a particular chord with commissioners Linda Dessau and Sam Mostyn, who both followed up with me to say how disappointed they were to hear that someone they admired and respected within the industry had been so badly affected by the way elements of the media chose to cover that story. The two most senior people in the room, Andrew Demetriou and Mike Fitzpatrick, didn't really react at all. I don't think they wanted to get caught in a media-bashing session.

I'm still embarrassed that's part of my story, but in retrospect, what would I have done differently? I could have definitely handled the aftermath differently too—laughed it off, not done the press conference angrily defending myself and my character, a move that was badly received. Maybe the whole thing would have died down. But it might not have either.

When the story of Dane Swan and Travis Cloke sending around nude pictures of themselves came out a couple of years later, everyone treated it as a bit of a joke. I didn't. I knew people would make the connection back to me. Even though my situation had been different, with the photos of myself and Nick Dal Santo effectively stolen. I feel bad for Cath and our boys that it's a part of my story.

As a footballer in the public eye you don't consciously work to maintain a clean image, but you know you have to do the right thing. I prided myself on doing that, and it still didn't spare me.

But I guess I should have become used to it. Because I played for St Kilda through a time when, rightly or wrongly, the whiff of scandal was never far away.

My career as a Saint started with a scandal of sorts, at least in a football sense. Fifteen rounds into my first season, 2001, Malcolm Blight was sacked as coach. My first game was his last.

Blighty played in North Melbourne's first premiership, coached Geelong to play revolutionary football that took the Cats within a kick of a flag, coached Adelaide to back-to-back premierships, and came to the Saints a much-loved legend of the game. When I arrived at training on the Tuesday after he'd been sacked, walking into a sea of cameras and media, it was the first time I saw what happens when a huge footy story breaks and your club is at the heart of it. That was the first time I really witnessed the media swing into action, and all I could say was, 'Wow!'

It would happen again less than three years later for different, far more worrying reasons. And to a degree, for the next nine years, it didn't go away.

We won the pre-season competition, then known as the Wizard Cup, on 14 March 2004. That success is remembered largely for the sight of our coach, Grant Thomas, and captain, Lenny Hayes, standing on the podium and lifting the trophy for the cameras, looking like they'd just been told they'd won the lottery and lost the ticket. Thommo had a certain contempt for games that ultimately didn't matter, and he'd made it clear we weren't to carry on like we'd won anything of substance. 'This isn't worth anything, don't you dare get wound up about this.' It made for a funny scene that night. Lenny looked like he was about to cry as he accepted the night premiership trophy.

The following day at Moorabbin was the annual family day. What happened a day after that would profoundly affect many people. In short, an allegation of sexual misconduct was made by one woman against two of my teammates, which they denied.

Two months later, after an investigation, Victoria Police announced there was insufficient evidence to launch a prosecution. Nine years later, in 2013, Stephen Milne was charged with rape. At the trial the following November he pleaded guilty to indecent assault, was fined, and no conviction was recorded.

As a teammate through those nine years I heard the things that were said to him over the fence. Not a week went by that he wasn't called a rapist, even on one occasion by Collingwood coach Mick Malthouse.

At the time, being exposed to the fallout of that situation at such an early stage of my career was instructive. As a professional athlete I don't think I went out as much, none of us did. We just didn't want to be out in the spotlight, because things would get said or you'd know people were talking about you as a St Kilda player.

A lot of the messaging and education we received around those situations asked you to imagine the woman as your sister.

It was about being conscious that you had that inner conversation in whatever situation you found yourself in. The entire situation was a trigger to run an audit on your life—what sort of behaviour are you getting up to, or what potentially dangerous situations are you putting yourself in? I was certainly more wary of the world after that. It didn't change my behaviour a great deal because there was no need, but I was even more conscious of being respectful. I was certainly more aware.

At the football club it took that media focus I'd first experienced after Malcolm Blight was sacked to a whole new level. For months, Moorabbin was home to a media circus. They set up camp out the back of the old grandstands, and the club in turn put in place protocols to deal with their presence. Our gym at the time was in the old change rooms, and you had to walk through the car park to get to the gym. Milney and Joey weren't allowed to be by themselves—someone always had to be with them, not to shield them from the cameras, just to support them so that they weren't left to deal with the throng on their own. I just remember it being constant for months. That's why, upon reflection, I regard them as two of the mentally strongest teammates I ever had.

Throughout my career I became accustomed to dealing with situations on the fly, having to straight bat questions with a bland 'No comment'. Over those months it felt like it happened every time you walked out the door. Of the various stories that sprang up like offshoots, I was disappointed with a piece Caroline Wilson wrote in *The Age* after Lenny and I appeared in court in support of Milney and his wife Melissa in 2014. It wasn't a last-minute, let's do it thing. I put on a suit, shirt and tie and went to show my support for a friend. Lenny and I had pretty good standing—I'd hope not just as footballers but as people. It disappointed me that somehow I'd become the story, almost as a way of getting the trial of someone who by then wasn't even an AFL footballer anymore onto the back page.

If I'd known the criticism was coming, I still would have gone to court. I saw Caro a while later at Seaford and told her I was disappointed, that I couldn't see how I could become the story. I wasn't condoning anything, I was simply supporting a friend. We get on well, and she accepted what I was saying. But it was just emblematic of a saga that rolled on for nearly a decade and felt like it would never go away.

As a club, and particularly as players, we knew from the outset what people were thinking, how things looked. Every day we saw the toll it was taking on two of our teammates. From a purely football perspective I don't think we could have handled an awful situation any better, and for that Thommo has to take huge credit. What he was able to do, bringing the group together in the face of incredible adversity, was special. We won the first ten games of the season in 2004. 'Galvanise' is a word that was used at the time—not that it was us against them, but there was a palpable sense that we were pouring all of our energy into each other.

Sadly, it wasn't my only exposure to that type of scandal in my time at the Saints.

Two nights before Christmas 2009, having just flown back to Melbourne after a tough pre-Christmas training camp on the Gold Coast, a group of us met at the Royal Saxon pub in Richmond. Among the gathering was our new recruit, former Bomber Andrew Lovett.

His drafting had already caused a bit of a stir, not least because of the 'history' between us. In a game the previous season I'd been picked up by an umpire's microphone, having a go at Lovett about his alleged assault of his former girlfriend. I rarely went out of my way to deliberately upset an opponent on the field. But that time I did, and bang, I was the worst bloke in the world.

I got his number, called him and apologised. When Lovett was asking for a trade at the end of the 2009 season, he actually came to my house to meet a group of players before we recruited him. We'd just lost a grand final by a kick, and he had something we desperately needed—outside speed, and an ability to use the ball and finish.

As the night rolled on at the Royal Saxon I did the 'smoke bomb'—said I was going to the toilet, snuck out, dived in a cab and went home. I was flying to Orford the next morning and had already had more than enough to drink. I get shocking hangovers, and I wasn't looking forward to how I'd wake up on Christmas Eve.

Scandal

I was living on my own at the time, in the early days of courting Cath, who was still in Texas. At about 3 a.m. I was woken by my phone ringing, with Sammy Fisher's name on the screen. I knew what was coming if I answered: 'Where are you? We're having a ball! Come back!' I hit decline, Sammy rang again, and on it went. One of the other boys tried, then Sammy's name came up again and I answered.

'Mate, I'm in bed asleep, leave me alone.'

And Fish said, 'The cops are here!'

I said something like, 'Yeah, good one mate.' I interpreted all the phone calls as simple, drunken attempts to get me to rejoin the party. I hung up, turned my phone off, rolled over and slipped back into a semi-coma.

The next morning I was violently ill. I stopped throwing up long enough to catch the one-hour flight to Hobart, and I was in Orford in the early afternoon before I realised my phone was still switched off. I turned it on and was trying to process all of the messages when Rossy Lyon rang. He told me a group of players had ended up back at Jason Gram's place in Port Melbourne, and a girl who was there had accused Andrew Lovett of rape.

My response was fairly predictable: 'Are you kidding?' It was unbelievable.

Early in the new year the club took the decision to delist Lovett, whose attitude and professionalism weren't consistently at the level required to play AFL. In 2011 the case went to trial and he was acquitted.

His time at the club lasted a matter of weeks, but it shone a light on us again for all the wrong reasons. It was all about perception; everywhere you turned people were saying, 'Of course it's St Kilda again.' That hurt me as a leader, because he wasn't a product of our environment. He'd been there for three weeks, and he left everyone associated with the club needing to defend us again. I was on the phone straight away to Cath to explain what was going on, in case she or her family saw another screaming headline on the internet: 'St Kilda footballer charged with rape'.

We were lumped with the same stigma six years later when we drafted Jake Carlisle, and before he'd even set foot in the place there was footage all over the TV news of him taking drugs. Once again it was, 'Look at St Kilda!' Jake made a mistake, and in our time as teammates I found him to be an absolutely professional and valued member of the team. But those things chip away at you, especially as we'd worked really hard on our culture and I was confident we'd built something special.

There are always exceptions, people who fall outside the group's ethos and values and tarnish everyone with their action. The message has always been clear: 'support the person, challenge the behaviour'.

I look at 'jock culture' now and think so much of it's pathetic. It's so ego-driven. But I also know there were times in my footy career that I was as guilty as anyone of being part of it—and essentially that's as good as driving it. If you're not stopping something from happening, you're driving it.

Hard lessons have been learnt along the way, which is a good thing. Where there's smoke there's fire. The dance between people with a certain level of fame and those who want to befriend them has always been fraught. People get hurt. I'm sure women have been hurt. In the age of social media, more than ever you have to be careful. And as always, you have to be respectful. That's the bottom line.

Reflecting on all the scandals that happened in my time at St Kilda, the lasting impression is that they made me hate the things I loved. In 2011 I rarely went a week without being mentioned in some way in relation to the photo scandal. But I still felt compelled to listen to everything, to read everything, to fight everyone. I was in such a combative, bad headspace. I'd had enough. I was mentally in a world of trouble.

I can see why the media lapped it up—it was just the perfect storm. The fact that it was St Kilda, the timing—just as the AFL had a serious focus on respect and responsibility. In the wash-up, we know there were so many lies told in the media. The story spiralled out of control and we were the worst in the world. It was just a perfect storm of shit, which came raining out of a bucket and landed on St Kilda. And on me.

When you're in that situation people say, 'Don't worry about it, it's not that big a deal.' But when you're in it, it's everything. It's all-consuming. At another AFL captains' day, only a couple of weeks after we'd lost Maddie and the cameras mercifully weren't pointed at me, I looked across at the huge scrum surrounding Jobe Watson. The Essendon scandal was at its height, and I could see in this good man's body language that he would have given anything to disappear.

I spoke to Jobe a bit around that time, and I know how seriously he considered giving the game away. Because he had reached the stage I'd reached before—where you're not sure if all the things you love about football still trump the negatives. Everything just compounds. Shit on shit on shit on shit. I know that feeling, and I could tell Jobe did too.

I probably didn't realise it until right at the end, but playing the last five years of my career without the cloud of scandal hanging over my club was such a relief it was almost invigorating. I'm grateful my career ended that way, because it reaffirmed for me how much I love the game.

16

FAMILY

Cath giving birth to James will forever be at the heart of the most profound period of my life, but not just for the usual reasons. I experienced the best thing that can happen to a person, and the worst thing, within the space of three months. James was born in December. Maddie died the following February. Incredible joy was followed by unimaginable grief. It feels like I'll never be able to separate one from the other.

I've always enjoyed being around kids. When I arrived at St Kilda, some of the older players like Robert Harvey, Stewy Loewe, Nathan Burke and Matty Young had kids. They were in the rooms all the time—at training, after games—and even as a teenager I got a kick out of playing and interacting with them. But I didn't give any consideration to the fact that those teammates were juggling a professional sporting career and parenthood. It would never have entered my head.

After James and then Will were born in the latter stages of my career, there would be days when I'd know Cath was under the pump and I'd be edgy about getting home and helping. Occasionally I'd leave training early, maybe even sneak off from Seaford, and I'd see the young boys watch me leave. I wondered what they were thinking, but I'm sure they were like I was, thinking their lives were so full and busy when all they really had to worry about was themselves. We all get consumed by our own worlds.

You're a young bloke, then all of a sudden you're a senior player thinking, 'What did I do with my time?' Then you get married and have a child and you think, 'Jeez, what did we do when it was just the two of us?' Then Cath and I had Will and I was like, 'What did we do when it was just us and James?' It's simply a progression.

At the start of my career footy clubs were more social places; it felt like there was more family interaction, more get-togethers with everyone involved. Grant and Kerry Thomas had a lot to do with that. We didn't know it at the time, but for a coach to welcome his players into his home like Thommo did us was unique. I haven't been exposed to it since, and I'm not sure there are many other coaches who would do that—especially not a coach who had eight kids of his own.

As I've already mentioned it was pretty much an open-door

policy at the Thomas household. It would be nothing for us to finish recovery on a Monday, have our team meeting and review, then all go back to Thommo's for a session in the steam room, a swim and a steak. His house almost became the central meeting point for a lot of us younger guys. Our team get-togethers would happen there, and end-of-season gatherings with forty-odd players and partners, their kids, his kids—a cast of thousands.

When I was drafted, Thommo and Kerry's youngest, Jamison, was a baby. Their oldest, Claye, is three years younger than me. Given my closeness to Grant and the amount of time I spent at their house, it was like I'd inherited another eight little brothers and sisters. Having that family connection, just being exposed to that sort of family life away from home, was incredibly important in my development. And it made me appreciate family all the more.

Not that I gave any thought at the time to becoming a father. Not many teenagers do; it just doesn't enter your stratosphere. When you're starting out, you don't even think about how long you're going to be playing the game, when you're going to meet the right person, you just live. At that stage of your life there are so many unknowns—and so many other priorities. Finding a wife and getting married was the last thing I was thinking about as an eighteen- or nineteen-year-old AFL footballer. It was enough to worry about what you were doing that night, or the next day.

THE THINGS THAT MAKE US

When he was nineteen, Stephen Milne was the first of our group—who came through together—to become a dad. We saw Tyson grow up, which was a really nice thing. After that there was a big gap until Justin Koschitzke and Alicia had Jack and then Ava. They'd be in the rooms after the game, and I'm glad I had the chance to experience that with James and at the very end with Will. Cath would bring them to the footy if the timing worked out, but if an afternoon game fell in the middle of nap time it was invariably too hard. Night games were no chance. As parents we're very structured; we don't stray too far from routine, because otherwise we pay for it. You reap the benefits of that, but you also sacrifice a bit.

We were married in 2012 and started talking about having kids at the start of 2014, just wondering if we should try. We were extraordinarily lucky that it happened straight away. We needed to be a bit strategic: 'We should start trying now, that way we can go back to Texas after footy finishes, get two months there, come back in November for the birth while you're still able to fly.' It's not fair that we were actually able to plan it that way, and we were totally naive about how hard it can be for others. But it just happened.

I remember going around to tell Mum and Dad that Cath was pregnant. It was around the time Maddie was getting booked in for a bone marrow transplant. Telling them they were going to be grandparents was so exciting, but deep down

Family

I wondered how the timing of it might be impacted by Maddie's transplant, and vice versa.

That year, going back to Texas was incredibly stressful. Cath was pregnant and Maddie was in hospital. That was a really challenging time. Cath had flown to the States a week or so before me to maximise the time she'd have at home. I won the best and fairest, went in to the hospital the next morning on the way to the airport and gave the medal to Maddie, told her I loved her and got on a plane. She was in ICU but in reasonable shape. I was away for six weeks. It's another of those times that stays with me—should I have stayed with her? Should I have been in Melbourne instead of Texas? Hindsight is 20–20.

•

People talk about juggling being a footballer and a new father. For me, throughout that initial period football didn't come into it. I'd go, I'd train, I'd clock in and clock out, but most of the time my head and my heart were somewhere else. I've always been really strong at compartmentalising, being able to park my emotions and not let them affect my performance. That was my MO my whole career: it's not how I feel, it's how I act. But it was just such a hard period—the joy around having a newborn baby, trying to raise that child, trying to support my wife. And the strain of trying to support my sister, of watching what she was going through and not being able to do anything about it.

There would be days where I'd leave home early, go to training, finish at Seaford and drive to the Royal Melbourne Hospital to be with Maddie. Getting back home from the hospital took over an hour. It was just so hard to juggle it all; all the time I felt like there wasn't enough butter to cover the slice of bread, I was spread so thin. I wasn't able to support Maddie the way I wanted to support her, and I didn't feel like I was supporting Cath the way she needed and deserved to be supported. And I felt like I wasn't spending enough time with James, let alone fulfilling my role as an AFL captain.

James's birth brought Mum and Dad a lot of joy, but even the night he was born was a juggling act. They came into the hospital with Alex, and there we all were, holding James, while less than two kilometres away in another hospital Maddie was fighting for her life. She should have been with us, but she was cytotoxic at the time and James would have been placed at risk if we'd taken him to see her in ICU.

•

I've always been a Mummy's boy. I get my emotional side from Mum—and from Dad, but Mum's an incredibly emotional creature. I guess she's a bit of an oxymoron. I think of her as being very delicate and fragile in a sense, but she's incredibly strong to have endured what she has. She's my hero in a lot of respects. She's inspired me with her courage and selflessness, but above all it's the balance between nurturing and challenging me that I'll always be most grateful for. That soothing mother's care at the right time, and the firm reassuring push when I needed to know what was right. Her maternal instincts have always been clear in her role as a mum and now a grandmother.

She's just a real mum: affectionate, emotional, protective. She has always made us feel safe. I guess that's part of what makes losing a child so devastating for a parent—you've spent their entire life trying to keep them safe, and in the end, sometimes it's not enough.

Dad's a huge personality: life of the party, a practical joker. He's a very emotional person too, a crier, but he has always tried to make everything light-hearted and fun, and has an ability unlike anyone else I know to go off on the most irrelevant tangents. But that's part of his charm. We could be talking about the blokes who were out the front of the house fixing the road and accidentally broke a pipe, cutting off our water supply, and Dad would say something like, 'Yeah, I was talking to one of them on the way in, and his grandfather . . . whatsisname? . . . yeah that's it, so-and-so, well anyway I saw him walking down the street once . . .'

And you'd have to cut him off and say, 'Dad, has this got anything to do with how we're going to get the water put back on?'

Alex is great at it. We'll be at lunch, Dad will go off on a tangent and start asking Mum to remind him the name of someone who's got some third-hand connection to the person you're talking about, and Alex will put his hand up and say, 'Irrelevant! Irrelevant!' But I love him. He's a storyteller, he's a joker. He's a worker too—he's always dug in and got things done to give Alex, Maddie and me every possible opportunity to achieve in life. He taught me to kick a footy, play cricket and, above everything, 'just do my best'. I don't think anyone enjoyed the ride of my career quite as much as Dad. He's been a huge support, always offering positive affirmation leading into a game or a glowing summary afterwards, regardless of how I performed.

Before every single game I played, Dad and I would speak on my way to the ground. Sometimes he'd grab a ride to the stadium with me, but I'd always give him a call before picking him up, just to keep the tradition alive. Going to the footy with Dad, Alex and our boys or having a beer with them in front of the TV on a Friday night is something I'm looking forward to.

One of the things I've loved most about becoming a parent is that sense of coming full circle, that you grew up experiencing so many things with your parents, and now you're the parent doing the same with your own children. There are certain emotions you can only feel with your family: the joy of shared milestones and accomplishments, the celebration of birthdays, the peace you find in something as simple as sitting down together to a family dinner, when the closeness of everyone at the table is so real you can almost taste it. Just knowing you're all together gives me a sense of calm. I have always felt that in those simple situations, and now I feel it with Cath and our children. And it's beautiful.

When I'm talking to James and Will, I might laugh a certain way and catch myself realising how much I sound like Dad. Sometimes I'll think, 'Gee, that's nice.' Other times it's like, 'Gosh, I sound like Dad!' I love that Alex will go through that now, since he and Roxy had little George midway through 2017. The connection you have with family, especially the connection with your parents, becomes so much stronger when you're a parent yourself. In a real sense, in a literal sense, they are the things that made me. I know that if they are okay, I'm okay.

•

After Maddie passed, we went through some family counselling sessions, grief sessions, where we were told how important it was to understand that we all grieve differently. Dad grieves totally differently from Mum. One way's not better or more correct than the other, but you have to understand and appreciate that we all deal with it in our own way.

It's so hard, because there's always that nagging feeling that you should be sad in the happy times: sad on birthdays, sad at Christmas, sad on every special occasion you can think of.

In a lot of respects there is a sense of dread, a feeling that those gatherings are something you have to get through. I love getting together with family and friends, that's who I am, but you have those thoughts. Obviously Christmas is exciting and fun now because we've got a young family of our own, but there's always going to be that hole.

After Will was born, just before our second Christmas without Maddie, we made a conscious effort to not go down the path of sadness. Christmas was Maddie's holiday, she just loved it. We made a pact to remember the good things. We know it's still going to be sad, that we'll always say a prayer for Maddie before we sit down to Christmas lunch. But we try to make it a happy time. It's the right thing to do, and we're getting much better at it.

•

Alex is my best friend. I know a lot of friends who have brothers, and I can't get my head around brothers not being as close as Alex and I are. Now that our situation has changed, I can't understand family disputes, or brothers who have fights. That's not to say we haven't had our fair share of arguments, particularly when we were growing up. I was the big brother, and I used to pick on Alex a bit.

If Alex ever whinged to Dad about me picking on him or hitting him, Dad's response was always the same: 'Alex, pick up a stick, and hit him with it. And he will stop. You'll only have to do it once, and he'll leave you alone.'

I still have the scar, and it wasn't from a stick. We must have been about fourteen and eleven. We were at the hairdresser's, waiting to get our hair cut. Alex was next but I pulled rank, pinned him down and said I was going before him. He'd had enough, so he picked up a pencil and went, 'Crack!' He stabbed me in the leg, just below the knee. That was his line-in-the-sand moment. He was next in the hairdresser's chair.

I'm incredibly proud of Alex's attitude to my career and its material benefits. In the warped world of AFL, it's commonplace for young men—many of whom were closer to the bottom than the top of the class at school—to reach nineteen or twenty and be earning more money than their parents. That can be hard to deal with. I know I had feelings of guilt associated with that imbalance, particularly with regard to Alex. The world's a tough place, and I saw how hard Alex had to work to get ahead.

He has a great job in real estate but, like most 30-somethings, he and Roxy had to wait to get into the Melbourne property market. And there I was, three years older, living in one of the best neighbourhoods in Melbourne. But there's never been even a hint of resentment or jealousy. He's only ever been proud of me, and incredibly supportive. I'm so proud of him for being like that, because I don't think everyone would be.

We talk about absolutely everything. Not to say I appreciate him more now that he's the only sibling I have left, but I do think a lot about the fact that I'll be an uncle to Alex's kids, but never to Maddie's. Maybe that's intensified our relationship.

For a long time we lived in each other's pockets. When Alex moved down from the Gold Coast he and his old housemate Jase lived with me in the terrace in South Melbourne, and they were there when Cath moved in. We'd sit upstairs, play stupid games, watch movies while Cath was at work. It came to a head one day when Cath came home. She was so admirable—moving to a foreign country, a big city, getting herself a good job, taking the tram to and from work. Anyway, she came home and there were Alex, Jase and I lounging on the couch like slobs, cracking jokes.

Cath walked in and quite reasonably asked, 'What are we going to do for dinner?'

And Alex just turned to her and said, 'If you're not gunna say anything funny, don't say anything at all.' He's always had that sense of humour, which I like. Cath jokingly gave me an ultimatum, and the boys were out a few weeks later. They were fine about it; it was time to go.

Alex and Roxy were on and off for a long time before they got their act together. In 2009 Alex was living and working in New York. He'd been seeing Roxy before he went, and then he flew back for the grand final. Maddie, Roxy and I drove out to the airport to meet him. We didn't really know Roxy, and I told the story of what happened that day at their wedding to highlight how tough Maddie could be with our girlfriends.

Family

In the car, on the way out to the airport, Roxy was saying how nervous she was. Maddie and I were looking at each other, thinking, 'What's she going on about? Nervous?' We got there and Roxy said, 'Do you think I can go and stand up the front so I'm the one he sees first?' She wandered off and Maddie turned to me and said, 'Who does she think she is?'

She made it really hard for Roxy in the beginning, then they ended up being such great friends. Everything that's transpired has made all of us reassess what's important, and maybe it even played a part in expediting Alex and Roxy getting married and having children. Roxy's the best; she's just such a huge part of our family now, and their little boy George is my beautiful first nephew.

Their wedding, at a winery in the Yarra Valley, is one of the best weddings I've been to. It was intimate, but the 70 or so who were there were the A-team. Everyone was so invested in their relationship and them as people, which meant that on the day everyone was into it. The dance floor was crazy, full of Mum and Dad's friends, our friends, relatives. Oma and Opa came up from Hobart and Oma was on fire. Opa had to drag her off the dance floor at one stage and get her to sit down and take a breath. She was 87, but we couldn't stop her.

Alex and Roxy had a place set for Maddie, an empty seat with a candle burning on the table in front of it.

I don't think there's been a single time since Maddie passed, or even in the last year of her life when she was so sick, that I've caught up with Mum and she hasn't become emotional. Most times she cries. If she doesn't, I can still see the emotion in her face, just beneath the surface, ready to overflow. Even if James or Will do something funny, she might laugh but I can tell she's seeing Maddie as a toddler, doing the same thing.

In one sense it was incredibly difficult having James around at that time, but he provided us with so much joy in the darkness too. It was weird, because at times I found myself thinking, 'I shouldn't be laughing, I shouldn't be enjoying this, because Maddie isn't here.' When we were in Orford for Maddie's funeral, James was three months old. One night he was on my lap in the bath and he just crapped all over me. I found myself lying there in a bath full of shit, and I couldn't stop laughing. I was in hysterics.

I look back and wonder how the hell I laughed at anything at that time. But you go into another space. You have to. When I cast my mind forward and envisage what I want for my children, it's quite simple: my family have created the platform and environment for me to be the best that I can, and all I can hope for is to do the same for my kids.

I know how lucky I am. I couldn't imagine a better wife for myself or mother for our children than Cath. What an incredibly beautiful soul she is. Cath's very practical and keeps me balanced. She's a voice of reason. I feel so centred and at peace when I'm around her and the boys. I love that friends have commented that we've been married five years and I still light up when she walks into the room. I'm not conscious of doing that—it's involuntary—which makes it even nicer to hear.

Without sounding preachy about what a great marriage we have, we have a rule we stick to. It's called the 60–60 rule, where each of us tries to do 60 per cent of the work in our marriage rather than 50. That means that if one of us is only running at 40 per cent, we've still got it covered. It's been a great pillar of our relationship.

Being with Cath and the boys fills me with pure joy, and I know that wherever we end up, if I'm with them I'll feel at home. I never thought it was possible to have as much fun with a two-year-old as I have with James. He's obsessed with basically every sport—be it baseball, soccer, footy, basketball—and is constantly begging me to join in his ball games. I've had to buy myself an adult-sized scooter just to keep up with him when we go to the park. It's actually been pretty handy for the morning coffee run. Every night before bedtime we lie on the couch together to read a book and watch part of a movie. He's reintroduced me to so many of the stories and films I treasured as a child. *The Very Hungry Caterpillar* and *The Sandlot Kids* are currently the flavours of the month.

As a baby, Will is far more chilled out than James was. I'm sure being born at more than four and a half kilos had something to do with that. To watch the boys interact and see their love for each other is the best feeling imaginable.

James and Will changed my purpose in every respect. It's amazing how quickly you go from number one to number four in your own mind. Every decision I make is made with them in mind, every job I do is done with a view to providing for them. Every holiday we go on, or experience we have, is about them growing and learning. Every day when I get home James comes screaming down the corridor, crying, 'Daddy, Daddy!' It's just the best feeling in the world.

In the weeks before I announced my retirement, James kept asking me, 'Daddy, are you going to football training?' To which I started replying, 'Not for much longer buddy. Do you want me to stay home with you?' And he'd say, 'Yes! Stay and play with me!'

I'll miss walking out to the car with my footy bag over my shoulder. But gee I'm happy with the alternative.

Conclusion

I went into the 2017 season very much wanting and expecting to play two more years of AFL football. My body was as good as it had been in five years, and my team was building a nice momentum towards challenging again for the thing that had driven me above all—playing in St Kilda's second premiership team.

Hurting my knee in the very first game of the season brought the future rushing up at me. For ten minutes, I thought my career was over. As it happened I missed only one game, but when my other knee needed more than just the mid-season break to get over its grumpiness, the 'noise' that accompanied my month on the sidelines was hard to take. It's funny how end-of-career discussions play out in football; for all the noise on the outside, within the football club there is only silence.

For the first time in my career there was complete uncertainty; I had no control over my future whatsoever. I could say I wanted to play on until I was blue in the face, but I knew the decision was out of my hands. I'd be lying if I said I wasn't doing it tough. The hardest thing was not knowing whether I had more to give, or if my tank was empty. I knew I couldn't replicate some of the things I'd always been capable of, but on occasions I played really well, which only confused things all the more.

It was alarming how quickly the landscape changed. On 8 July, I was arguably best afield against Richmond in the second Maddie's Match. Then I had two quiet games and the 'noise' around my future was turned up to ten. I didn't have the 'fall off the cliff' epiphany so many retiring athletes speak of. I fought it, told myself I was just being weak, that I'd found a way countless times before to overcome adversity.

Ultimately my body decided for me, and the people closest to me guided my path. On 25 July, I told the club I would retire at the end of the season.

I'm at peace, I know I'll be okay. I have built the foundations of a great life for myself, Cath, James, Will and anyone else we might be lucky enough to welcome into our family.

As for the future, not knowing what's next is exciting. For seventeen years I've had certainty: I've known what I'm doing tomorrow, what I'm doing next weekend, what I'm doing in six weeks' time. There's nervousness in no longer having that,

Conclusion

but there's excitement as well. Cath and I can take the kids to Texas in the summertime now; we can go and live there for a stretch if we choose to. A whole new range of possibilities about how we want to live our lives has opened up. What's possible for us as a family? What's possible for our kids? What's possible for me? Who knows? But it's exciting. For most people, a career comes to an end at 60 or 65. It's happening in my thirties, and it feels like I still have a lifetime in front of me.

I've been an AFL footballer for half my life. The structure, the routine, everything that's happened around me being a footballer has helped shape me. In some ways the game has been a great support. In others—the spotlight, the scandal, the stress—it's been a burden.

Midway through my last season, when the 'noise' was building a deafening momentum, we beat Gold Coast in a forgettable game on a Sunday evening at Docklands. I played okay, but in the last quarter I got run down after playing on and running into an open goal. We hadn't even left the rooms after the game and Joey Montagna was showing me on his phone the things that were being said, the comparisons to the Heath Shaw incident in the replayed 2010 grand final.

I felt sick, dirty even—because I hadn't been perfect. I was pretty happy with the way I'd played—eight marks and three goals, you'd take that every week—but I ended up totally consumed by that one thing. I hate being that way. That's something about the game and what it did to me that I won't miss at all.

Surrendering control is something I've been working on, and it's not easy. I've always been a control freak—not about people, but outcomes, my destiny. I know I'll be a better person if I'm a bit lighter, if I just let things happen. I did everything in my power to make myself and my team the best over seventeen years, and I still walk away without a premiership. That's life I guess—prepare as best you can, give everything, and accept whatever the outcome is.

As much as playing the game worked me into a lather at times, I'll miss it enormously. Right to the end, I'd still get goose bumps running onto the ground. The great moments—doing something well, hearing the call of 'Roooooo' come over the crowd—they were priceless. But I'll miss the simple things too. I'll miss the team environment, and the hundred little conversations you'd have daily at the footy club. The sound of the final siren when we're in front. Walking in arm-in-arm, preparing to sing the team song. Running out at training in the middle of winter when it's sunny, still and cold, and it might take you ten minutes to warm up, but once you get there and can see the smoke on your breath, the steam rising off your body, that's a feeling like no other. They were great days.

Above all else, I hope I'm well placed to make my children better versions of their father. We're all products of our family and our environment, and I hope mine have given me that

Conclusion

insight, that strength, that gift to help my children be the best people they can be. Better versions of me, of Mum and Dad, of Cath and her family, of my brother Alex and my sister Maddie.

They'll grow up with Alex and Roxy's son George, their cousin, living just around the corner. They'll have their little pack running around like the Riewoldt boys—Dad and his three brothers—did in Tasmania all those years ago. There's a beautiful circle there.

And they'll grow up knowing their Aunty Maddie was as tough as can be, because we'll never stop telling them about her.

The end is the beginning. I'm not scared about what's next, but I am sad about what I'm leaving behind. Such is the athlete's lament. Ultimately, I don't want to be defined by footy. I want to immerse myself in the real world, and I can do that with confidence and with my head held high. There are a lot of people and a lot of experiences—good and bad—to thank for that.

They are the things that made me.

Acknowledgements

I've never been an avid reader of non-fiction, so I thank you for making it this far. I embarked on this project wanting others to find it informative or relatable, so I hope there has been something within these pages for you. Regardless, thank you for taking the time to read it.

Peter Hanlon, thank you for stepping into the unknown and taking the risk to go on this journey with me. I'm not sure what the final product would have been like without your wisdom, patience, eloquence and sensitivity. I started this book with a ghostwriter, and ended it with a friend.

Catherine, James and Will, when I reflect on all the wonderful times documented in this book, the moments each of you came into my life are the greatest. Thank you for providing me with the love, support and inspiration to help me live my dreams. And for making the next chapter so exciting to contemplate.

Mum, Dad, Alex and Maddie, thank you for your unconditional and unwavering love and support. Exploring my past has rammed home to me just how fortunate we are to share such a special bond. I'm truly grateful for your strength, courage and selflessness.

Nanny Fay, Oma and Opa, thank you for allowing me to share your incredible stories. I love you all very much.

Carlie Merenda, thank you for steering the ship. For holding me accountable and challenging me to be the best possible version of myself. Above all, thanks for being a loyal friend.

Tom Gilliatt and Allen & Unwin, your guidance and vision gave me the confidence to embark on something I otherwise wouldn't have contemplated. I'm so proud of the final product and grateful that when my children are old enough they'll be able to read it.

To all those individuals and families fighting bone marrow failure, you are not alone. Be brave and #FightlikeMaddie.

To every Saints fan, thankyou for the way you embraced, included, supported and ultimately farewelled me. You are the embodiment of our club's motto, *Fortius quo fidelius*—strength through loyalty.

Finally, to all my friends, teammates, coaches and everyone else I've encountered throughout my career, thank you for the impact each of you has had on me and for the relationships we share.

Maddie Riewoldt's Vision

On 24 February 2015, 26-year-old Maddie Riewoldt tragically lost her five-year fight against a type of bone marrow failure called aplastic anaemia. In June 2015, with overwhelming support from the AFL community, the Riewoldt family established 'Maddie Riewoldt's Vision' (Maddie's Vision), in collaboration with the Snowdome Foundation. Maddie's Vision aims to raise funds to find a cure—honouring Maddie's legacy and her wish that nobody else would share her devastating experience.

Bone marrow failure syndromes (BMFS) are life-threatening conditions diagnosed in approximately 5 million people globally each year—a figure that translates into about 140 young Australians diagnosed each year. The majority of patients are young, otherwise well, people. The relative rarity of these conditions has traditionally been a barrier to comprehensive research into the biology and optimal treatment of bone marrow failure. Bone marrow failure syndromes can be randomly acquired, or to a lesser extent, genetically inherited; there is not enough known about them and people affected are constantly concerned about their future.

Current therapies are not well tolerated—there is only a 60 per cent success rate—and are very disruptive to daily life. While bone marrow transplantation is the most effective treatment, there are numerous barriers to a successful outcome. Obtaining a suitable, matched bone marrow donor is a huge obstacle and the preparation for transplantation is often quite toxic, especially for younger people. The bone marrow transplant is followed by over a hundred days of isolation in hospital. Maddie was frustrated by this simply unacceptable situation for children as young as two and their families.

There is an urgent need to understand more about BMFS. Since launching on 10 June 2015, Maddie's Vision has raised $1.87 million for investment in medical research, with $1.085 million already committed to innovative medical research projects. It is with huge thanks to the AFL community (particularly St Kilda Football Club), a number of generous individuals, sporting clubs, businesses and the community at large, that we have already raised significant funds towards making a difference.

Fortunately, we are in an era of improved medical technology and access to tools to increase understanding. This is where Maddie's Vision is singularly focused—on collaboration to bridge the gap between the need for answers and the ability to uncover them. In all instances of medical practice-changing, research is the most effective means by which to dissect the biology and improve treatment.

As at June 2017, we have commitments to fund the following projects being conducted in partnership with institutes across Australia: creation of The Australian Aplastic Anaemia Registry; prevention and treatment of bone marrow failure in *Fanconi anaemia* and other inherited disorders; identification of miRNA biomarkers, which play a functional role in disease pathogenesis; genome editing of haematopoietic stem and progenitor cells to uncover novel therapeutics; predicting malignant transformation of bone marrow failure syndromes; influences of clonal haematopoiesis in allogeneic bone marrow transplantation (co-funded with Snowdome Foundation).

Our future fundraising will work towards the establishment of a world-first National Biobank and the first National Centre of Excellence in Bone Marrow Biology. We won't stop until we provide sufferers and their loved ones more certainty of a cure.

To follow our progress, or learn more about our generous donors and how to become involved, visit **mrv.org.au** or **@maddiesvision** on social media.

Index

Adelaide Football Club 71
AFL Players' Association 224
The Age 316, 335
Akermanis, Jason 52
All-Australian team 237, 293
Allan, Graeme 66
Angwin, Laurence 65
anxiety 122, 221, 224–5
    attacks 222–3
aplastic anaemia 188, 189, 213, 218
The Australian 134
Australian Football League (AFL) 21
    under-18 national carnival 2000 64–5
    under-18 national carnival 1999 64
Australian Light Horse regiment 16

Baker, Dicky 19
Baker, Steven 253
Bakers Milk Tasmania 19
Baldock, Darrel 328
Ball, Luke 57, 80, 138, 140, 256, 257, 258, 266, 311
    captaincy 315–16, 318
    move to Collingwood 256
Bana, Eric 280, 283–4, 285, 305
Barbour, Tim 228, 240, 241, 298
Barker, Trevor 275–6, 328
Bartel, Jimmy 57
Bartlett, Nathan 249
Batten, Jerome 173, 209, 248

Battery Point 38, 207
Battle of Berlin 11–12, 14
Battle of Fromelles 16
Beetham, Caydn 79
Bellerive 6
Bellerive Oval 20
Berlin 11–12, 13
Bernacchi, Diego 29
best and fairest awards 99–100, 293, 310, 318, 345
Beveridge, John 68–9, 289
Billings, Jack 236
Black, Simon 62
Blake, Jason 259
Blight, Malcolm 71, 129, 332
Boak, Travis 327
body language 85, 92
bone marrow failure syndromes (BMFS) 365–6
Boonah 60–1
Bradshaw, Daniel 62
Brady, Tom 233
Brand, Russell 106
Breen, Barry 274
Brisbane Lions Football Club 61, 65, 66
    2005 season 90
Broadbeach Junior Cricket Club 57
Bromley, David 45
Brown, Jonathan 57, 235, 293, 326
Brown, Nathan 107, 263–4

Brown, Tony 41
Brownlow Medal 88, 99, 234, 237
Bruce, Josh 234, 267, 319
Bryant, Martin 49
Buckland, Aaron 53
Buckley, Nathan 99, 311
Bugg, Tom 211, 212
Burke, Nathan 71, 267, 341
Butterss, Rod 129, 130, 136, 282

Callaghan, Craig 70
Campbell, Wayne 264
captaincy 88, 103, 127–8, 140, 250, 316–20, 323, 328
  rotating 134, 315
captains' day 267, 326–8, 329
Capuano, Matthew 70, 71
Carey, Wayne 100, 304
Carlisle, Jake 338
Carrol, Neale 'Cowboy' 274
Casey, Clinton 52–3
Channel Seven 269, 270
Chapman, Paul 299
Chizik, Brandon 125–6
Christmas 6–8, 118, 350
  Boxing Day barbecue 118–19
Clarke, Jan 207
Clarke, Lloyd 207
Clarke, Xavier 80
Cloke, Travis 302, 331
clothing and style 102, 245
club culture 246, 275
coaches 126–9, 139–45
collarbone break 2005 88, 92–3, 260, 316
Collingwood Football Club 33, 66, 256, 269–70, 295, 300, 301
Cometti, Dennis 304
competitiveness 73–5, 77–8
concussion 2015 137, 240–1
Connors, Paul 65, 70
Copeland, Robbie 64
Corr, Cathal 133
Cousins, Ben 262
Crawford, Shane 52

cricket career 57–61, 64, 76–7
Crismani, Dr Wayne 218
Cunningham, Geoff 275

Daffy, Nick 264
Dal Santo, Nick 80, 105, 106, 138, 141, 144, 154, 205, 252, 255
  friendship with 258, 259
  nude photo scandal 108, 252, 331
Darcy, Luke 99
Davis, Luke 61
Davis, Michael 65, 72
Dawson, Zac 108, 111, 154, 278, 304
Day, Georgie 287, 305
Demetriou, Andrew 134, 329, 331
Dempster, Sean 299
Dessau, Linda 330–1
diaries 84–5, 263
Dickson, Peter, *The Chosen Few* 327
diet 235
Dillon, Chris 39
diphtheria 10
Ditterich, Carl 52
Dodge's Ferry 7, 47
Doohan, Mick 150
draft 66–8, 98–9, 317
Dunleavy, Virginia 69, 129
Dunstall, Jason 53

Eddy, Robert 143
Essendon Football Club 255, 325
Everitt, Peter 'Spida' 71, 313
expectation, weight of 86, 87

Facebook 111, 118
faith 193–4, 225
fans 97–8, 280, 287–8
Farrar, John 104–5
Farrar, Sam 105
Finnis, Matt 217, 288
Fisher, Leigh 311
Fisher, Sammy 337
fishing 28, 31, 35, 42
Fitzpatrick, Mike 329, 331
flag football 167

Index

Flavorite 217
Flying Start 69, 116–17, 261
Flynn, Errol 33
The Footy Show 20, 51–2, 99, 245, 269
Form Four clearances 20, 21
Fox, Andrea 170, 262
Fox, David 126, 217, 262
Fox, Lindsay 126, 204, 207, 217, 262, 263
Fox, Mem 90
Fox, Paula 204, 207, 217, 262
Fox Footy 229
Franklin, Lance 'Buddy' 304
Frawley, Danny 328
friendships 243–4, 259–63, 268
    teammates 245–6, 250–1, 256–9
Frost, Ray 59, 60
Fuglsang, Bridget 'Biddy' 206, 207, 208
Fuglsang, Christopher 206, 208
Fuglsang, Madeleine 215
Fyfe, Nat 145

Gale, Brendan 49, 264
Gale, Mark 70, 264
game day 81–3, 186, 291, 321–3
games, number played 68
Gardiner, Michael 257–8
Gdanski, John 214, 215
Geary, Jarryn 267, 301, 323
Geelong Football Club 295, 299, 300, 305
Gehrig, Fraser 70, 71, 79, 81, 134, 267
Gibson, Tom 55
Gilbert, Sam 109, 110, 115, 116, 154
Gleeson, Brian 274
Goddard, Brendon 173, 198, 209, 253–6, 264, 301, 311
    move to Essendon 255, 278
Gold Coast 38, 56–7, 180, 248
Gold Coast Bulletin 68
Gold Coast Suns 48, 271, 359
Google 112
GPS reading 135, 227
Graham, Ben 84

Gram, Jason 154, 337
grand final replay 2010 108, 113, 161, 188, 257, 301, 303–5
grand final week 297–8
Green, Brad 63
Greene, Toby 237
Grenier, Adrian 104
Gresham, Jade 246
grieving 213, 226, 349–50, 353–4
Gudinski, Michael 280–1
Gwilt, James 57, 259
GWS Giants 48, 319

Hale, David 66
Hall, Barry 71, 313
Hall of Fame 52
Hamill, Aaron 'Sammy' 47, 70, 267, 313–15, 319
hamstring injuries 140, 159–60, 212, 239, 300
Harvey, Robert 71, 141, 267, 293, 312, 323, 328, 341
Hawaii 2005 245
Hawkins, Tom 235, 288, 305
Hawthorn Football Club 53, 142, 236, 270, 295, 304
Hayes, Lenny 88, 138, 140, 145, 229, 253, 302, 319
    captaincy 315, 318
    Wizard Cup 2004 332
Heard, Caroline 155–6, 162, 164–5
Heard, Catherine 36, 82–3, 95, 108, 111–12, 137, 224, 230
    Australian visit 2010 156–9
    children, births 341–2
    family life 354–5
    Maddie, relationship with 185
    marriage proposal 170–3
    meeting Nick 150–5
    move to Australia 160, 161, 352
    Texas ranch 45, 163–4
    wedding 22, 137, 173–6
Heard, John 162, 173
Heard, Larry 156, 162, 163, 164–5, 168, 171, 225

Heard, Vivian 162, 171
   wedding 225, 231
Henderson, James 49
Herald Sun 110, 113–14
   'The One You Want' 99
Hill, Bradley 236
Hine, Derek 271
Hobart 6, 49
   Cheverton Parade 34, 37
   Duke Street 33–4
Hodge, Luke 57
Hollywood 104
Hosseini, Azim 240, 241–2
Houston 163, 165, 167, 170
Howell, Verdun 274
Hudghton, Max 90
Huggins Stand 276
hunting 168–9
Hutchins Old Boys 48, 55, 56
Hutchison, Greg 120
hydro-electric schemes 17

immigrants 17
injuries 238–9
   ankle 239
   calf 216
   collarbone 88, 152, 239, 260, 316
   concussion 62, 137, 239, 240–1
   facial surgery 239
   hamstring 140, 159–60, 212, 239, 300
   knee 79, 83, 113, 146, 227–30, 232, 238–9, 357
Ireland tours
   International Rules tour of Ireland 2015 87, 228, 264–5
   International Rules tour of Ireland 2004 263

Jeans, Allan 21, 135
Johnson, Mitchell 58
Jones, Austinn 'Aussie' 88
Judd, Chris 229, 294

Kane, George 'Gee' 168, 169
Kane, Harrison 168, 169

Kernahan, Stephen 311
King, David 107
Kingsley, Adam 92, 121, 210
knee injuries/surgery 79, 83, 113, 146, 227–30, 232, 238–9, 357
Korn Ferry 160
Koschitzke, Justin 47, 64, 70, 79, 154, 302, 311, 317
   competitiveness with 78–81
   draft 2000 68, 69
   father, becoming 344
   friendship with 102, 209, 258, 259
   living with 75, 129, 292
Koutoufides, Anthony 99

Lachman test 230, 231
Lake, Brian 271
Lane, Tim 89
Las Vegas 150–1, 153, 156
Lawrence, Stevie 70, 71, 79
leadership 37, 127–8, 309–12, 325, 327
Levine, Adam 105
Lion Cubs 61
Little Athletics 57
Lockett, Tony 274
Loewe, Stewart 267, 312–13, 341
Long, Nicky 214, 217
Longer, Billy 47
longevity 267
Longmire, John 69
Lovett, Andrew 336–8
Lyon, Ross 36, 122, 126, 136, 139–45, 284, 296, 300, 318
   match reviews 141–2
   move to Fremantle 146–7

McCartin, Paddy 234
McDonald, James 127
McGuire, Eddie 20, 269–71
McIntosh, Stephanie 103–4, 160
McLachlan, Gillon 329
McLeod, Andrew 99
McNabb, Bob 160
McQualter, Andrew 143
McVeigh, Jarrad 327

Index

Maddie's Match 215, 216, 259, 358
Maddie's Vision 87, 123, 213–19, 220–1, 285, 365–7
  contact 367
  'Fight Like Maddie' 215–16
  formation 214–15
  logo 217, 367
  Maddie's Match 215, 216
  projects funded 367
  purpose 218, 365
Maguire, Matt 'Goose' 80, 138, 245, 257, 311
Malthouse, Mick 66, 256, 333
Maria Island 29, 35, 36, 43
Matthews, Leigh 62, 66
Maxwell, Nick 301
media career 269
media coverage 106–7, 330–1, 332, 334, 338–40
Melbourne 177
Melbourne Cricket Ground (MCG) 140, 304
Melbourne Football Club 80, 127
Meldrum, Ian 'Molly' 280, 281, 285
mentors 125–48
Mercury 54
Meredith, Louisa 29
Merenda, Carlie 202, 205, 217, 261–2
MG ZT sponsored car 100
Miami 109, 152, 154
Michael, Mal 88, 89
mid-season breaks 131
Milicia, Adrian 218
Millington/Hean family 8
Millington, Fay 26–33, 39, 40, 175, 183, 202
Millington, Harold Charles 27, 29–30, 33
Millington, Kitty 27, 28, 29, 31–2
Millingtons Beach 30, 33
Millingtons Funeral Homes 206
Milne, Stephen 70, 89, 141, 251, 252, 253, 302
  father, becoming 344
  rape charge 333, 334

Montagna, Leigh 'Joey' 80, 91, 105, 119, 138, 154, 238, 323
  friendship with 127, 224, 258–9
  house-sharing 75
  Milne rape charge 334
Moorabbin 276–80, 314
Mostyn, Sam 330–1
Moyle, Brett 70
Murphy, Bob 87, 228, 231, 264–6

Nation, Jarrod 39, 126, 215
Neeld, Mark 127
Neighbours 103
Nettlefold, Michael 111
New England Patriots 233
New Zealand training camp 2010 115
Newman, Sam 69
Newnes, Jack 201
Newton-John, Olivia 104
Nike 88
Nixon, Ricky 69, 70, 100, 108, 110, 111, 116–17, 261, 264, 271
Norm Smith Medal 271
North Melbourne Football Club 77, 100, 304
Notting, Tim 62
nude photo scandal *see* 'The St Kilda Schoolgirl' scandal

Ogilvy, Geoff 284–5
On The Couch 318
One Small Step Collective 216
Orford 7, 18, 25–6, 27, 30, 35, 44–6, 191
  Maddie's farewell 209
  Nick Riewoldt house 39–41
  Sunways 27–8, 30, 38
Osborn, Michael 61, 76

Pastor Sean 194, 202, 223, 225
Pavlich, Matthew 326
Peckett, Justin 313
perfectionism 91
Petroro, Tom 261, 272
Picken, Marcus 62

polio 28, 31
Ponting, Ricky 49
Port Adelaide Football Club 135, 295
Port Arthur 36, 49
post-football career life 139, 359
post-traumatic stress 223–4
Powell, Robert 70
pre-season
   2017 323
   2015 210
   2012 146
   2009 142
   2004 332
   2001 71
pre-season camps 131
premiership 293–4, 295, 360
Presley, Luke 248
Prince, Professor Miles 187, 214
pub trivia 254
Puma 100

Queenborough Oval 56
Queensland 38, 49, 56–7
   under-16s football team 61
Queensland Australian Football League (QAFL) 61, 65

racism 17–18
Ray, Farren 185
reputation 111, 112, 114, 233, 242, 331
retirement 358
   thoughts of 122, 228–9, 231, 232–3, 358
Rhode, Andreas 22
Rhode, Bianca 22
Rhode, Fabienne 22
Richardson, Alan 41, 126–8, 148, 200, 210
Richardson, Matthew 49
Richardson, Sean 143
Richmond Football Club 52, 215
Riewoldt, Alex 5, 6, 35, 37, 59, 74–5, 82, 158, 230, 260
   fatherhood 349, 353
   friendship with 249, 350–2
   Maddie's death and funeral 202, 209
   Maddie's Vision 215
   marriage 352–3
   Nick's wedding 175
   Queensland, move to 247–8
Riewoldt, Carly *see* Ziegler, Carly
Riewoldt, Catherine *see* Heard, Catherine
Riewoldt, Christover 8, 20–1
   football career 48
Riewoldt, Fiona 10, 32, 39, 175, 202, 209, 230, 346–7
   Maddie's Vision 213, 215
Riewoldt, George 349, 353, 361
Riewoldt, Heinz 7, 8, 18–19
   childhood 9–10
   migration to Australia 17
   World War II 13, 14–16
Riewoldt, Helga 7, 8, 19
   World War II 11–13
Riewoldt, Jack 8, 19, 21, 198, 215, 216
   friendship with 259–60
Riewoldt, James 9, 26, 166, 199, 202, 230, 234, 341, 354
Riewoldt, Joerg 'Joe' 8, 20, 37, 41, 42, 175, 202, 209, 23, 347–8
   football career 48
   football coach 54–5
   Maddie's Vision 215
Riewoldt, Madeleine 'Maddie' 5, 37, 61, 113, 158, 175, 179–202, 250
   ashes 26, 208, 209
   bone marrow transplants 192–3, 195, 197, 344
   childhood 179–82
   death 202, 203–4, 225, 341
   funeral 47, 207, 208, 214
   illness 187–202, 346
   Maddie's beach 26, 182
   Maddie's Vision *see* Maddie's Vision
   Orford 25–6, 41, 46, 182–3, 209

Index

Oscar the dog 205, 210
skull fracture 181, 184
Riewoldt, Nick
  career achievements 293, 305–6, 318
  childhood 6, 24, 38, 53–7
  collarbone break 2005 88, 92–3, 260, 316
  colour blindness 91–2
  eulogy for Maddie 207
  fatherhood 341–2, 344, 345–6, 348–9, 355–6
  funeral and wake 207–8
  German heritage 6–24
  German passport 23
  high school 75–6
  honeymoon 176
  marriage proposal 170–3
  Milne, support in court 251, 335
  Orford house 39–43
  Queensland 38, 56–7, 180, 247, 310
  St Kilda life membership 115
  university 67
  wedding 22, 137, 173–6
Riewoldt, Peter 10, 20
Riewoldt, Ray 8, 9, 20, 21
Riewoldt, Roxy 202, 349
Riewoldt, Will 9, 26, 45, 166, 342, 355
Rimmington, Nathan 58
Rising Star award 79–80, 99
Ritchie, Professor David 192, 193, 201, 215
Roach, Danny 64
Roobound Enterprises 39
Rooke, Max 305
Ross, Seb 324
Roughead, Jarryd 87, 264–5, 266, 267
Rusca, Shannon 62
Ryan, Gerry 125, 217, 263

St Kilda Football Club 33, 215, 251, 270, 271–3, 305–6
  2017 season 227, 357
  2016 season 233, 234
  2015 season 211, 212–13
  2011 season 119–20, 135, 146, 306
  2010 season 109, 113, 159, 161, 188, 295, 301–3, 305
  2009 season 88, 103, 109, 143, 286, 295, 296–300, 305
  2008 season 141, 142
  2007 season 140
  2005 season 295
  2004 season 295
  2002 season 79, 80, 99, 100
  2001 season 71
  1996 season 273
  AGM 2011 115–16
  club facilities 276–8
  draft 2000 68–9, 98–9, 317
  history 273–5
  Maddie's Match 216–17
  members 287
  one-club player 271–3
  Orford pre-season 41–2, 44–5
  Saints disco 277
  Saints Man 323–6
St Kilda Heritage Museum 287
'The St Kilda Schoolgirl' scandal 107–13, 118, 121, 234, 284, 330
Saints Man 323–6
Seaford 116, 119, 276, 278–9
separation anxiety 221–2
spotlight 95–7, 100–2, 112–13, 115, 118, 121, 122–3
Sandy Bay juniors 34, 53
Scarlett, Matthew 298
Schneider, Adam 75, 200, 259, 304
Scott, Chris 88, 89
Shadforth, Tony 214, 215
shark attack 43
Shaw, Heath 359
Sheahan, Mike 318
Smith, Clay 229
Smith, Isaac 236
Smith, Patrick 134
Snowdome Foundation 214–15, 365

social media 87, 110, 242
Southport reserves 61–3
Spirit of Tasmania 158, 206
sponsorships 100
Spring Bay Hotel 44–5, 247
Stanley, Rhys 320
Steven, Jack 267
Stewart, Ian 274
Stone, Dr Ian 230, 240, 241, 260
Summers, Peter 217
Swan, Dane 310, 331
Sydney Swans 100, 295

Tandy, Rob 214
Tarrant, Chris 66
Tarrant, Robbie 47
Tasmania 25–6, 35, 46–7, 49
Tasmanian Football League (TFL) 20, 21
Taylor, Harry 299
Taylor, Simon 119
teammates, relationships with 245–6, 250–1, 256–9, 268, 335
Texas 45, 108, 149, 163–4, 165–9, 176, 177
Thomas, Claye 343
Thomas, Grant 47, 52, 80, 100, 101, 122, 126, 137, 148, 295
   match day coaching 134
   mentor, as 129–39, 342
   open house 132, 342–3
   sacking 135–6
   Wizard Cup 2004 332
Thomas, Jamison 343
Thomas, Kacey 135–6
Thomas, Kerry 132, 133, 136, 342
Thompson, Alex 35, 39, 41, 55, 118, 173, 247
Thompson, Andrew 323
Thompson, Elle 56
Thompson, Leith 35, 39
Townsend, Luke 240
training 91, 235, 297, 314
Trethewey, Jennifer 215

Trevor Barker medal 293
Tyson, Frank 'Typhoon' 58

Vallane, Holly 105
Victorian Football League (VFL) 21
Voss, Brett 62, 70
Voss, Michael 99

Wade, Matthew 20
Wade, Scott 20
Waldron, Brian 72
Wallis, Andrew 228, 240, 241, 298
Walls, Robert 89
Warne, Shane 130, 150, 280, 282–3, 285
Waterside Hotel 264
Watson, Jobe 326, 327, 340
Watson, Shane 58
Watson, Tim 316
Watters, Scott 270, 272
Weekend Australian 21
Weller, Luke 61
Wellman, Sean 264
West, Justin 157, 174
West Coast 294
Western Bulldogs 228, 266, 295, 304
Whiffin, Kenny 274
Wigney, Stuart 264
Willis, Anthony 214
Wilson, Caroline 335
Wilson, Terry 68
wing position 235–6
winning 292–3, 294, 304, 306
Wizard Cup 2004 332
Wizel, Mark 218
World War I 16
World War II 11–13, 14, 16
Wulf, Daniel 70

Yoemans, Paul 126
Young, Matty 341

Ziegler, Carly 259